VISIT US AT

www.syngress.com

Syngress is committed to publishing high-quality books for IT Professionals and delivering those books in media and formats that fit the demands of our customers. We are also committed to extending the utility of the book you purchase via additional materials available from our Web site.

SOLUTIONS WEB SITE

To register your book, visit www.syngress.com/solutions. Once registered, you can access our solutions@syngress.com Web pages. There you may find an assortment of value-added features such as free e-books related to the topic of this book, URLs of related Web sites, FAQs from the book, corrections, and any updates from the author(s).

ULTIMATE CDs

Our Ultimate CD product line offers our readers budget-conscious compilations of some of our best-selling backlist titles in Adobe PDF form. These CDs are the perfect way to extend your reference library on key topics pertaining to your area of expertise, including Cisco Engineering, Microsoft Windows System Administration, CyberCrime Investigation, Open Source Security, and Firewall Configuration, to name a few.

DOWNLOADABLE E-BOOKS

For readers who can't wait for hard copy, we offer most of our titles in downloadable Adobe PDF form. These e-books are often available weeks before hard copies, and are priced affordably.

SYNGRESS OUTLET

Our outlet store at syngress.com features overstocked, out-of-print, or slightly hurt books at significant savings.

SITE LICENSING

Syngress has a well-established program for site licensing our e-books onto servers in corporations, educational institutions, and large organizations. Contact us at sales@syngress.com for more information.

CUSTOM PUBLISHING

Many organizations welcome the ability to combine parts of multiple Syngress books, as well as their own content, into a single volume for their own internal use. Contact us at sales@syngress.com for more information.

SYNGRESS®

Linksys® WRT54G Ultimate Hacking

Paul Asadoorian

Larry Pesce

Raúl Siles Technical Editor

SYNGRESS®

KEY	SERIAL NUMBER
001	HJIRTCV764
002	PO9873D5FG
003	829KM8NJH2
004	GHJ923HJMN
005	CVPLQ6WQ23
006	VBP965T5T5
007	HJJJ863WD3E
008	2987GVTWMK
009	629MP5SDJT
010	IMWQ295T6T

PUBLISHED BY
Syngress Publishing, Inc.
Elsevier, Inc.
30 Corporate Drive
Burlington, MA 01803

Linksys WRT54G Ultimate Hacking

Printed in the United States of America
1 2 3 4 5 6 7 8 9 0
ISBN: 978-1-59749-166-2

Publisher: Amorette Pedersen
Acquisitions Editor: Andrew Williams
Technical Editor: Raúl Siles
Cover Designer: Michael Kavish

Project Manager: Jay Donahue
Page Layout and Art: Patricia Lupien
Copy Editor: Audrey Doyle
Indexer: Michael Ferreira

For information on rights, translations, and bulk sales, contact Matt Pedersen, Commercial Sales Director and Rights, at Syngress Publishing; email m.pedersen@elsevier.com.

Acknowledgments and Dedications

Paul Asadoorian

Dedicated to my wife Shannon and mother Paula who stuck by me and supported me throughout the entire project, and to my grandfather who always said, "You get out of something what you put into it."

Larry Pesce

Dedicated to my wife Kristin and my mother Pam, who stand by me to pick up the slack when I put too many irons in the fire, and for all of their support and encouragement.

Thank you!

Paul and Larry would like to collectively thank the following for their support, inspiration, hard work and encouragement in the concept and execution of this book: Mike Baker, Andrew Williams, Raúl Siles, The OpenWrt developers, Mike Kershaw, Jay Beale, Renderman, Andrew Lockhart, members of irc.freenode.net #pauldotcom, #openwrt, everyone who contributed to the OpenWrt Wiki, Rocco, Victor, Joshua Wright, David Cook, anyone else we forgot to mention, and everyone who has ever hacked a WRT54G and put information about it on the Internet.

Book Web Site

For updates, new tutorials, and all new things related to WRT54G hacking by the authors, please visit www.wrt54ghacks.com.

Co-authors

Paul Asadoorian (GCIA, GCIH) is the Lead IT Security Engineer for a large University in the New England area. In the past 6 years he has been responsible for intrusion detection, firewalls, VPN, and networking assessments/penetration testing in the educational IT space. He speaks frequently on topics such as wireless security at various events, such as the MIT Security Camp. Paul's research has been featured in numerous publications such as *Network Intrusion Detection, 3rd Edition*, Securityfocus.com, and the SANS Reading Room. In addition to owning and operating an independent security consulting company, Defensive Intuition, Paul is also the host of PaulDotCom Security Weekly (http://pauldotcom.com), a weekly podcast discussing IT security news, vulnerabilities, hacking, and research, including interviews with some of the top security professionals. Paul graduated from Bryant College with a degree in Computing and Information Systems, and is currently on the SANS GIAC advisory board. When not trying to hack something Paul can be found spending time with his wife and pug, Rocco.

Larry Pesce (CCNA, GCFA Silver, GAWN Gold) is the Manager for Information Services Security at a mid-sized healthcare organization in New England. In the last 13 years in the computer industry, Larry has become a jack of all trades; PC repair, network engineering, Web design, non-linear audio and video production and computer security. Larry is also gainfully employed as a Penetration Tester/Ethical Hacker with Defensive Intuition, a Rhode Island-based security consulting company. A graduate of Roger Williams University in Computer Information Systems, Larry is currently exploring his options for graduate education. In addition to his industry experience, Larry is also a Security Evangelist and co-host for the PaulDotCom Security Weekly podcast at www.pauldotcom.com. More of Larry's writing, guides and rants can be found on his blog at www.haxorthematrix.com and the SANS Reading Room.

Technical Editor

Raúl Siles is a senior Independent Security Consultant specializing in advanced security solutions and prevention, detection and response services in various industries including government, defense, telecom, manufacturing, and financial. Raul's expertise and service offerings include security architecture design and review, penetration testing, incident handling, forensic and malware analysis, network, system, database and application security assessments and hardening, code security reviews, wireless security, honeynets solutions, intrusion detection/prevention, expert witness, information security management and security awareness and training through The SANS Institute.

Contents

## Chapter 1

WRT54G Fundamentals

Solutions in this chapter:

- **Our Approach to This Book**
- **History of the Linksys WRT54G**
- **Linksys WRT54G Series Hardware**
- **WRT54G Buyer's Guide**

☑ **Summary**

☑ **Solutions Fast Track**

☑ **Frequently Asked Questions**

Introduction

The road to third-party firmware has been a long one, at least where the computer industry is concerned, and the changes to the WRT54G series of hardware have been many. In this chapter, we will discuss our approach to this book, the history of the WRT54G product line and its variations, and the history behind the development of third-party firmware.

Our Approach to This Book

This book is meant to document many of the features, projects, and interesting and fun things in general that you can do with the WRT54G series of routers from Linksys. Everyone should read this chapter in its entirety before moving on to other chapters in the book. Whether you own one WRT54G router or one of each model number in the series—or even if you have yet to purchase a WRT54G—you should read this chapter before reading any further. It will give you a map and a history of this hardware platform and it will help you to decide which model to purchase and/or whether your current hardware will do what you want it to do. If you do not yet own a WRT54G, or you just have an old dusty one in the corner, please note that we believe everyone should have at least two WRT54Gs at their disposal. Many of the projects we cover in this book either will require two routers, or will benefit performance-wise with at least two routers because you'll be able to split the processing load among them. And don't worry; the prices of these devices have come down over the years, making them affordable for even penny-pinching college students.

In this book, we have taken a "top-down" approach to teaching you how to make the most of the WRT54G platform. For instance, we show you by example how to configure and use these devices in various ways. In addition, we selected and documented each project and example carefully to ensure practical usage. Yes, we could show you how to use your WRT54G series router to run your entire Web site, database and all, but this is certainly not advisable. There are proper uses for your WRT54G, and there are some which stretch the limits so far that they are not practical. On the flip side of practical is, well, just plain fun, and we've made certain to include fun projects in this book as well. In each instance, we attempt to fully document the use case, based on extensive testing we've conducted in our own home and work environments. We included enough details about embedded devices, operating systems, and software engineering as we thought you would need, and we provide resources for those of you who want more details in these areas. We want this book to expand the audience of the WRT54G platform, and embedded device usage as a whole, unlocking the potential that this platform has to offer.

We want this book to be your road map to using WRT54G devices to your advantage in many different environments, including work and home. We've found so many uses for them that we know others can benefit as well. Hence, this book will guide you on your journey to unlocking all of the potential of the WRT54G hardware and software platforms.

> **NOTE**
>
> There are a few different perceived meanings of the word *hacking*. In this book, hacking means to use things for a purpose for which they were not originally intended. For example, Linksys did not intend to allow users to add a Secure Digital (SD) card reader to a WRT54G. However, we will show you how to "hack" the WRT54G and add an SD card reader to expand the WRT54G's storage capabilities. Hacking also refers to the act of gaining access to computer systems and/or networks (i.e., using the systems or software in a way that the creators did not originally intend), which should always be done with written permission. Along those lines, we will show you how to use WRT54G routers to aid in your legitimate hacking and security practices, such as penetration testing and performing network/system audits. You must always perform this testing with permission, preferably written, from appropriate parties.

History of the Linksys WRT54G

Linksys began selling version 1.0 of the WRT54G in late 2002 as a home router, firewall, and wireless networking product. In the beginning, it was primarily intended to support wireless networks, and inclusion of additional features merely complemented the wireless capabilities. At that time, the device was relatively commonplace; it featured a wide area network (WAN) port, a four-port 10/100 switch, and 802.11b support. The device also shipped with a Web interface for configuration—a practice that had become popular with consumer devices in earlier years. Since the initial launch in 2002, Linksys has revised the hardware of the WRT54G several times to provide upgrades to the base unit. The device has proven popular enough that Linksys has spawned several similar models in the WRT54G series to deliver various features, speed enhancements, and form factors. We will discuss a number of the models later in this chapter, and we will begin to see the natural progression that developments in technology have afforded the product line.

This particular product line has been a very good seller for Linksys. Although sales figures for the device are typically not broken out from sales figures for Linksys as a whole, company executives have been quoted as saying, "We sell literally hundreds of thousands per month." This popularity may be due, in part, to the ease with which you can modify the device, and as such a community of open source advocates and hardware hackers alike has embraced it readily.

With the recent official support from Linksys of third-party firmware through the release of the WRT54GL, Linksys is poised to sell even more units. We are currently seeing additional hardware revisions of the WRT54GL which, from an initial observation, seems to be following the trend of the original WRT54G series of hardware. With this continued development of the WRT54GL, and further adoption of open source methodologies, it appears clear that Linksys is committed to keeping the product line alive and well. This is good news for all of us who are tearing them open, and making them submit to our will!

History of the WRT54G Open Source Firmware

At some point in early 2003, Andrew Miklas posted several times to the Linux Kernel Mailing List (http://lkml.org/lkml/2003/6/7/164) about his discovery that Linksys was using General Public License (GPL) code in the firmware for the Linksys WRT54G. As part of the GPL, anyone who modifies the open code is required to release her modification back to the community, and Andrew was unable to locate the source for the modifications. Andrew opened communication with Linksys in order to get the modified software released back to the community, and he gathered some significant support in this endeavor.

Linux enthusiasts were made aware of Linksys' use of open source software by several postings to Slashdot in June 2003. The Slashdot and Linux communities rallied to support the GPL, and made their opinions known that Linksys should comply with the GPL. Given the enormous pressure from the community, and a group of executives that understood the GPL at Linksys, Linksys released its modified code to the public under the GPL.

In June 2003, Rob Flickenger posted to his O'Reilly blog about work that he had been performing during Hack Night sessions with Seattle Wireless. During these postings, Rob linked to the start of the tools for building your own custom firmware. Additionally, Andrew made some additional postings to the Linux Kernel Mailing List on methods and issues with cross-compiling code for the Linksys WRT54G.

From this point forward, we were able to create our own firmware, and many individuals did just that. This resulted in a number of different firmware versions, all with different add-ons. We will discuss a number of these firmware versions throughout this book.

Linksys WRT54G Series Hardware

WRT54G Series: Common Features

Although there are many models and variations of the Linksys WRT54G, most models have the same basic features. Let's explore these common features so that we have a solid foundation for understanding the differences among versions, which will allow us to become better WRT54G hackers. This book covers many projects which require some knowledge of the WRT54G internal hardware. Also, we will be referring to many parts of the WRT54G throughout this book, so it is important that we establish a common foundation of embedded device hardware knowledge. We'll start with an overview of the hardware inside the WRT54G. In this case, we will use WRT54GL, version 1.1, as shown in Figure 1.1.

Figure 1.1 Overview of the WRT54GL Hardware Components

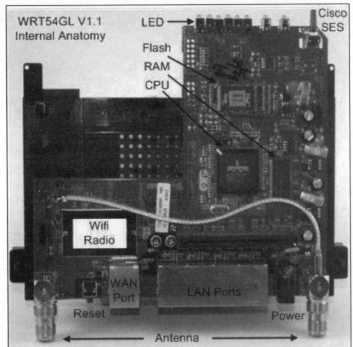

Power

Aside from WRT54G, version 1.0, all power requirements are the same, using 12V DC 1.0A. The power requirements are standard for embedded devices and wireless access points, making them compatible with Power over Ethernet (PoE). We will cover "power supply hacking" in greater detail in Chapter 7, where we'll show you how to make a battery pack for your WRT54G devices, which you'll need if you want to take advantage of the WRT54G's capabilities in mobile scenarios such as war-driving activities.

The Reset Button

This button, by default, will reset the device to factory defaults. It is programmable and has many different uses, depending on when and how long you press it, which router version you have, and which firmware you are running. You will need a small instrument (such as a ballpoint pen) to press this button. Be careful not to press it by accident, because doing so could cause the device to reboot or it could reset the router's settings. We discuss the use of the Reset button in depth in Chapter 8.

LED

The LED lights differ on the various models, and combinations of the LED light states indicate different conditions. Figure 1.2 depicts the most common configuration of LEDs on a WRT54G.

Figure 1.2 WRT54G Front Panel LEDs

The Power light indicates whether the device is receiving power. This light will be a solid green when the device is powered on. When the device is booting, or when you're applying new firmware, the Power light will typically flash. DMZ light usage varies among different firmware. For example, OpenWrt uses it to indicate its progress in the boot process. The WLAN LED and the Ethernet LEDs numbered 1–4 are activity lights, and they are a solid green when connected and a flashing green when indicating activity. The Internet LED indicates a connection to the WAN port, and it is a solid green when a connection is made and a flashing green to indicate activity. Once you've successfully installed third-party firmware on your device, you will be able to manipulate the LED status simply by changing values in the contents of system files.

Secure Easy Setup Button

The button in Figure 1.2 labeled "Cisco Systems" (yes, the Cisco logo on the left-hand side of the front panel is a button) is referred to as the Secure Easy Setup button, or the Cisco SES button, or simply the SES button. The SES button first appeared in WRT54G, version 1.1, and was originally intended to allow users to easily set up an encrypted wireless network, provided that they used hardware from vendors participating in the SecureEasySetup program (those vendors being Linksys, Gateway, and HP). Third-party firmware allows you to reprogram this button to do anything you want; for example, turn off the wireless interface or enable/disable a virtual private network (VPN) connection.

NOTE

SecureEasySetup is being replaced by a new standard developed by the Wi-Fi Alliance. Wi-Fi Protected Setup, or WPS (because we needed yet another wireless acronym), was made available as an optional standard for wireless vendors to provide a push-button setup for encrypted wireless networks. WPS also adds the capability to provide a PIN number, instead of a physical button, that the user would enter to enable the setup of a secure wireless network. The PIN number method will allow device manufacturers to enable WPS on older devices that do not provide a hardware facility for WPS. For more information, see the Wi-Fi Alliance Web site at http://wi-fi.org.

Here are some common operational indicators for the LED lights:

- **Flashing Power light** By itself, this is not a cause for concern. The Power light will flash at various points in the startup process, and may also flash to indicate other states.
- **Solid DMZ light** This indicates that the device is booting.
- **Flashing Power light and slowly flashing DMZ light** This indicates that your flash image is corrupt. You can resolve this by using the Trivial File Transfer Protocol (TFTP) to upload a new flash image; we give you the instructions in Chapter 2.

Processor Architecture

All processors that ship with the WRT54G models use a Broadcom MIPS (Microprocessor without Interlocked Pipeline Stages) processor, common to embedded devices and game consoles. These processors are based on the Reduced Instruction Set Computer (RISC), meaning they have a smaller set of instructions than most processors from Intel (which feature a Complex Instruction Set Computer, or CISC, architecture). MIPS processors are used by SGI, by Sony for its PlayStation and PlayStation 2 game consoles, and by Cisco Systems in its routers and switches. Speeds will vary throughout the different models; however, all feature the same architecture and all are manufactured by Broadcom. So, why do we care? Most Linux-based open source software is made for the Intel x86 platform, which is a completely different architecture. This means we will need to "port" or "cross-compile" software to allow it to run on this platform, or be certain that we are using software that has already been ported. Two primary families of Broadcom processors are used in all WRT54G models: BCM47xx and BCM5352.

BCM47xx

There are two distinct models in the BCM47xx family. The BCM4704 series was released to be used in small wireless access points to be targeted toward the home or SOHO user. It provided only CPU functions and relied on separate chips to control the Ethernet Media Access Control (MAC) and Wireless MAC. You can see in earlier versions of the WRT54G, such as the version 1.0 and 1.1 models, that they do, in fact, contain separate chips for all three functions. The BCM4712 series processors not only contained CPU functionality, but also were able to provide Wireless MAC capability (integrating with the BCM2050 wireless radio). This design is referred to as SoC, or System-on-Chip. The BCM47xx series always relied on a separate processor for Ethernet MAC in the form of the ADM6996 and BCM5325 series processors. The latest revision of this processor was used in WRT54G, version 2.0, which also increased CPU speeds from 125 MHz to 200 MHz.

BCM5352

The BCM5352 family of processors is a next-generation SoC architecture that combines the CPU, Wireless MAC, and Ethernet MAC onto one chip (see Figure 1.3).

Figure 1.3 Broadcom BCM5352 Chip from a Version 1.1 WRT54GL

Notes from the Underground...

Overclocking Your WRT54G

You can find many different tutorials and articles online describing how to overclock your WRT54G. Overclocking allows your processor to run at a speed that is faster than that to which it was originally set or for which it was designed. At first glance, this may seem like an easy change to gain some speed (in essence, it is as easy as making a change to an NVRAM variable). However, you need to be very cautious if you are going to attempt this hack. It is a dangerous hack to perform, as it could cause your router to overheat and/or become "bricked." Your CPU frequency capacity is defined by the router version, processor, and processor version. You can determine which processor (CPU) and version a specific device uses by executing the following command (tested on OpenWrt and DD-WRT):

```
root@openvpn:~# grep cpu /proc/cpuinfo
cpu model           : BCM3302 V0.8
```

So, just what is a BCM3302 v0.8? It's the actual CPU associated with a WRT54GL model router. Table 1.1 lists the different CPU types and versions.

Continued

Table 1.1 CPU Types and Versions

Model	CPU Type and Version	Default Speed	Max Speed*
WRT54G 1.0	BCM4710 V0.0	125 MHz	216 MHz
WRT54G 1.1	BCM4710 V0.0	125 MHz	216 MHz
WRT54G 2.0	BCM3302 V0.7	200 MHz	250 MHz
WRT54G 2.2	BCM3302 V0.7	200 MHz	250 MHz
WRT54G 3.0	BCM3302 V0.7	200 MHz	250 MHz
WRT54G 3.1	BCM3302 V0.7	200 MHz	250 MHz
WRT54G 4.0	BCM3302 V0.8	200 MHz	250 MHz
WRT54G 5.0	BCM3302 V0.8	200 MHz	250 MHz
WRT54G 5.1	BCM3302 V0.8	200 MHz	250 MHz
WRT54G 6.0	BCM3302 V0.8	200 MHz	250 MHz
WRT54GL 1.0	BCM3302 V0.8	200 MHz	250 MHz
WRT54GL 1.1	BCM3302 V0.8	200 MHz	250 MHz
WRTSL54GS	BCM3302 V0.6	266 MHz	300 MHz

The BCM3302 processor is part of the BCM5352 family of SoC processors. Speeds in the "Max Speed" column were reported by various users and in online documentation, and were gleaned from the source code that determines the CPU clock frequency. You can go higher in most cases, but going higher than the values listed will most likely cause problems with overheating and routers locking up. This is one reason we are covering this only briefly and are not providing a full tutorial. For those of you who just have to do it because, well, you can, the following commands will change the CPU clock frequency:

```
nvram set clkfreq=250

nvram commit

reboot
```

On the other hand, overclocking has some added advantages, such as increasing I/O when using SD cards, and using applications that are CPU-intensive. We disclaim all responsibility for melted routers that come as a result of overclocking.

Storage

Storage on all WRT54G-based devices comes by way of flash memory, a form of nonvolatile storage commonly used in small electronic devices, such as your digital camera (see Figure 1.4). One of the limiting factors we will have to work with is limited storage, which defines just how much software we can load onto the device. However, have no fear: We will show you how to upgrade the capacity of your flash memory in Chapter 7 through the use of other storage technologies.

Figure 1.4 Intel 4 MB Flash Chip from a Version 1.1 WRT54GL

The more flash storage you have, the better, because it means you can load more software (kernel and software packages) onto the device. WRT54GS models with version numbers from 1.0 through 3.0 and the WRTSL54GS series contain the most on-board flash in the entire WRT54G family, with 8 MB.

Memory

RAM

The WRT54G series routers use Synchronous Dynamic Random Access Memory (SDRAM) for their main memory system. However, this is a different kind of SDRAM than you would put into your PC. RAM on the WRT54G series is soldered directly to the printed circuit board (PCB) instead of using a standard PC DIMM format (see Figure 1.5).

Tutorials on the Web discuss how you can upgrade the memory on your WRT54G. However, they require special tools (such as an air rework station) and special skills (such as adding and removing surface mount components) in order to execute properly (above and beyond what we will cover in this book).

Figure 1.5 RAM Memory Chip from a Version 1.1 WRT54GL

Wireless and Ethernet Networking

The WRT54G platform has a very powerful networking architecture, which includes an Ethernet switch, virtual LAN (VLAN) configuration, and bridging capabilities. It provides a five-port Ethernet switch, which by default is broken out into two VLANs (VLAN0 and VLAN1). The wireless interface, although separate, is bridged by default to the Ethernet switch, and you can use it just like another Ethernet interface and place it on any VLAN. You also can use the wireless interface to serve wireless clients when the device is acting as an access point (Master mode), to serve as a client and connect to other wireless networks (Managed mode), to provide direct connectivity to other wireless clients, Peer-to-Peer network (Ad Hoc mode), and to act as a wireless bridge (Client Bridge mode).

Figure 1.6 shows the architecture of the WRT54G (specifically, the WRT54GL). Starting with the WiFi component, it has an 802.11 b/g radio chipset, the BCM2050. The device uses a diversity chip to balance signals between the two built-in antennas. The WiFi radio connects to the CPU Wireless MAC on eth1, which is bridged to VLAN0 via the br0 interface. The Ethernet MAC in the CPU provides the tagging functions for the two default VLANs, and carries this information to the switch via port 5, the internal port associated with eth0. The VLANs are then assigned to the appropriate ports, putting, by default, the WAN port (VLAN1) and local area network (LAN) ports (VLAN0) on different VLANs. The Ethernet switch then controls the Ethernet (LAN) and Internet LED lights, whereas the Power, DMZ, and WLAN lights are controlled by a General Purpose Input/Output (GPIO) port on the CPU.

Figure 1.6 WRT54GL Block Diagram

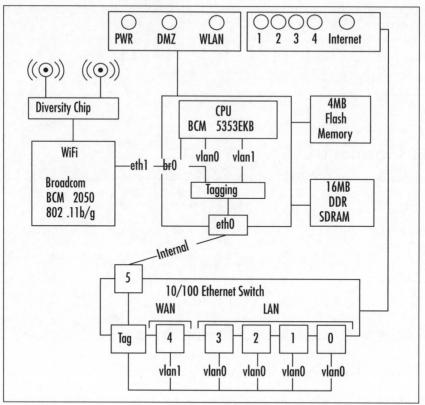

Throughout this book, we will be customizing this configuration to suit our needs, so it is important that we discuss some of the basic concepts in more detail:

- **VLAN tagging** VLANs allow us to, in essence, create multiple Layer 2 segments on the same switch. You can think of this as a switch within a switch. WRT54Gs come with a standard VLAN setting, and for the WRT54GL it sets up two VLANs by default. VLAN0 is referred to as the Ethernet VLAN (LAN), and tags ports 0, 1, 2, and 3 with this VLAN tag, which corresponds to the physical ports labeled 1, 2, 3, and 4, respectively (i.e., tagged port 0 is physical port 1). The tagged port numbers will be of significance when we cover how to manipulate VLANs in various projects throughout the book.

- **Bridging** The WRT54G, by default, creates a networking bridge between the wireless interface and the LAN ports, known as br0. If you have used a Linksys brand router before, even in its default configuration with the Linksys firmware, you know that when you associate to the wireless network you end up on the same subnet as though you were plugged directly into a LAN port. Br0 is also the interface assigned to the actual switch itself, which is the LAN Internet Protocol (IP) address that you connect to in order to manage the router (192.168.1.1 by default).

- **WAN port** The WAN port, as it is labeled on the outside of the router, is assigned to VLAN1 and its internal port assignment is 4. When you plug your cable modem into this port, it will typically pull a Dynamic Host Configuration Protocol (DHCP) address from your Internet service provider (ISP). Because the WAN port and all LAN assigned ports are on separate VLANs, they act as two physically separate networks linked by the WRT54G routing capabilities. The firewall prevents traffic flowing from the WAN network to the LAN network by default, but allows all traffic initiated from the LAN to exit via the WAN port.

Antenna Connectors

One of the common features of all WRT54G models (with the exception of the WRT54SLGS, which does not feature a removable antenna) is the external antenna connectors. Shown in Figure 1.7 without antennas connected, this connector is referred to as an RP-TNC (Reverse Polarity–Threaded Neill-Concelman, named after its creators). This connection type is standard for use in 802.11 wireless networking.

Figure 1.7 RP-TNC Antenna Connector from a WRT54G

The RP-TNC connector allows you to easily upgrade antennas, or replace damaged antennas, simply by unscrewing the existing ones and screwing on new ones. Many add-on antenna options are on the market that will increase gain; see Chapter 7 for more information.

Determining Your Hardware Version

So you've got a WRT54G sitting on the shelf or the floor that you've had for years. Maybe someone gave you an old WRT54G because he bought a new one and he knows you're a geek and might be able to use it. Before we can go down the WRT54G hacking path, we need to be certain of the router version number, as different firmware will be applied according to the version number. This is important, as applying the wrong firmware to your device will cause "bricking." Many other hacking projects, add-ons, and upgrades will very heavily depend on version number. For example, in Chapter 6, we will show you how to add an SD card reader to your WRT54G for increased storage. This hack will be very different in terms of solder points and drivers, depending on the model that you own.

You can usually determine the router version in one of two ways: by looking at the "Model No" field, which should list the router type and version, or by using the first four characters and numbers of the serial number. Both are located on the bottom of your device, as shown in Figure 1.8.

Figure 1.8 WRT54G Labels and Versions

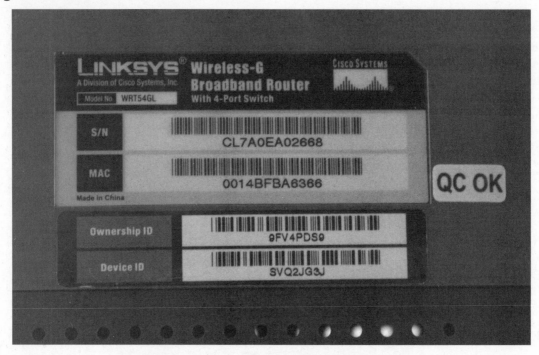

Figure 1.8 shows the "Model No" field as being "WRT54GL," which indicates the type of device. But which version of the WRT54GL are we looking at? For that information, we need to look at the first four characters in the serial number—in this case, "CL7A"—and then refer to Table 1.2.

Table 1.2 WRT54G Series Serial Numbers and Versions

Serial Number Prefix	Router/Version
WRT54G	
CDFF	WRT54G v.8.0
CDF0, CDF1	WRT54G v1.0
CDF2, CDF3	WRT54G v1.1
CDF5	WRT54G v2.0

Continued

Table 1.2 continued WRT54G Series Serial Numbers and Versions

Serial Number Prefix	Router/Version
WRT54G	
CDF7	WRT54G v2.2
CDF8	WRT54G v3.0
CDF9	WRT54G v3.1
CDFA	WRT54G v4.0
CDFB	WRT54G v5.0
CDFC	WRT54G v5.1
CDFD	WRT54G v6.0
CDFE	WRT54G v7.0
WRT54GL	
CL7A	WRT54GL v1.0
CL7B	WRT54GL v1.1
WRT54GS	
CGN0, CGN1	WRT54GS v1.0
CGN2	WRT54GS v1.1
CGN3	WRT54GS v2.0
CGN4	WRT54GS v2.1
CGN5	WRT54GS v3.0
CGN6	WRT54GS v4.0
CGN7	WRT54GS v5.0
CGN8	WRT54GS v5.1
CGN9	WRT54GS v6.0
WRTSL54GS	
CJK0	WRTSL54GS v1.0

Table 1.2 shows that "CL7A" corresponds to WRT54GL v1.0. Now that we can easily identify model numbers, serial numbers, and router versions, let's take a look at some of the differences among them.

WRT54G Models

The WRT54G is one of the first devices to integrate a router, firewall, Ethernet switch, and wireless access point into a single device. The original design and goal of this product was to sit behind your cable modem and provide wireless Internet access to your mobile clients, such as laptops or handhelds, as well as give you the ability to plug in four desktop computers for Internet access.

WRT54G, Version 1.0

WRT54G, version 1.0, is easily distinguishable from its later siblings. Most notably, it sports 20 front-panel LED lights, as shown in Figure 1.9, and it uses a mini PCI slot to hold the wireless chipset, something no other WRT54G comes with. Table 1.3 lists the specifications for version 1.0 of the WRT54G.

Figure 1.9 Front Panel of the WRT54G, Version 1.0

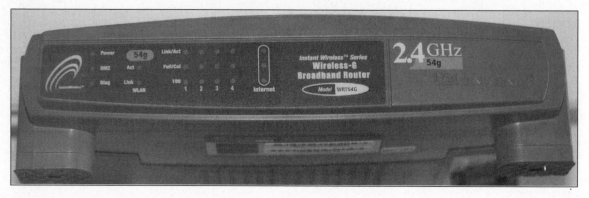

Table 1.3 Specifications for the WRT54G, Version 1.0

CPU speed	125 MHz
RAM	16 MB
Flash	4 MB
Serial number prefix	CDF0
	CDF1

The wireless radio is the standard BCM2050 from Broadcom; however, you could use the mini PCI to install any wireless device you wish, provided that you are able to install the appropriate driver or develop one on your own.

Figure 1.10 shows the inside of version 1.0 of the WRT54G. You can see the mini PCI card and slot in the lower right-hand corner. Attached are the two antenna connectors. Another interesting characteristic of version 1.0 is the power supply, which runs at 5V DC 2.0A, a sharp contrast to all other WRT54G models that run at 12V DC 1.0A. Running at 5V DC 2.0A offers compatibility with the Linksys WAPPOE, which provides PoE capabilities using the Ethernet cable unused pairs. However, this is not the standard, so your options for PoE will be limited with this version.

Figure 1.10 Internals of the WRT54G, Version 1.0

You can find more PoE information in Chapter 7.

WRT54G, Version 1.1

Version 1.1 of the WRT54G isn't very different from version 1.0. In what most people believe was an effort to cut manufacturing costs, Linksys has replaced the mini PCI slot with an on-board wireless chip, but is still using the same wireless radio, the Broadcom BCM2050, which will be prevalent throughout the WRT54G models. Linksys also changed the power supply to a 12V DC 1.0A. On the outside, there are some noticeable visual changes, primarily the removal of 12 of the 22 LED lights and the addition of the "Cisco Systems" logo, as shown in Figure 1.11. The internals are not shown here, as they are similar to other models shown later in this section. Table 1.4 lists the specifications of the WRT54G, version 1.1.

Figure 1.11 The Front Panel of the WRT54G, Version 1.1

Table 1.4 Specifications of the WRT54G, Version 1.1

CPU speed	125 MHz
RAM	16 MB
Flash	4 MB
Serial number prefix	CDF2
	CDF3

The LED lights in the front of the device are much simpler to interpret. They blink when there is activity and stay solid green to show a link. The Power light should be solid green; if it is blinking, that could spell trouble. Many other LED states indicate problems, or opportunities to do something, such as push the Reset button. We will cover all of these throughout this book.

NOTE

In March 2003, networking giant Cisco Systems announced it would purchase Linksys in a stock deal valued at $500 million. Cisco decided to leave the Linksys branding, but conveniently added the "Cisco Systems" logo you see depicted in Figure 1.11. Cisco still owns Linksys as of the time of this writing.

WRT54G, Version 2.0

Version 2.0 of the WRT54G is the last version to use the ADMTec ADM6996 Ethernet MAC as a separate chip, in favor of having it built into the CPU; see Figure 1.12. We do not show the front panel for this model due to its similarities with other models described in this section. Table 1.5 lists the specifications of version 2.0 of the WRT54G.

Figure 1.12 The Internals of the WRT54G, Version 2.0

Table 1.5 Specifications of the WRT54G, Version 2.0

CPU speed	200 MHz
RAM	16 MB
Flash	4 MB
Serial number prefix	CDF5

The SoC in version 2.0 can power a six-port 10/100 Ethernet switch. The most significant change from the 1.0 and 1.1 WRT54G series is the new and improved CPU, which boosts the speed from 125 MHz to 200 MHz. You will also notice in the upper right-hand corner of Figure 1.12 that the circuit board has the model and version number screen printed in white.

WRT54G, Version 2.2

Version 2.2 of the WRT54G sports the first appearance of the BCM5325 chipset for the Ethernet MAC. It also uses Hynix memory, which will become standard on most model WRT54Gs from this version forward. Table 1.6 lists the specifications of the WRT54G, version 2.2

Table 1.6 Specifications of the WRT54G, Version 2.2

CPU Speed	200 MHz
RAM	16 MB
Flash	4 MB
Serial number prefix	CDF07

TIP

Attention, owners of WRT54G version 2.2 model routers: Linksys shipped this version and advertised it as having 16 MB of RAM. However, the memory chips inside are IS42S16800A-7T, which support 32 MB of RAM. Although this is not an officially supported configuration, many people have reported that they have successfully enabled the other 16 MB of RAM (after all, the word *hacking* is in the title of this book). If you have this particular version, we recommend that you verify the model number on the RAM chip, and if it matches IS42S16800A-7T, you can use the following nvram commands to enable the extra memory:

```
nvram set sdram_init=0x0008
nvram set sdram_ncdl=0x0000
nvram commit
reboot
```

NOTE

You can verify that the memory is being recognized with the following command (note the *MemTotal* line, which should be about 2 MB less than the actual total):

```
# cat /proc/meminfo
        total:   used:   free:  shared: buffers:  cached:
Mem:  31453184 12652544 18800640 0    2080768 6393856
Swap:     0      0      0
MemTotal:     30716 kB
MemFree:       1830 kB
MemShared:        0 kB
Buffers:      2032 kB
```

```
Cached:        6244 kB
SwapCached:       0 kB
Active:        4100 kB
Inactive:      5716 kB
HighTotal:        0 kB
HighFree:         0 kB
LowTotal:     30716 kB
LowFree:      18360 kB
SwapTotal:        0 kB
SwapFree:         0 kB
```

Wasn't that much easier than using expensive soldering tools and a magnifying glass?

WRT54G, Versions 3.0 and 3.1

Versions 3.0 and 3.1 of the WRT54G are almost identical to the version 2.0 and 2.2 model routers. In fact, all of the internal workings are exactly the same, with the exception of the new Cisco SES button. Formerly the "Cisco Systems" logo, it has been converted into a button, as shown in Figure 1.13.

Figure 1.13 The Front Panel of the WRT54G, Version 3.1

The button has an LED behind it, which you can see in the upper right-hand corner of Figure 1.14.

Figure 1.14 LED and SES Button Layout in the WRT54G, Version 3.1

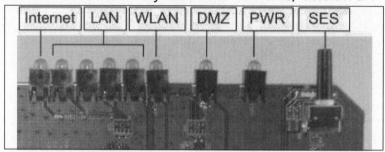

In Figure 1.14, you can see the LED lights for the WAN, LAN, and WLAN ports, and then the DMZ and power indicators. The button is the larger post all the way to the right. You can change this button programmatically to perform different functions, such as disabling your wireless connection when not in use.

Table 1.7 lists the specifications of the WRT54G, version 3.*x*.

Table 1.7 Specifications of the WRT54G, Version 3.*x*

CPU speed	200 MHz
RAM	16 MB
Flash	4 MB
Serial number prefix	CDF8 (version 3.0) CDF9 (version 3.1)

WRT54G, Version 4

The WRT54G, version 4, was the first router to integrate the CPU, Ethernet MAC, and Wireless MAC onto a single chip (SoC). The Broadcom BCM5352 series processor was utilized for this purpose and became the standard on most WRT54G series routers from this version forward (the GS model versions 4.0 and higher, and the WRT54GL versions 1.0 and higher, used this processor as well). This design was carried forward into the WRT54GL series routers; aside from a few small differences, such as the brand of memory, these routers are exactly the same. Table 1.8 lists the specifications of the WRT54G, version 4.0.

Table 1.8 Specifications of the WRT54G, Version 4.0

CPU speed	200 MHz
RAM	16 MB
Flash	4 MB
Serial number prefix	CDF0 CDF1

Tools & Traps…

Which Hardware Do I Have?

You'll see when we cover the hardware in version 4.0 of the WRT54G that the lines separating all the routers in this series moving forward will begin to blur. There are few notable differences between the WRT54G hardware after version 4.0 and the hardware in version 2.0 of the WRT54GS. To dig a bit deeper, it is important to understand some of the subtle differences, as they may be significant depending on which WRT54G hack you are trying to perform.

The WRT54G devices, in addition to other devices, store information in NVRAM related to the type of hardware. You can view this information by using the following commands to list the pertinent NVRAM variables, such as board information:

```
# nvram show | grep board | sort
size: 13076 bytes (19692 left)
boardflags2=0
boardflags=0x2558
boardnum=42
boardrev=0x10
boardtype=0x0467
```

You can then compare this information to the table provided by the OpenWrt project, located at http://wiki.openwrt.org/OpenWrtDocs/Hardware/Linksys/WRT54G, Section 1.1.8, "Table Summary." First let's look at the *boardflags* variable and find it on the table. We can see that WRT54G versions 4.0 through 6.0 have this same value. Upon closer inspection, we can see that the same versions also have the same *boardnum* and *boardtype*. However, the *boardrev* in our case is *0x10* and it corresponds to a version 4.0 WRT54G, according to the table. We just established that the WRT54GL is the same hardware, and we can verify this as the variables in the preceding example did, in fact, come from a WRT54GL (version 1.1, to be specific). It is not possible to differentiate between the version 5.0 and 6.0 models with this table.

Another important detail is the process version. You can obtain the processor type and version by running the following command:

```
# grep cpu /proc/cpuinfo
cpu model               : BCM3302 V0.8
```

Versions 4.0 through 6.0 of the WRT54G also share the same CPU model: the BCM3302, version 0.8.

WRT54G, Versions 5.0 and 6.0

For a brief moment, the entire WRT54G hacking community stood in shock and awe when Linksys released the WRT54G, version 5.0. Indeed, the company ended a long series of hackable routers by introducing a model based on VxWorks rather than Linux, but it quickly followed this with the release of the WRT54GL, which was intended for WRT54G hackers. However, versions 5.0 and 6.0 of the WRT54G routers contain several significant architectural changes, as listed here and shown in Figure 1.15:

- **Decreased flash** The amount of flash was reduced from 4 MB to 2 MB. This was a major factor in the crippling of the device, as it greatly limits the amount of software that users can install.

- **Decreased memory** The memory was also cut in half, from 16 MB to 8 MB. Even before this change, you could easily push the WRT54G platform to its limits with respect to available memory, and cutting it in half makes the problem twice as bad. For example, the popular port scanning tool, Nmap, has a difficult time running on the WRT54G platform, even with 16 MB of RAM.

- **Transition to the VxWorks operating system** The final blow was the migration from a Linux-based operating system to VxWorks, a proprietary OS from Wind River used in embedded devices which include printers, private branch exchange (PBX) telephone systems, digital cameras, and even the Mars Exploration Rover! VxWorks is a true Real Time Operating System (RTOS), which means it is intended to have a small footprint for embedded devices, yet still provide a multitasking environment.

Other than these changes, there are few notable differences between the devices. The type of RAM used is slightly different, with version 5.0 using an ISSI brand and version 6.0 using Samsung-branded memory. Most other models use an Intel-branded flash device, whereas versions 5.0 and 6.0 use a different brand. It has been speculated that the company transitioned to this platform to reduce manufacturing costs.

On the plus side, you can still hack these versions! And thanks to a great effort from some dedicated folks in the WRT54G hacking community, doing so is actually a fairly simple process. Please note, you will be limited to the DD-WRT micro edition; however, we believe this firmware has much more to offer than VxWorks. We provide full and detailed upgrade instructions in Chapter 2.

Table 1.9 lists the specifications of versions 5.0, 5.1, and 6.0 of the WRT54G.

Figure 1.15 The Internals of the WRT54G, Version 6.0

Table 1.9 Specifications of the WRT54G, Versions 5.0, 5.1, and 6.0

CPU speed	200 MHz
RAM	8 MB
Flash	2 MB
Serial number prefix	Version 5 CDFB CDFC
	Version 6 CDFD

Are You 0wned?

Applying the Latest Linksys
Firmware for the WRT54G, Versions 5.0 and 6.0

The average consumer will purchase a router, and many will end up with a version 5.0 or 6.0 router, plug it in, make it work, and forget about it. Usually somewhere down the line, problems begin to occur. Maybe the router is locked up and you have to power-cycle it before it becomes operational again. Maybe operation is slow, either randomly or on an ongoing basis. What could all this mean?

The most common cause is that the firmware has not been kept up-to-date, and with respect to the version 5.0 and 6.0 platforms, the consequences can be truly disastrous. Because these models were the first to use the new VxWorks-based firmware, they tend to contain bugs. In fact, the initial firmware version was 1.00.0, and those of us familiar with software development life cycles know that 1.0 revisions are typically full of bugs, and this is no exception. The release notes provided by Linksys document numerous bug fixes as the version numbers increase. Some of the fixes include:

- Resolves issues with slow downstream speeds
- Resolves issues with instability when using BitTorrent
- Resolves SSH issue of disassociation due to inactivity
- Resolves issue with accessing online game servers

And those are just a sample of the problems that have been fixed! The first one, slow downstream speeds, is pretty obvious and could also be related to the problem of instability when using BitTorrent. We will provide some tips and details on these issues throughout the book; for now, note that you can solve most of these issues simply by installing third-party firmware. Losing your terminal (SSH, Telnet) connections can be very annoying, and it is a problem most often immediately reported by end users, in addition to not being able to play games online.

Another excellent reason to stay current with firmware upgrades is security. On August 4, 2006, a security researcher going by the name of "Ginsu Rabbit" posted a vulnerability to the Full-Disclosure mailing list that describes two vulnerabilities in the VxWorks 1.00.9 firmware release (http://lists.grok.org.uk/pipermail/full-disclosure/2006-August/048495.html). One of these vulnerabilities allows anyone with HTTP Web GUI access to make configuration changes to your router. Linksys silently fixed the vulnerability in the 1.00.10 firmware release (by *silent*, we mean it was not mentioned in any of the release notes). An attacker would need access to the LAN network assigned to the WRT54G in order to exploit this vulnerability. However, an attacker can easily craft a Web page that sends the crafted HTTP request to the router to exploit

Continued

the vulnerability. Code examples that implement this exploit are readily available on the Web.

Keeping up-to-date with your firmware is extremely important, especially if you are running a version 5.0 or higher WRT54G that runs the VxWorks firmware, as it tends to be very buggy. We hope you decide to experiment with third-party firmware as well, which you also need to keep up-to-date. The following Web site keeps track of the latest firmware releases for many different hardware platforms and firmware projects, including the WRT54G, versions 5.0 and higher, running VxWorks, and the stock Linksys US firmware versions:

www.linksysinfo.org/forums/showthread.php?t=47159

Although you may be good at keeping your firmware up-to-date, maybe your friends and neighbors are not. Be a responsible citizen and help them out by applying the latest firmware for them. Deep down, they will be eternally grateful, and probably call you a lot less often.

WRT54G, Version 7.0

Little is known about this model at the time of this writing. There are reports that it has 2 MB of flash memory and 4 MB of RAM. According to specifications, it uses an Atheros AR2317 chipset, which is still an 802.11b/g-only radio. Although the move to an Atheros-based chipset is intriguing; the reduced flash/RAM will inhibit the hackability of this platform.

WRT54GL Models

Linksys has proposed that its WRT54GL series of routers should appeal to the hacking community, and therefore most of the hacks covered in this book will be based on this platform. The average cost is between $59 and $79; slightly higher than the average WRT54G with the same hardware (which is one of the complaints we hear about this series). For the extra cost, you get a model that is intended to be hacked; however, Linksys will not offer support for third-party firmware. We will cover this model extensively throughout the book, documenting its internals, showing you how to install firmware on it, taking it apart, and showing you where to add SD card readers, JTAG cables, and serial ports. If you plan to do some hacking on the WRT54G platform, this is the model for you. Table 1.10 lists the specifications of versions 1.0 and 1.1 of the WRT54GL.

Table 1.10 Specifications of the WRT54GL, Versions 1.0 and 1.1

CPU speed	200 MHz
RAM	16 MB
Flash	4 MB
Serial number prefix	Version 1.0: CL7A
	Version 1.1: CL7B

WRT54GL, Version 1.0

This is the first release of the WRT54GL series router, and it is almost identical to the WRT54G, version 4.0. The only difference we could find visually was a slightly different part number on the memory chip, the Hynix 166 MHz DDR SDRAM chip.

WRT54GL, Version 1.1

There are very minor differences between the version 1.0 and 1.1 WRT54GL routers. The processor appears to have a slightly different model number associated with it; however, we could find no documentation that describes the actual differences. One notable difference is the software loaded on the devices out of the box. Version 1.1 has a slightly newer firmware, which does not matter because our goal is to replace it with something better anyhow!

Linksys WRT54GS Hardware

WRT54GS Models

The WRT54GS series of routers are very similar to the WRT54G routers in many ways. These similarities include the physical characteristics, as well as many of the electrical components. In the following sections, we will indicate the capabilities of the WRT54GS series of routers.

The WRT54GS series of routers are typically more desirable for modification, as most routers in this series contain double the amount of RAM and flash of the WRT54G series. As we mentioned earlier, this will provide more computing and storage resources.

One unique feature of the WRT54GS series of routers is a technology known as SpeedBooster. SpeedBooster is the Linksys branding for the technology known as AfterBurner, developed by Broadcom, the maker of many of the chips in the WRT54G series of routers. AfterBurner is a technology that allows for increased wireless speeds. With a typical 802.11g wireless connection, the maximum theoretical operating speed is 54 megabits per second (Mbps). Broadcom claims that with the use of SpeedBooster/AfterBurner, an 802.11g connection can operate at a theoretical throughput of up to 125 Mbps! It should be noted that AfterBurner will deliver performance gains only when utilizing a compatible client device that also contains AfterBurner technology.

The AfterBurner technology has been licensed to a number of companies for use in their wireless products, including Belkin, Buffalo, Dell, Gateway, HP, Motorola, and U.S. Robotics. In addition, a number of companies have rebranded the AfterBurner technology under their own names; however, they are interoperable. Clearly, we would not be tied to only Linksys wireless cards to obtain higher-speed 802.11g connectivity.

Notes from the Underground...

SpeedBooster/AfterBurner Available Only on GS Models?

Linksys does charge a premium of about $20 for the GS series of routers, ostensibly for the inclusion of the SpeedBooster technology, and the increased flash and RAM. Through our descriptions of the GS models in this section, you will probably note extensive similarities in the chipsets. Our original thought when we began writing this book was that SpeedBooster/AfterBurner was a function of the chipsets themselves, and we figured that if there was some overlapping hardware, the technology would be available on both the G and GS models. We were partially right.

SpeedBooster/AfterBurner is supported on all of the Broadcom BCM4712 and BCM5352 processors, and on the BCM2050 and BCM2050KML wireless chips. However, this support is not a function of the hardware; it is based on the wireless driver provided by Broadcom on the GS units! As Broadcom does not provide the source code for the drivers, developers are forced to utilize the precompiled drivers included with the stock Linksys firmware. The OpenWRT (and DD-WRT) developers have included the GS wireless driver by default in the firmware installations. As a result, SpeedBooster/AfterBurner can be enabled on G series routers!

The Broadcom driver does verify that the hardware can support SpeedBooster/AfterBurner through the reading of some NVRAM variables. Under many third-party firmware installations, we can change our NVRAM settings through the command-line interface. We will cover the use of NVRAM in more depth in Chapter 3.

In order to enable SpeedBooster/AfterBurner support on most G series routers, we need to set the *boardflags* NVRAM variable from the default value of 0x0188 to 0x0388. After setting the proper *boardflags* variable and reloading the wireless driver (*wl*), we then need to tell the wireless driver to enable SpeedBooster/AfterBurner. We can accomplish these steps with the following commands:

```
nvram set boardflags=0x0388
nvram commit
rmmod wl
insmod wl
wl gmode 6
```

After you have issued these commands, SpeedBooster/AfterBurner should be enabled on your G series router.

WRT54GS, Version 1

The WRT54GS, version 1.0, much like version 1.1 of the WRT54G, contains the BCM2050 wireless chipset, which will be prevalent throughout most of the WRT54G models.

With the introduction of the WRT54GS series, the Cisco Systems logo has been a fixture, as the WRT54GS models were released after Cisco acquired Linksys. Additionally, all of the GS models utilize the same 12V DC 1.0 A power supply, prevalent in many other G and all GS models.

The LED lights in the front of the device are very similar to those on the G models, and they exhibit the same characteristics. They blink when there is activity and stay solid green to show a link. The power light should be solid green; if it is blinking, there could be trouble. Many other LED states indicate problems, or opportunities to do something, such as push the Reset button. We will cover all of these throughout this book.

This model is also the only WRT54GS router to utilize the ADMTec ADM6996L chipset to power the Ethernet switch built into the router. Other unique characteristics of this GS model are that Linksys has elected to use 32 MB of Etrontech SDRAM.

Version 1.0 of the GS model also features 8 MB of Intel flash memory and the Broadcom BCM4712 processor. Table 1.11 lists the specifications of the WRT54GS, version 1.0.

Table 1.11 Specifications of the WRT54GS, Version 1.0

CPU speed	200 MHz
RAM	32 MB
Flash	8 MB
Serial number prefix	CGN0 CGN1

WRT54GS, Version 1.1

Although not a radical departure from version 1.0, there are some differences in version 1.1 of the WRT54GS. For example, Linksys opted to replace the SDRAM for DDR-SDRAM, utilizing a 32 MB Hynix module, and has dropped the ADM6996L Ethernet MAC in favor of the Broadcom BCM5325.

Version 1.1 still utilizes the Broadcom BCM4712 processor and the Broadcom BCM2050 wireless chipset, as well as 8 MB of Intel flash. Table 1.12 lists the specifications of the WRT54GS, version 1.1.

Table 1.12 Specifications of the WRT54GS, Version 1.1

CPU speed	200 MHz
RAM	32 MB
Flash	8 MB
Serial number prefix	CGN2

WRT54GS, Version 2.0

Additional hardware upgrades of the WRT54GS series introduce the SES button (and two associated LEDs) to the front panel of the GS series. The SES button is featured in all GS models from this version forward. The new SES button adds two LEDs, amber and white, on the board behind the button to indicate its status. Figure 1.16 shows the SES button.

Figure 1.16 The SES Button in the WRT54GS, Version 2.0

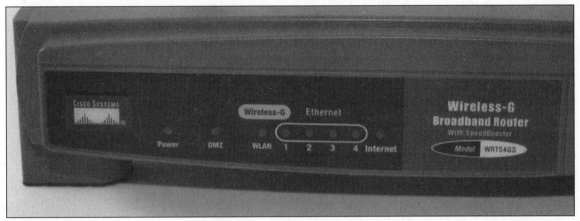

Except for the addition of SES button, version 2.0 of the WRT54GS is identical to its version 1.1 counterpart. The GS version still utilizes the Broadcom BCM4712 processor, 8 MB of Intel flash, 32 MB of Hynix DDR-SDRAM, the Broadcom BCM5325 Ethernet MAC, and the Broadcom BCM2050 wireless chipset. Table 1.13 lists the specifications of the WRT54GS, version 2.0.

Table 1.13 Specifications of the WRT54GS, Version 2.0

CPU speed	200 MHz
RAM	32 MB
Flash	8 MB
Serial number prefix	CGN3

WRT54GS, Version 2.1

There is one small change to the GS line with the 2.1 version of the WRT54GS: an update to the Broadcom BCM2050KML wireless chipset. Due to the proprietary nature of Broadcom's chips, it is unknown what the actual differences are between the BCM2050 and the BCM2050KML. Testing and implementation during the course of this book have not revealed any noticeable differences in functionality between the two chipsets.

The rest of the components in version 2.1 of the WRT54GS remain the same, including the SES button, the Broadcom BCM4712 processor, 8 MB of Intel flash, 32 MB of Hynix DDR-SDRAM, the Broadcom BCM5325 Ethernet MAC, and the Broadcom BCM2050 wireless chipset. Table 1.14 lists the specifications of the WRT54GS, version 2.1.

Table 1.14 Specifications of the WRT54GS, Version 2.1

CPU speed	200 MHz
RAM	32 MB
Flash	8 MB
Serial number prefix	CGN4

WRT54GS, Version 3.0

The WRT54GS, version 3.0, introduces a significant change in the design of the WRT54GS series of routers. This change replaces the Broadcom BCM4712 processor with the Broadcom BCM5352 processor. With this new processor, the Ethernet MAC is contained in the new BCM5352, and as a result, we no longer have a separate Ethernet MAC, nor do we have a BCM5325 chipset! The same applies to the Wireless MAC and the Broadcom BCM2050 wireless chipset. This consolidation of parts likely reduces the overall cost to manufacture the router. Even with the upgraded processor, the upgrade does not come at any speed increase, as the new BCM5352 still operates at 200 MHz. The real upgrade is found with the chip consolidation.

The rest of the components do remain the same, including the 8 MB of Intel flash, 32 MB of Hynix DDR–SDRAM, and continued inclusion of the SES button. Table 1.15 lists the specifications of the WRT54GS, version 3.0.

Table 1.15 Specifications of the WRT54GS, Version 3.0

CPU speed	200 MHz
RAM	32 MB
Flash	8 MB
Serial number prefix	CGN5

WRT54GS, Version 4.0

The WRT54GS, version 4.0, reveals a disappointing trend with the GS series. Version 4.0 features half of the flash and RAM of previous GS models. These routers have been reduced to 4 MB of Intel flash and 16 MB of Hynix RAM.

NOTE

Some version 4.0 models of the WRT54GS do contain 8 MB of Intel flash and 32 MB of Hynix RAM; however, Linksys elected not to create different hardware versions for each variety. Unfortunately, there is no method to determine these amounts based upon the serial number.

The rest of the components, aside from the flash and RAM, remain identical to those in version 3.0 of the WRT54GS, including the new BCM5352 processor and the inclusion of the SES button. Table 1.16 lists the specifications of the WRT54GS, version 4.0.

Table 1.16 Specifications of the WRT54GS, Version 4.0

CPU speed	200 MHz
RAM	16 MB
Flash	4 MB
Serial number prefix	CGN6

WRT54GS, Versions 5.0, 5.1, and 6.0

Much like version 5.0 of the WRT54G, the entire WRT54G hacking community stood in shock and awe when Linksys released the WRT54GS, version 5.0, and subsequent models. The new version ended a long series of hackable routers, but was quickly followed with the release of the WRT54GL, which was intended for WRT54G hackers. This version marked several significant changes to the WRT54GS architecture:

- **Decreased flash** The amount of memory was again reduced, this time from 4 MB to 2 MB. This was a major factor in the crippling of the device, as it greatly limits the amount of software you can install.

- **Decreased memory** The memory was also cut in half, this time from 16 MB to 8 MB. The WRT54GS platform could easily be pushed to its limits with respect to available memory in the 16 MB models, and cutting it in half makes the problem twice as bad.

- **Transition to the VxWorks operating system** This final blow was the migration from a Linux-based operating system to VxWorks, a proprietary OS from Wind River used in embedded devices which include printers, PBX telephone systems, digital cameras, and even the Mars Exploration Rover! VxWorks is a true RTOS, which means it is intended to have a small footprint for embedded devices, yet still provide a multitasking environment.

Additional differences include a slightly different type of RAM, with version 5.0 using the NECI brand and versions 5.1 and 6.0 using RAM from undefined manufacturers. Most other models use an Intel-branded flash module, whereas versions 5.0, 5.1, and 6.0 use a generic, unbranded chip. It has been speculated that the transition to this platform was to reduce manufacturing costs.

On the plus side, you can still hack these versions! And thanks to a great effort from some dedicated folks in the WRT54G hacking community, doing so is actually a fairly simple process. Please note, you will be limited to the DD-WRT micro edition; however, we believe this version of firmware has much more to offer than VxWorks. We cover this in more detail in Chapter 2.

Table 1.17 lists specifications for the WRT54GS, versions 5.0, 5.1, and 6.0.

Table 1.17 Specifications for the WRT54GS, Versions 5.0, 5.1, and 6.0

CPU speed	200 MHz
RAM	16 MB
Flash	2 MB
Serial number prefix	Version 5.0 CGN7
	Version 5.2 CGN8
	Version 6.0 CGN9

Other Linksys WRT54G Hardware to Hack

WRT54GC Models

This model router has only 1 MB of flash and 4 MB of RAM, and it uses a Marvell wireless and Ethernet chipset (not Broadcom). Unfortunately, given the hardware differences and greatly reduced amount of flash and RAM, this model does not lend itself to being very hackable. We mention it here to make you aware that you should not purchase this model unless you intend to use it as it comes out of the box (but what fun is that?).

WRTSL54GS Models

The WRTSL54GS model is very different from most other routers we will cover in this book. Figure 1.17 shows the router's internals, documenting the various components that comprise this device.

The most notable addition is the Universal Serial Bus (USB) controller, the NEC D720201 USB 1.0/2.0, which connects to the external USB port. The USB port was originally intended to let users attach USB hard drives to add external storage. However, using third-party firmware, we can attach all sorts of USB devices (including USB hard drives) to interact with, provided we have the appropriate software or drivers. The antennas on this model are very different as well. We are given only one antenna that is not easily interchangeable; in fact, it is soldered directly to the board, as shown in Figure 1.18. To account for the loss in signal, the wireless antenna is powered by a 21dBm amplifier, which should provide adequate coverage in most environments. For more information on antennas, including a full description of the power measurements, refer to Chapter 7.

Figure 1.17 WRTSL54GS Block Diagram

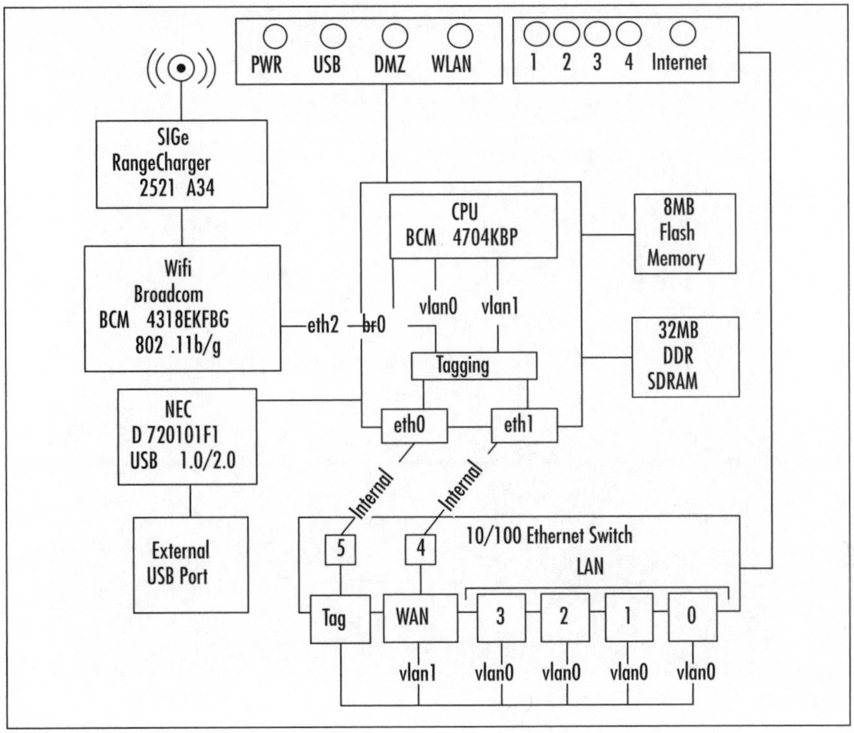

You will also notice that unlike the other WRT54G models, two adapters connect the CPU to the Ethernet switch on this model: eth0 and eth1. The WAN port is given its own physical interface, no longer sharing the same interface as the LAN. This will equate to better throughput and faster network speed through the router, applying to traffic that travels between the WAN port and any of the LAN assigned ports. The RAM and flash are among the highest capacity, with 8 MB of flash (version 1.0) and 32 MB of RAM. The CPU is also the fastest, using the BCM4704 chipset and a frequency of 266 MHz.

The outside appearance is drastically different. The rear view of the WRTSL54GS, as shown in Figure 1.19, contains the four LAN, WAN, USB, and power ports.

Figure 1.18 WRTSL54GS Internals

Figure 1.19 WRTSL54GS Rear View

The front view displays the LED lights, as shown in Figure 1.20, which are the same as the LEDs available in other models, except for the addition of the USB light. The USB light will be solid green if there is a device attached to it.

Figure 1.20 WRTSL54GS Front View

This model also includes the Cisco SES button; however, it is not labeled "Cisco". The button is yellow in color and is simply labeled "Secure Easy Setup," as shown in Figure 1.20.

TIP

If you have, or are planning to install, OpenWrt on this device and you wish to use the USB port to access a USB disk drive, you will need to install the appropriate software packages through the following commands:

ipkg install kmod-usb-ohci
ipkg install kmod-usb-storage
ipkg install kmod-vfat
Then you will have to reboot the device.

Table 1.18 lists the specifications of the WRTSL54GS, versions 1.0 and 2.*x*.

Table 1.18 Specifications of the WRTSL54GS, Versions 1.0 and 2.*x*

CPU speed	266 MHz	
RAM	32 MB	
Flash	Version 1.0	8 MB
	Version 2.00.5	4 MB
Serial number prefix	Version 1.0	CJK0
	Version 2.00.5	CJK1

WRT54G Buyer's Guide

One of the questions we hear most often is "Which WRT54G should I purchase?" The answer is always "It depends." Of course, if we kept answering this question with "It depends," we would not be winning any popularity contests anytime soon, nor would that help anyone. In response to this question, and to help you make more informed purchasing decisions, we have created a chart that you can reference when buying a WRT54G and subsequently deciding which firmware to install on it.

Table 1.19 lists four columns, the first being "User Type." In order to get the most out of your WRT54G and associated hacking activities, you need to identify with yourself. Without getting too philosophical, we merely want you to put yourself in a category that best defines the ways in which you will use WRT54Gs. You could also fit into multiple categories. For example, while at home you may need a stable and secure wireless network to which you can connect and do your work. Your day job may be that of a penetration tester, so you can review the recommendations in that category as well. The next column is "Features Desired," where we attempt to list the main features we think each user type will want. This is based on feedback we have received over the past several months, and our experience in general. Based on the data we include in the "User Type" and "Features Desired" columns, we list the recommended WRT54G models, under "Recommended Model(s)" and "Recommended Firmware".

We then expand on each user type and offer some suggestions and recommendations for various network setups. Some may seem elaborate or complex; however, they are built using only the projects we cover in this book. You may choose to implement them as shown, or implement only some of the suggestions. Whatever you decide, we hope the following information provides a useful guide for all of your WRT54G hacking needs.

Table 1.19 WRT54G Buyer's Guide

User Type	Features Desired	Recommended Model(s)	Recommended Firmware
Average user	Standard wireless access point, firewall appliance to protect cable modem setup	WRT54G, version 5.0, 6.0, or 7.0	Linksys, DD-WRT micro, HyperWRT
Power user	Increase signal strength, better performance using WPA-PSK or WPA2-PSK	WRT54GL	OpenWrt, HyperWRT
Typical geek	Tinker, play with different firmware images, experiment with many different features	WRT54GL; WRT54GS, versions 1.0 through 4.0; WRT54G, versions 1.0 through 4.0	OpenWrt
Speed freak	Installing many different software packages, penetration testing, intrusion detection	WRT54GS, versions 1.0 through 3.0; WRTSL54GS	OpenWrt
Hardware hacker	Adding serial ports, SD cards, antennas, general GPIO usage	WRT54G, versions 1.0 through 4.0; WRT54GL; WRT54GS, versions 1.0 through 4.0; WRTSL54GS	OpenWrt
Penetration tester	Using Nmap, Nessus, Snort, Kismet, and so on	WRT54GS, versions 1.0 through 3.0; WRTSL54GS; WRT54GL	FairuzaWRT, OpenWrt
Bargain shopper	Best deal for the money, minimal hacking features, ability to adjust signal strength with third-party firmware	WRT54G, version 5.0, 6.0, or 7.0	Linksys, DD-WRT
IT professional	Remote VPN, wireless troubleshooting.	WRT54GL; WRTSL54GS	OpenWrt

Average User

The average user of the WRT54G is someone whose primary usage is to check email and browse the Web. Such users may have only one computer—or two if there is a laptop in use. A laptop may also be the primary computer. They may require one Ethernet port for the home PC which will plug in directly. Wireless may also be required for the laptop, which will connect via the wireless interface. The network may look as shown in Figure 1.21.

Figure 1.21 Average User Network Layout

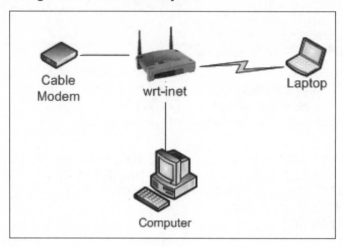

Recommended Models

We recommend that average users purchase the off-the-shelf, standard Linksys WRT54G, version 5.0, 6.0, or 7.0. This device will serve as a firewall, protecting the home PC and/or laptop from the Internet. It will also serve as the DHCP server, providing IP addresses for the one or two systems that are connected to it. The wireless network should be configured with WPA-PSK or, preferably, WPA2-PSK (if the client wireless card and driver support it) to provide adequate security.

Notes from the Underground...

Peer-to-Peer Traffic and the WRT54G

If you have ever used peer-to-peer software with your Linksys router (or other similar routers), you may have encountered a problem described by many as "freezed connections" or "frozen routers." One person even suggests that increasing your transmit power to 200 mW will help to solve the problem! (Please do not attempt to do this without first reading this book and the countless warnings about increasing signal

Continued

strength.) Even more frustrating are the people who try to blame it all on Linksys and give its routers a bad name. Rest assured that more people misunderstand the problem than understand it.

To understand the problem you have to understand some Transmission Control Protocol/Internet Protocol (TCP/IP) fundamentals and how peer-to-peer networking protocols work. All TCP communications (a.k.a. sessions) have a lifetime associated with them, sometimes called a **timeout**. In addition to timeouts, devices have limits on the number of connections they can handle simultaneously. These two factors are important for devices running firewalls. All the Linux-based devices we will be talking about throughout this book use iptables (Linux netfilter). iptables uses connection tracking to limit the number of sessions and timeouts.

Peer-to-peer software typically creates more simultaneous sessions than most other software. When you start up peer-to-peer software, it connects to hundreds, sometimes thousands, of hosts looking for other machines that have information about the file you are looking for, or portions of the file you are looking for. It's generally a noisy protocol, which in turns loves to create large numbers of sessions, some of which even cause problems with enterprise-level firewalls.

The default settings on Linksys routers using older versions of the stock firmware would, among other things, set the default established session timeout to *five days*. After some period of time, your router will run out of connections and stop passing traffic. Admittedly, Linksys did not do a very good job of tuning these default settings. Even some of the third-party firmware packages include settings that cause the routers to hang. However, we did not find that this problem existed in OpenWrt.

In any case, the fix for this problem equates to the following commands on older WRT54G firmware that uses Linux kernel versions previous to 2.4.23:

```
# echo "600 1800 120 60 120 120 10 60 30 120" >
/proc/sys/net/ipv4/ip_conntrack_tcp_timeouts
```

These values correspond to TCP/IP parameters as follows:

Timeout (Seconds)	TCP/IP Connection State
600	NONE
1,800	ESTABLISHED
120	SYN_SENT
60	SYN_RECV
120	FIN_WAIT
120	TIME_WAIT
10	CLOSE
60	CLOSE_WAIT
30	LAST_ACK

The preceding TCP/IP parameters control many of the properties and timeouts associated with TCP/IP connections. For example, "60 – SYN SECV" refers to how long

Continued

the operating system should wait for a TCP three-way handshake to complete once the initial SYN packet is received. For more information, refer to http://forum.utor-rent.com/viewtopic.php?pid=29675.

Firmware using kernel version 2.4.23 or later should change the following:

```
# echo '4096' > /proc/sys/net/ip4v/netfilter/ip_conntrack_max
```

The preceding command puts a value of 4096 as the maximum number of connections that the kernel can track. A "connection" in this case is any attempt to initiate a TCP/IP connection to another host that requires passing through the WAN port of the router. If you are using OpenWrt, the default value is already set to an even higher value of 5953. For DD-WRT, the default value is set to 512. You may want to experiment with these values and/or check the current connection count. You can check the number of current connections by using the following command in OpenWrt and DD-WRT:

```
# wc -l /proc/net/ip_conntrack
```

Although these configuration changes are not the only ones mentioned to fix "peer-to-peer problems," they are the most effective as they address the root cause of the problem. Each distribution has its own take on this problem. For further information, refer to the following links:

OpenWrt (http://forum.openwrt.org/viewtopic.php?pid=39508) OpenWrt Forum, *"How to Debug router crash & reboots?"*

DD-WRT (www.dd-wrt.com/wiki/index.php/Router_Slowdown) *"Router Slowdown"*

HyperWRT/Thibor (www.utorrent.com/faq.php#Special_note_for_users_with_Linksys_WRT54 G_GL_GS_routers) *"Special note for users with Linksys WRT54G/GL/GS routers, there are severe problems with them when running any P2P app (read for fix)"*

Recommended Firmware

No third-party firmware is required to perform the basic functions described earlier, and the stock Linksys firmware is more than capable, provided it is the latest version and the revision is kept up-to-date with regular firmware upgrades. Average users will most likely run the standard Linksys firmware. However, the most common feature in third-party firmware sought after by this user class is the ability to increase the wireless signal strength. Many users will place an access point in their homes and will want to connect wirelessly throughout. Due to the dynamic nature of 802.11 wireless networks, and the high level of interference that could occur, signal strength may not always be optimal. An increase in radio transmit power could solve some of these issues (although not all them) and is more cost-effective than adding large antennas. This feature is, of course, not available in the stock Linksys firmware (Linksys most likely does not want to be held responsible for users melting their WRT54G routers). However, an upgrade to DD-WRT micro edition on the WRT54G, versions 5.0, 6.0, and 7.0, is an excellent way to increase signal strength and gain features not available in the stock Linksys firmware. Throughout this book, we will warn you of the dangers of increasing radio transmit power to avoid damaging your router.

Power User

A power user is someone who may have a desktop computer and a laptop, or even two desktop computers and a laptop. She uses the Internet to download music and movies (legally, of course) and to transfer large video files, and she allows others to use her system to surf the Web or use the Internet in some way at any given time. The power user may also use some sort of home media extender and have one or more video game console systems.

Recommended Models

For this setup, we recommend purchasing at least two WRT54GL series routers. Two routers will help to separate wireless traffic (and the associated processing required to perform encryption/decryption) from wired traffic. The WRT54GL also provides the option of upgrading firmware, which will allow for better performance on its own, and tuning, if necessary. Also, with third-party firmware, you will be able to utilize the VLAN features inside the router to separate traffic, and numerous other features to enhance your setup. Figure 1.22 shows what this setup may look like.

Figure 1.22 Power User Network Layout

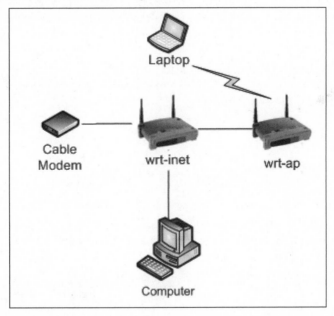

Figure 1.22 shows one WRT54GL, called "wrt-inet," connected via an Ethernet cable to the cable modem. This would connect to the WAN port on the WRT54GL. Connected to the LAN ports are the home computer and another WRT54G, labeled "wrt-ap". "wrt-ap" is placed on a separate VLAN from the home computer. This allows "wrt-ap" to provide wireless connectivity to the

laptop, passing it along the Ethernet connection to "wrt-inet" for Internet access. This setup helps increase performance by putting all of the wireless processing, including encryption and decryption of wireless frames, on the "wrt-ap" access point.

Recommended Firmware

Because a power user may not be a computer professional proficient in command-line usage, we recommend DD-WRT be installed on both of these routers. It will easily allow you to set up a WPA-PSK wireless network, and separate traffic through VLANs via the Web interface.

Typical Geek

The typical geek is someone who has everything in the power user setup, and more, including the urge/need/desire to tinker with the hardware and experiment with different software. First, let's define the practical need. A typical geek has multiple computers, laptops, gaming devices, media extenders, and/or handheld devices. Typical geeks also have typical geek friends who visit on occasion and require access to the Internet, either with a laptop or with a handheld device. The purpose of the visits could be specific as well, such as hosting a LAN party or recording a podcast (such as PaulDotCom Security Weekly, http://pauldotcom.com/security_weekly).

Recommended Models and Firmware

This setup can be pretty elaborate. For practical usage, we recommend WRT54GL model routers, which are made for hacking and support all the popular third-party firmware packages. The setup described in Figure 1.23 utilizes four WRT54GL routers.

Figure 1.23 Typical Geek Network Layout

Figure 1.23 shows four WRT54GL routers in use. The "wrt-inet" router is providing Internet access for the entire setup, in addition to providing connectivity between wired and wireless clients via the "wrt-ap" access point. Wireless connectivity is being provided by "wrt-ap" and is using WPA encryption. WPA-capable wireless clients are able to connect and get Internet access. The "wrt-bridge" WRT54GL is being used in bridging mode, with the wireless capabilities being used as a client to "wrt-ap" to provide Internet access for a gaming system. The fourth WRT54GL is labeled "wrt-CP" and is a captive portal implementing technology similar to WiFi hotspots (such as T-Mobile hotspots). "wrt-CP" has the sole purpose of providing Internet access for guests. The connection from "wrt-CP" to "wrt-inet" is an Ethernet connection and could conceivably be put on a separate VLAN to prevent guests from accessing the internal network. The firmware recommended for this setup is OpenWrt.

Speed Freak

If it's speed you're after, we have just the router for you. You are considered a speed freak if you are planning to make the most out of one router and want it to be fast for a variety of tasks. These tasks could include using it for general Internet access, or experimenting with the numerous software packages that have been ported to the WRT54G platform, such as Asterisk, OpenVPN, Snort, or Nessus. There are also uses for penetration testing, which have dedicated third-party firmware installations such as Fairuza-WRT.

Recommended Models and Firmware

Versions 1.0 through 3.0 of the WRT54GS contain the most flash and the most RAM of any other models. They have a whopping 8 MB of flash and 32 MB of RAM. If you plan to run memory-hungry applications such as the ones listed earlier, this is the router for you. The firmware recommended for this setup is OpenWrt.

Hardware Hacker

The hardware hacker is someone who wants to push the physical limits of the WRT54G platform. Examples of hardware hacking include overclocking (which usually requires adding your own heat-sync and fan to the processor), adding additional antennas, adding serial ports, adding more flash memory, and even adding USB ports.

Recommended Models and Firmware

Hardware hackers can really do all the hardware hacking they wish with any of the WRT54G series routers. However, the type of hack you are trying to perform may require a specific model and version number, so be certain to research the hack in advance. All of the hardware hacks in this book will indicate the proper model and version number required to do the hack. As general guidance, the firmware recommended for this setup is OpenWrt.

Penetration Tester

This is a relatively unexplored usage of the WRT54G series routers, and one we wish to explore throughout this book. The challenges presented to today's penetration testers are much different from those of years ago, and we believe the WRT54G series routers can help. The WRT54G series routers with custom firmware can allow you to deploy wireless access points to trap clients, sit behind the organization's perimeter firewall, and act as a gateway for your attacks, sniff traffic off the wireless network, map the wireless network, map the internal wired network, and perform various other tasks to help with your assessments.

Recommended Models and Firmware

As a penetration tester, the activities for which you may want to use your WRT54G require the most RAM and flash, so the WRT54GS model routers, versions 1.0 through 3.0, are well suited to the task. Also, the WRTSL54GS router has a good amount of RAM and flash, in addition to a USB port, so it can be more flexible and allow you to perform even more tasks remotely (such as analyze the 2.4 GHz spectrum, perform Bluetooth hacking, and even perform RFID analysis). The firmware recommended for this setup is OpenWrt and, from a security perspective, Fairuza-WRT.

Bargain Shopper

You're a bargain shopper if you want all the features and technology, but do not want to spend a dime more than you have to. We very much admire your type, as we purchase many WRT54G series routers and are encouraging you, the reader, to do the same.

Recommended Models and Firmware

If you're after deals, the WRT54G model routers, versions 5.0, 6.0, and 7.0, seem to have the best price point. You can typically find them on sale, usually after a rebate, for $39. There are many ways to shop for deals on WRT54G series hardware. What follows is a list that will help guide you:

- **Your local computer store** This can be a good place to look; pay special attention to the Sunday paper advertisements.

- **Online Web sites** Many online merchants carry all of the WRT54G series devices. Some popular ones are www.amazon.com, www.buy.com, and www.newegg.com.

- **eBay** eBay is the best place to find older model routers (even internationally). Some even include the original box, with the best being an unopened package, proving the router has never been used. Older routers will actually cost more money, especially the WRT54GS, versions 1.0 through 3.0, which were selling for around $80 at the time of this writing. If you do plan to purchase WRT54G hardware on eBay, be certain to beware of eBay scams and use caution as you would with any other auction.

- **Your local craigslist** craigslist (www.craigslist.org) is an online classified ads Web site that will typically have listings in your area. The URL for your area would be <*your city*>.craigslist.org. For example, http://providence.craigslist.org is the Web site for this author's local area (several people were selling Linksys routers there at the time of this writing). It even provides international links. For example, for Spain the Web page is http://geo.craigslist.org/iso/es.

■ **Neighbor/family/friend** Have you ever heard the expression "One man's trash is another man's treasure"? This couldn't be truer when speaking of Linksys wireless routers. Many people are willing to trade or simply get rid of their WRT54G series hardware. Consider this scenario: You've found a version 5.0 or version 6.0 series WRT54G on sale for $40. You know someone who has an older version 2.0 WRT54G series router. He may want to get rid of his old router (it's old and dusty, and the warranty has expired). This is a golden opportunity for you to trade the brand-new router still in the box for the older one with more flash and RAM. You might be asking about the warranty on the old router; we're just going to show how to violate the warranty anyway, so don't lose sleep over it!

TIP

There are many places to shop for electronics online, and each online retailer will always run its share of specials and deals. These can be great places to find a deal on the WRT54G series hardware. To aid you in your search, here is a list of Web sites that track deals being offered by online merchants:

www.dealmac.com Dealmac, by far, has the best slogan of all the deal Web sites: "How to go broke saving money." It offers a steady stream of deals on all electronic goods on the Internet, including computers and, more important, wireless routers. Using its search feature, search for "wrt54g" and stare in amazement at all of the wonderful deals.

www.techbargains.com This Web site offers a huge assortment of tech deals, is very timely, and even has hooks to eBay.

www.slickdeals.net This is a daily deals Web site, which not only offers online deals, but also will inform you of deals in newspapers, coupons, and other nononline deal happenings.

http://digg.com/tech_deals Using the power of the "collective," Digg users post deals they have found for all to see. Most Digg users are geeks, so this Web site typically has some of the best tech deals going. However, get there fast, as either these will be limited in quantity or the online shopping Web site will suffer from the "DiggEffect" and stop responding due to the sheer volume of visitors.

Each of the preceding Web sites also has an RSS feed that you can subscribe to that will push the deals to your computer if you have an RSS reader. More advanced RSS readers will let you search all feeds for a particular keyword, such as "wrt54g," so you can always be informed when deals are happening for your favorite router.

Resources

www.linuxdevices.com/news/NS4729641740.html An excellent article announcing the release of the WRT54GL, including quotes from a Linksys executive on the success of the WRT54G platform.

www.wifinetnews.com/archives/006101.html More coverage of the WRT54GL release, VxWorks, and Linksys hardware hacking.

http://en.wikipedia.org/wiki/WRT54G The Wikipedia page covering the WRT54G, including a complete table of all the different versions, including ones not covered in this book.

http://wiki.openwrt.org/TableOfHardware The listing of hardware supported by the OpenWrt project, including the WRT54G models.

www.linksysinfo.org/forums/showthread.php?t=47124 The now infamous article, "Autopsy: Linksys WRT54G and WRT54GS Hardware Versions Under the Knife," which contains some of the most detailed information about the WRT54G series hardware, with full pictures.

http://wiki.openwrt.org/OpenWrtDocs/Hardware/Linksys/WRT54GL The OpenWrt project's page dedicated to development and support of the WRT54GL series hardware.

http://wiki.openwrt.org/OpenWrtDocs/Hardware/Linksys/WRT54G The OpenWrt project's page dedicated to development and support of the WRT54G series hardware.

http://wiki.openwrt.org/OpenWrtDocs/Hardware/Linksys/WRTSL54GS The OpenWrt project's page dedicated to development and support of the WRTSL54GS series hardware.

http://wiki.openwrt.org/OpenWrtDocs/Hardware/Linksys/WRT54GS The OpenWrt project's page dedicated to development and support of the WRT54GS series hardware.

www.bitsum.com/openwiking/owbase/ow.asp?WRT54G An article focused on overclocking the WRT54G, specifically the WRT54G, version 4.0, using a BCM3302 version 0.8 processor.

www.hynix.com/datasheet/eng/dram/details/dram_02_HY5DU281622ET.jsp Hynix semiconductor page which contains the technical specifications to the memory used in many WRT54G models, including the WRT54GL.

www.necel.com/usb/en/product/upd720101.html The product page for the NEC processor that handles the USB subsystem on the WRTSL54GS.

www.sige.com/wireless/se_2520_wlan.html The product page from SIGe that details the specifications for the wireless front-end module on the WRTSL54GS.

www.linksysinfo.org/forums/archive/index.php?t-41153.html A posting to the Linksysinfo.org forums that lists the different WRT54G/GS devices and their internal parts.

www.wrtrouters.com/documents/wrt54g/v7 Information and photos of the WRT54G, version 7.0.

www.linux-mips.org/wiki/Broadcom_SOCs A complete write-up and extensive resource for all Broadcom SoC hardware.

www.hotchips.org/archives/hc15/2_Mon/11.broadcom.pdf Detailed specifications on the Broadcom BCM2050 wireless radio (PowerPoint presentation in PDF format).

Solutions Fast Track

Our Approach to This Book

- ☑ Please read this chapter first, it will help you decide which Linksys router to purchase, and previously unknown features about any Linksys WRT54G routers that you currently own.

- ☑ We provide you with real-world examples of how to use WRT54G routers throughout the different projects in this book.

- ☑ "Hacking" refers to the way in which we use something for a purpose other than what it was originally intended. Always get written permission from appropriate parties before you engage in performing security assessments.

History of the Linksys WRT54G

- ☑ The Linksys WRT54G series routers have been available since 2002, and have sold well.

- ☑ Linksys used modified GPL source code, and in early 2003 was forced to release this to the public due to Andrew Miklas? discovery of this practice

- ☑ Once the source code to the WRT54G was released, many people began to create their own firmware and cross-compile applications.

Linksys WRT54G Series Hardware

- ☑ All WRT54G series routers have common features, such as Flash, RAM, RP-TNC antenna connectors, CPU, Ethernet MAC, Wireless MAC, and wireless radios.

- ☑ All WRT54G series routers use a Broadcom MIPS CPU.

- ☑ The model, version, and serial number can be obtained from the sticker on the underside of the device.

- ☑ The WRT54G, version 1.0, was the only WRT54G series router to use a mini PCI slot for the wireless card.

- ☑ The WRT54G, version 2.2, came with 32 MB of RAM; however, Linksys activated only 16 MB of RAM in its default configuration.

☑ The WRT54G, version 4.0, was the first device to combine the CPU, Wireless MAC, and Ethernet MAC onto a single chip (SoC, or System-on-Chip).

☑ The WRT54GL is produced by Linksys specifically for hacking.

☑ The WRTSL54GS contains the fastest processor (266 MHz) that we will cover in this book. It also offers a USB port and is the only router we will cover that does not use RP-TNC connectors for the wireless antennas.

WRT54G Buyer's Guide

☑ The average user might not require third-party firmware, and therefore use a WRT54G version 5.0 or 6.0. However, if such a user requires a boost in wireless signal strength, he can install the DD-WRT micro edition to gain this ability.

☑ Power users and typical geeks will want to purchase the WRT54GL model routers and use OpenWrt firmware.

☑ Speed freaks will want to purchase routers with the most memory and flash, so versions 1.0 through 3.0 of the WRT54GS, or the WRTSL54GS, are good choices.

☑ The hardware hacker should buy any WRT54G he can afford, as they all contain GPIO ports and can be hacked in some way, shape, or fashion.

Frequently Asked Questions

The following Frequently Asked Questions, answered by the authors of this book, are designed to both measure your understanding of the concepts presented in this chapter and to assist you with real-life implementation of these concepts. To have your questions about this chapter answered by the author, browse to **www.syngress.com/solutions** and click on the **"Ask the Author"** form.

Q: What is the difference between the WRT54G and WRT54GS?

A: There are few differences between the two models. However, the major difference is that most WRT54G models contain 16 MB of RAM and 4 MB of flash. Most WRT54GS models contain 32 MB of RAM and 8 MB of flash, and have the SpeedBooster/AfterBurner technology enabled by default.

Q: Why would I want to put third-party firmware on my WRT54G?

A: For the same reason people climb mountains?because you can! Also, you are able to unlock many of the hidden features inside your WRT54G series routers, such as the ability to adjust the wireless radio transmit power, access all of the firewall features, change the default port assignments, and install a wide variety of open source software.

Q: How do I know which version of the WRT54G I own?

A: You can determine your router version by looking at the underside of the device and reading the "Model No" field, using the first four characters of the serial number to cross-reference the table in this chapter, or comparing your *boardflags* NVRAM variables to the table located at http://wiki.openwrt.org/OpenWrtDocs/Hardware/Linksys/WRT54G, in Section 1.1.8, "Table Summary."

Q: Is there third-party firmware support for the WRTSL54GS?

A: Yes, this device has excellent support from the OpenWrt project. See http://wiki.openwrt.org/OpenWrtDocs/Hardware/Linksys/WRTSL54GS for more information.

Q: I have a WRT54G, version 5.0 or 6.0. Can I install third-party firmware on it?

A: Yes, you can, and we will cover this in Chapter 2. You will be limited to the DD-WRT micro edition, or OpenWrt micro edition, however.

Working with WRT54G Firmware

Solutions in this chapter:

- **Installing Third-Party Firmware**
- **Introduction to Firmware Used in This Book**
- **Other Firmware Worth Mentioning**

☑ **Summary**

☑ **Solutions Fast Track**

☑ **Frequently Asked Questions**

Introduction

This chapter will walk you through the various methods of installing third-party firmware on the Linksys WRT54G. This process is usually fairly simple, provided you verify certain information properly (such as router model and version) and follow the instructions *exactly* as they are written. Most of the problems people have when installing third-party firmware stem from loading the incorrect firmware image for their hardware. Refer to Chapter 1 for more information about determining your hardware version.

> ## WARNING
>
> Installing third-party firmware on your Linksys WRT54G voids the manufacturer's warranty. If you "brick" your WRT54G (i.e., render it unusable), Linksys will not provide you with a new one. We do include full instructions on how to recover from a firmware upgrade gone bad in Chapter 8; however, do realize that you are doing this at your own risk and we hold no responsibility.

The installation instructions for the various firmware and WRT54G models may differ slightly, which is even more reason to be certain that you check and double-check your installation procedures. We promise that this effort will pay off. Although we call it "installing third-party firmware," some call it "upgrading firmware" because of the increased functionality. We cover quite a bit of the added functionality you will gain in this chapter, and continue to expand on it throughout this book. Your diligence and caution in the beginning will be worth it in the end.

Installing Third-Party Firmware

The following sections will show you how to install third-party firmware via the Web interface and the Trivial File Transfer Protocol (TFTP). We will also cover the concepts you will need in order to do an installation via a Joint Test Action Group (JTAG) cable in Chapter 7. Before you begin, refer to Table 2.1 as a guide to the potential upgrade paths.

Table 2.1 Firmware Installation Methods

Method	Description	Tools Required
Web interface	Use this method when upgrading from the Linksys firmware for the first time, because no TFTP server is readily available. This is the easiest way to apply firmware updates (either from Linksys or from a third party).	PC, Web browser, network cable

Continued

Table 2.1 continued Firmware Installation Methods

Method	Description	Tools Required
TFTP	Utilizing the CFE/PMON *boot_wait* checking process, you can upload new firmware via TFTP. This method works best once you have already installed third-party firmware and can manipulate the *boot_wait* settings.	PC, TFTP client, network cable, networking hub or switch (optional)
JTAG	This method is for recovery purposes only and you should use it only if you have a "brick," meaning there is no other way to recover the firmware. Applying firmware updates via JTAG can take several hours.	PC, JTAG cable, specialized software; refer to Chapter 7 for more information.

WARNING

To ensure a smooth and successfully upgrade you must abide by the following guidelines:

- Be certain that your router and computer are plugged into a reliable power source. This doesn't have to be a UPS powered outlet, although that would be the best option. Make certain that the plugs are firmly in place, and that the cords are not placed where someone could easily trip and unplug them. If you are using a laptop, be certain it is plugged in and not relying solely on battery power.
- Connect your computer to any local area network (LAN) port on the WRT54G using any standard Ethernet cable.
- Assign a static Internet Protocol (IP) address to your computer Ethernet adapter. *Do not* use a Dynamic Host Configuration Protocol (DHCP) address. Using a dynamic address could cause you to lose contact with the router. You may not retain the DHCP address long enough to communicate with the router. Even worse, you could lose your connection while transferring the new firmware images. This would "brick" your router. Refer to Chapter 8 for recovery procedures.

Installing Firmware via the Web Interface

The easiest way to install firmware images on a stock WRT54G is via the stock Linksys Web interface. Out of the box, this will be the place where the most casual user will begin the upgrade process. This method of installation is quite safe, as after the firmware is uploaded and before it is applied, the Linksys firmware checks the validity of the new firmware image. Certainly many of the other third-party firmware distributions will contain a Web interface for upgrading firmware, and will contain the same protections against corrupt firmware.

TIP

To avoid installing a corrupt firmware image on your WRT54G, be certain to verify the Message Digest 5 (MD5) hash. This ensures that the firmware image distributed from the developer's Web page is in fact the same as the one you've downloaded. For example, the OpenWrt project stores MD5 hashes of all firmware images for the Whiterussian RC6 version in http://downloads.openwrt.org/whiterussian/rc6/bin/md5sum. Here is a sample:

        4492c775f13b52eea90723b5e283079a openwrt-wrt54g3g-squashfs.bin
        53a5d69d7a7df2b7a578a90bca533e2b openwrt-wrt54g-squashfs.bin
        e941c3448b13d067af5a56270a088bd0 openwrt-wrt54gs-squashfs.bin

The MD5 hashes of all firmware images for the Whiterussian 0.9 version are available at http://downloads.openwrt.org/whiterussian/0.9/MD5SUMS.

To check the MD5 hash, say you downloaded opwrt-wrt54g-squashfs.bin. Now you need to use an MD5 hashing utility to generate the MD5 hash and compare it against what the OpenWrt project has published. Here is how you do that on various platforms:

Mac OS X:

$ md5 openwrt-wrt54g-squashfs.bin
MD5 (openwrt-wrt54g-squashfs.bin) = 53a5d69d7a7df2b7a578a90bca533e2b

Linux:

$ md5sum openwrt-wrt54g-squashfs.bin
53a5d69d7a7df2b7a578a90bca533e2b openwrt-wrt54g-squashfs.bin

Windows:

Download md5sums from http://www.pc-tools.net/win32/md5sums/
C:\tools>md5sums.exe "c:\downloads\openwrt-wrt54g-squashfs.bin"
MD5sums 1.2 freeware for Win9x/ME/NT/2000/XP+
Copyright (C) 2001-2005 Jem Berkes - http://www.pc-tools.net/
Type md5sums.exe -h for help
[Path] / filename   MD5 sum

[c:\downloads\]openwrt-wrt54g-squashfs.bin
53a5d69d7a7df2b7a578a90bca533e2b

Not only will this help to ensure that your firmware image is not corrupt, but also it will prevent you from contracting malware, in the form of a Trojan, by verifying that the file you've downloaded is in fact the same file published by the OpenWrt project. Although it's not 100 percent guaranteed against malware, it is still an important step to take.

You will want to be certain that if you've made changes to the Linksys firmware—in other words, you were not taking it out of the box for the first time—you restore to factory defaults. You can do this from the Web interface by going to your router, http://<IP address of Router> (typically http://192.168.1.1), logging in, and going to **Administration | Factory Defaults** (see Figure 2.1).

Figure 2.1 Resetting to Factory Defaults

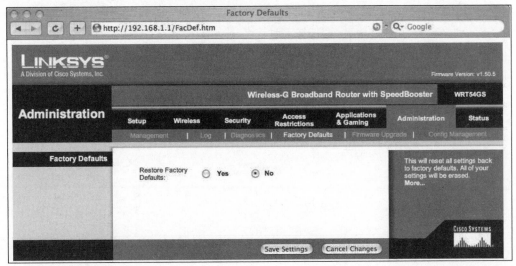

Now click the radio button labeled **Yes**, and then click the **Save Settings button**. You will then be taken to a screen indicating that the settings were changed successfully. Your router, regardless of its previous settings, will be accessible from 192.168.1.1 and the default username and password will now be reset to *admin* and *admin*, respectively. In some older versions of the Linksys firmware, the username is blank and the password is set to *admin*.

To upgrade the firmware using the Web interface of the default Linksys firmware, you will need to access the router with a Web browser at http://192.168.1.1. Before you do, you need to be certain that you have a static IP address assigned to the machine that will send the image over TFTP on the same subnet as the router. This can be any static IP address in the 192.168.1.0/24 subnet (/24 = 255.255.255.0), except for 192.168.1.1, which is the address of the router. Once connected via the Web browser, you'll be presented with the default Linksys login page, as shown in Figure 2.2. Log in with the default username and password.

Upon login, utilize the menus to navigate to the firmware upload page by selecting **Administration | Firmware Upgrade**. You will be presented with the Upgrade Firmware page, as indicated in Figure 2.3.

Figure 2.2 Linksys Login Page

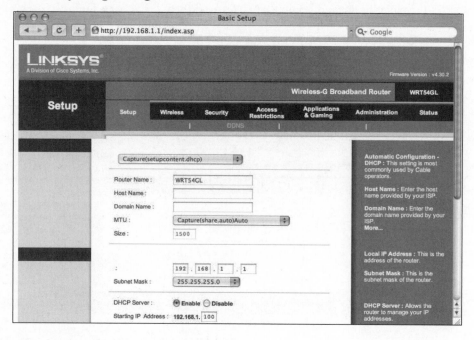

Figure 2.3 Linksys Firmware Upgrade Page

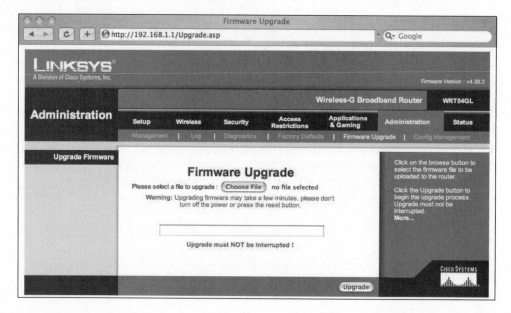

On the **Firmware Upgrade page**, select the **Browse** (or **Choose File**) button to display the file selection dialog box. Within the file selection dialog box, select the appropriate firmware image file that you would like to upload to the WRT54G and then select **Upgrade**, as seen in Figure 2.3.

The upgrade process will comprise uploading, verification, and installation. You should see the box labeled "Upgrade must NOT be interrupted!" begin to fill with black vertical bars. At this point in the process, it is extremely important that network connection or power not be compromised, as this can result in a bricked WRT54G. Refer to Chapter 8 if this happens. Once completed, you will see a screen displaying the message "Upgrade is successful." Click the **Continue button** to go to the default firmware Web page.

Installing Firmware via TFTP

In this section, you will learn how to upgrade firmware via TFTP, which will entail the following:

- Understanding the WRT54G boot process
- Resetting the WRT54G to factory defaults
- Understanding what *boot_wait* does and how to enable it
- Applying firmware via TFTP in Linux, Windows, and OS X

Aside from using the JTAG method (covered next), installing your firmware images via TFTP is the safest and most reliable method (and does not require hardware modifications). In order to use this method, you must be able to access the TFTP process that is part of PMON (PROM MONitor)/CFE (Common Firmware Environment).

When a WRT54G boots, the PMON (for WRT54G, versions 1.0 and 1.1) or CFE (for all versions after 1.1) bootloader takes control of the boot process. The PMON/CFE is similar to a CMOS in PCs and ROMMON in Cisco routers, performing the basic functions upon device startup to get the operating system (in this case referred to as *firmware*) loaded. One of the first things that PMON/CFE does is check that the NVRAM partition exists. If it does not exist, it is created using the NVRAM values stored in the PMON/CFE. Whether it is a new NVRAM partition or an existing one, the bootloader then reads the *boot_wait* parameter. If its value is set to *on*, it will start a TFTP server waiting for incoming connections for the specified period of time (approximately three seconds). Next, it will perform a cyclic redundancy check (CRC) on the firmware. If the firmware image is not corrupt, booting will proceed normally. If the firmware does not pass the CRC (i.e., it is corrupt), the bootloader will go into the wait state until new firmware is received via TFTP. Refer to Figure 2.4 for a graphical representation of the boot process.

In the wait state, whether a result of *boot_wait* being enabled or corrupt firmware, the router does a few interesting things to get itself on the network and provide a TFTP server:

- The PMON/CFE loads a very limited IP stack, which does two things. First, it responds to ARP requests for 192.168.1.1 and listens for ARP broadcasts. This mode will also respond to Internet Control Message Protocol (ICMP) ping echo requests.
- The PMON/CFE starts the TFTP server with no password. This is very different from the TFTP server that is available when the router is booted normally. In fact, many people get confused between the two, and try to upload firmware when the router is booted normally and they are stumped by the password.

Tools & Traps…

Stale ARP Caches and TFTP Usernames/Passwords

Because of the way in which the PMON/CFE handles limited network connectivity during the boot process, you may want to either clear your ARP cache or set a static ARP entry. When in the wait state, the router will answer for ARP requests to 192.168.1.1, regardless of the IP address configured. However, if you are on a system that has an existing entry for 192.168.1.1, your packets will never get to the router. In order to solve this problem, you can clear your ARP cache using the following command, which works on Linux, OS X, and Windows:

```
# arp -d 192.168.1.1
```

Alternatively, you could set a static ARP entry. This would require that you note the Media Access Control (MAC) address on the bottom of the router and add the entry using your operating system's *arp* command. For example, if the MAC address is 01:02:03:04:05:06, the command would look like this:

```
# arp -s 01:02:03:04:05:06 192.168.1.1
```

This will ensure that you have the appropriate ARP entry and that your new firmware image gets copied over properly.

Another common mistake is confusing the PMON/CFE TFTP server with the WRT54G operating system's TFTP server. The PMON/CFE TFTP server does not require a password. The operating system's TFTP server requires a username and password and has a different purpose. So, if you initiate the TFTP process and you receive the error message "Invalid Password," your router is not in the appropriate wait state and you should double-check all of your steps and possibly use the JTAG method covered in Chapter 8.

Some other interesting notes about the boot process are that the kernel will protect the PMON/CFE bootloader partition by not allowing anything to write to it. This will prevent the bootloader from becoming corrupt, which would brick the router. Also, you can exploit the fact that an NVRAM partition will be created if one does not exist by wiping it and rebooting the router. Sometimes a brick is created even when the firmware image is good; for example, you've rolled your own firmware that passes a CRC, but does not boot properly, or you've changed your NVRAM variables and rendered the device unusable. For complete coverage of these features see Chapter 8.

Figure 2.4 The WRT54G Boot Process

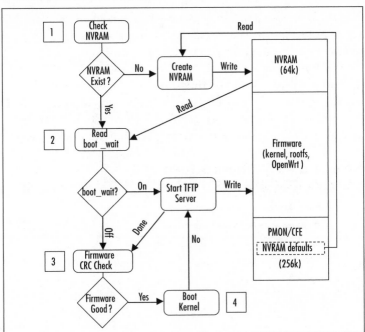

Once the system has booted normally (i.e., not with the TFTP listener), the contents of the NVRAM partition are copied into memory. Using the *nvram* command available in most third-party firmware, you can manipulate these settings. However, these changes will exist in memory only until they are committed back to the NVRAM partition using the *nvram commit* command. Your setting may still not take effect until you execute scripts or programs that will reread the NVRAM variables on the NVRAM partition. We will see many examples of this in the sections that follow, and throughout this book.

Before choosing and executing the TFTP upgrade method, you will need to restore the factory defaults on the Linksys firmware installed on the router prior to installing third-party firmware. You can do this by going to **Administration | Factory Defaults** (refer Figure 2.1). Keep in mind that this will reset the *boot_wait* parameter to its default setting, so depending on what operating system is installed, you may need to reset this value to activate its functionality. From here, your TFTP instructions will differ depending on the operating system of the client machine you are using to upload the image.

The concept of *boot_wait* is very important. The TFTP installation process will exploit this feature to get the new flash image onto the router. In addition, it is a vital part of the recovery process if something should go wrong when applying new firmware or working with the device in general. Given its importance, let's go through the various ways in which to set this parameter:

- The "Ping Hack"
- Using the operating system's *nvram* command
- Directly in the PMON/CFE

The Ping Hack

Linksys WRT54G stock firmware versions prior to 1.42.2 contained a vulnerability in the ping.asp Web page that allowed remote arbitrary code execution. This method is used only for older routers and is no longer required. However, it is important to understand some of the historical items surrounding it. Using the vulnerable Linksys firmware, you need to browse to http://192.168.1.1/Ping.asp (or by using the menu in the Web interface, click **Administration | Diagnostics | Ping**). The original intent of this page was to allow the user to send ping packets via the Web interface. However, due to a programming flaw, you can run commands of your choosing by enclosing them in "`", and sending the output to /tmp/ping.log. Figure 2. 5 provides an example of the Ping Hack Screen.

Figure 2.5 Example of the Ping Hack Screen

For example, consider the following command:

```
;ls${IFS}>/tmp/ping.log
```

If you were to put that command into the **IP Address or Domain Name field** and then clicked **Ping**, it would execute and list the contents of the current directory in the text box. The **${IFS}** is an interfield separator, a UNIX/Linux environment variable that inserts a space so that the command can run properly. With some modifications, you can write a set of commands that will enable the *boot_wait* parameter:

```
;cp${IFS}*/*/nvram${IFS}/tmp/n
;*/n${IFS}set${IFS}boot_wait=on
;*/n${IFS}commit
;*/n${IFS}show>tmp/ping.log
```

The first command copies the NVRAM information to /tmp/n in order to make a backup. The next two commands enable *boot_wait* and save the changes to NVRAM, using */n as the command, which is a copy of the *nvram* binary. You must execute the command this way because Web application vulnerability does not let you execute commands outside of /tmp. The last command dumps the contents of NVRAM, so you can verify that *boot_wait* is set properly.

Using the Operating System nvram Command

If you already have an operating system installed that gives you access to the command line, you can simply enable *boot_wait* using the following commands:

```
# nvram set boot_wait=on
# nvram commit
```

By setting the *boot_wait* parameter to *on*, and committing the changes to the NVRAM partition, the system will go into a boot wait state upon the next reboot. We recommend that you *always* do this once you've installed third-party firmware, in case you want to either revert to Linksys stock firmware or apply a new/different firmware image.

Directly in the PMON/CFE

You can access the PMON/CFE variables directly by adding a serial port on /dev/tts/0 and connecting via a serial terminal session (see Chapter 7). Once you have command-line access, you can enable *boot_wait* in the PMON/CFE by entering the following commands:

```
CFE> nvram set boot_wait=on
*** command status = 0
CFE> nvram commit
*** command status = 0
CFE>
```

This setting will be used only if the NVRAM partition does not exist (either due to user error, or because you want to re-create it because the NVRAM values are wrong, causing the device not to function). You can remove the NVRAM partition using the OpenWrt command line with *mtd*. The *mtd* command allows you to manipulate partitions. The following command will reformat the NVRAM partition and reboot the device:

```
# mtd -r erase nvram
```

WARNING

The *mtd –r erase nvram* command is dangerous. It worked on all of our WRT54GL series routers over the course of writing this book. However, if your hardware model, version, and CFE somehow are unable to write a clean NVRAM partition, or if they write a corrupt NVRAM partition, you will be in serious trouble. Use this only as a last resort and not as a regular course of business.

These commands, and more, will be covered in Chapter 8. You will want to thoroughly read that chapter before executing these commands, making certain that you understand what they mean, and their implications, before trying them out.

The time that the router will wait for TFTP connections during boot depends on the model, version, and firmware settings. Simply setting *boot_wait* to *on* will cause the router to pause for anywhere from one to five seconds (depending on model and version) before booting the image on the flash.

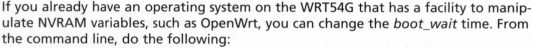

TIP

If you already have an operating system on the WRT54G that has a facility to manipulate NVRAM variables, such as OpenWrt, you can change the *boot_wait* time. From the command line, do the following:

```
# nvram set wait_time="30"
# nvram commit
```

This will tell the bootloader to wait 30 seconds upon each boot (even if the firmware image is not corrupt) for a new firmware image. This should give you enough time to initiate a TFTP transfer to load a new image. Be aware that *wait_time* does not exist by default, which means the command *nvram get wait_time* will return no results until you create the variable with the *nvram set* command.

Linux TFTP Instructions

From a Linux command-line window, enter the following:

```
$ tftp
(to) 192.168.1.1
tftp> bin
tftp> trace
Packet tracing on.
tftp> timeout 60
tftp> rexmt 1
tftp> put openwrt-wrt54g-squashfs.bin
```

When you first execute the *tftp* command, it should ask you the IP address of the host in which you want to send the image—in this case, 192.168.1.1. Next, you will issue the *bin* command, telling the TFTP program to transfer the image in binary format, as it is a binary file and not a text (or ASCII) file. In general, it is always a good idea to transfer files in binary mode, as it will ignore the file format (in ASCII mode it will try to accommodate the file format with regard to carriage returns and line feeds). The *trace* command will display send and receive messages (with byte counts) to indicate the file transfer progress, which helps to reassure you that the file is actually transferring (and the command itself reassures you that it is activated by displaying "Packet tracing on." after completing the command). The *timeout 60* parameter indicates how long, in seconds, it should continue to attempt to transfer the file once you've initiated the connection. The *rexmt 1* command tells it to keep retrying every second within the specified timeout. Finally, you will need to execute the *put* command, specifying the image file as a parameter. When you press **Enter** after this command, it will execute, sending the file to the router at 192.168.1.1. When it is completed, you should see the following:

```
received ACK <block=2769>
sent DATA <block=2770, 512 bytes>
received ACK <block=2770>
sent DATA <block=2771, 0 bytes>
received ACK <block=2771>
Sent 1418240 bytes in 12.4 seconds
tftp>
```

Once completed, simply enter the *quit* command to exit the TFTP client.

Windows TFTP Instructions

The Windows TFTP command behaves a bit differently than the Linux and OS X TFTP commands. It does not support interactive mode, and you must run it as a single command. Following the instructions for connecting your router as before, you can upload a new image using the Windows TFTP command as follows:

```
C:\firmware> tftp -i 192.168.1.1 put openwrt-wrt54g-squashfs.bin
```

where 192.168.1.1 is the IP address of your router, and openwrt-wrt54g-squashfs.bin is the image file located in the same directory where you ran the *tftp* command. When the transfer has completed, you should see something similar to this:

```
Transfer successful: 1418240 bytes in 5 seconds, 283648 bytes/s
```

In addition, graphical tools are available for Windows, which should work as well.

Tools & Traps…

Windows Interfaces and boot_wait

While performing the upgrade via TFPT under Windows (and in some cases, even with Linux or OS X, depending on your hardware and driver), it can be beneficial to connect your computer to an additional hub or switch, and then connect the WRT54G LAN port to the same switch.

Depending on the amount of time that *boot_wait* is set to, it is possible to miss the TFTP upload time window, because when the WRT54G is booting, Windows will not have completely brought up the Ethernet interface. Unfortunately, Windows will

Continued

not keep an interface in the up state when it does not detect an active Ethernet connection, and when the WRT54G is booting, that connection is not considered active by Windows, and Windows will take several seconds to make the Ethernet interface available for use. During the time that Windows does not have the interface available it is possible to miss the *boot_wait* time window.

With some older WRT54G models, *boot_wait* is enabled by default, but with a very short wait period. The additional hub or switch in these instances can save you considerable amounts of time troubleshooting.

OS X TFTP Instructions

For OS X, you can use the same commands as you would use in Linux, with only a slight change in the way you tell the TFTP client to connect to a specific IP address:

```
pdc:~ nologin$ tftp
tftp> connect 192.168.1.1
tftp> bin
tftp> trace
Packet tracing on.
tftp> timeout 60
tftp> rexmt 1
tftp> put openwrt-wrt54g-squashfs.bin
```

The OS X *tftp* command, by default, does not ask you to which IP address you would like to connect using TFTP. So, using the *connect* command, you specify 192.168.1.1. You may also run into the same problem as with Windows Ethernet interfaces and have to put a hub in between the WRT54G and your Mac. Also, you may want to hard-code the speed and duplex settings on your adapter in OS X. They should be set to Manual, 10baseT/UTP, full-duplex. You can do this by going to **System Preferences | Network** and double-clicking on **your Ethernet adapter** in the **Network Status screen**. Now, click on the **Ethernet tab** and select **Manually (Advanced)** from the **Configure menu**. Here you can change the **Speed** and **Duplex settings**, and then click **Apply**. You must have administrator rights in OS X to make these changes, or provide administrator credentials when prompted.

Completing the TFTP Installation

WARNING

Regardless of your operating system, it is extremely important that once the TFTP transfer is complete, you do not remove the power or disrupt the router in any way. It will come back on its own after a few minutes and should happily boot your new firmware. This part requires patience, up to six minutes in some cases, so it's a good opportunity to get a fresh energy drink or catch up on your Slashdot reading.

TFTP Firmware Installation Step by Step

We have gone through many of the details surrounding TFTP installation, which we will use throughout this book. Completing the projects throughout this book will mean installing firmware on many different routers. We have found that the TFTP method is best suited for this task. To be certain that it is successful, here is a consolidated guide to installing firmware via TFTP in a WRT54G:

1. Locate and download the third-party firmware image to the computer that will be used in the upgrade process. Verify the MD5 checksum to be certain that the image is not corrupt.

2. Connect the computer and WRT54G to a reliable power source.

3. Connect the computer to the WRT54G with a reliable Ethernet cable. Verify the link lights on the computer (if available, typically they are solid green) and the WRT54G. For most WRT54G models, the LED associated with that port should be solid green and flashing when there is activity.

4. Assign a static IP address to the computer in the 192.168.1.0/24 subnet (e.g., 192.168.1.10/24, or anything that is not 192.168.1.1 and a valid IP address) and disable any DHCP clients on the host in accordance with the operating system instructions.

5. To ensure that there are no stale ARP entries, remove the entry for 192.168.1.1 by issuing the command *arp –d 192.168.1.1*. This command should work in OS X, Linux, and Windows; however, refer to your operating system-specific documentation for more details.

6. On the computer, if you are using Linux or OS X, issue the appropriate TFTP commands outlined in the preceding sections, being certain to use 192.168.1.1 as the destination. Do not yet send the image (via the TFTP *put* command) to the WRT54G.

7. Unplug the WRT54G from its power source.

8. Send the firmware image via TFTP. For Linux and OS X, run the TFTP *put* command. For Windows, run the *tftp* command.

9. Plug the power source back into the router, making sure that you do not unplug the router while the TFTP transfer is taking place or in the time thereafter.

10. Once the firmware transfer completes, the router will then reboot on its own and you should be able to ping it (using the command *ping 192.168.1.1*).

Installing Firmware via JTAG

Firmware installation via the JTAG connector is not recommended for the faint of heart, nor for standard installations. If you need to install firmware via JTAG, chances are you have totally hosed your WRT54G. Ideally, the only time you would ever want to install via JTAG is when recovering from a bricked router. We discuss the construction of an unbuffered JTAG cable for use with your WRT54G in Chapter 7. We also discuss the use of the unbuffered JTAG cable and the HairyDairyMaid WRT54G Debrick Utility in Chapter 8.

Although we wanted to mention this installation method for consistency, it should be noted that this installation method is a somewhat advanced procedure (i.e., it will require the use of a soldering iron), and you should treat it as such.

Introduction to Firmware Used in This Book

In this section, we will discuss some of the countless versions of third-party firmware for nearly every model of the Linksys WRT54G. We want to take you through the background and features of all common third-party firmware. This will give you a good foundation for the rest of this book. Now that you know how to install firmware, you may be inclined to grab whichever firmware your friend told you about most recently and install it on your WRT54G. Please try to hold off from doing this until you read the rest of this chapter. What follows is a guideline that will help you choose the right firmware for you. Many distributions are based on the OpenWrt firmware, so much of this chapter focuses on installing, configuring, and using OpenWrt. With this knowledge, you should be able to master any of the OpenWrt-based firmware available. We use OpenWrt extensively throughout this book, for this reason and many others. OpenWrt, as you will see, is very robust, has excellent package management, documentation (http://wiki.openwrt.org), community support (http://forum.openwrt.org), and IRC (available at #openwrt on irc.freenode.net). Furthermore, it offers an easy-to-use development environment (buildroot). Many other firmware distributions did not have these features at the time of this writing.

Linksys Original Firmware

Background

This firmware is the version that has been the inspiration for the entire WRT54G hacking movement. As discussed in Chapter 1, this firmware is Linux-based, and much of the components have been released under the GNU General Public License (GPL). Although this firmware is not hackable or extensible directly, it has served as the basis of many of the other third-party firmware solutions in terms of either code or design.

Features

The original firmware from Linksys does not have as many features as the third-party versions. However, the later versions do support WPA-PSK and WPA2-PSK, which should offer adequate protection for most Small Office Home Office (SOHO) environments. Many of the original versions of the firmware did not contain support for Wi-Fi Protected Access (WPA), so if you want to retain the original firmware and avoid the weak Wireless Encryption Protocol (WEP) encryption, you should upgrade the WRT54G to the latest official Linksys version.

Who Should Use This Firmware

The original Linksys firmware is perfectly suitable for use by the casual user that is satisfied with the operation of the WRT54G out of the box. This firmware will provide many of the features required by the average user, including network address translation (NAT) and moderately powered wireless with good security when appropriately configured. Chances are you purchased this book because you are looking to get more from your WRT54G for one of many purposes.

Latest Linksys Firmware (VxWorks)

Background

This is the new firmware from Linksys, available only on series 5 and later WRT54G and WRT54GS model routers. This firmware is not Linux-based, but rather a proprietary UNIX-like real-time operating system from Wind River designed for embedded devices, called VxWorks (www.windriver.com/vxworks). The version 5.0 and later routers, therefore, have limited hackability, with the DD-WRT micro edition being one of the only supported VxWorks-based third-party firmware solutions.

> **NOTE**
>
> Remember, the WRT54G series 5 and later model routers have significantly less flash and RAM than previous versions, as specified in Chapter 1. They are not ideal for installing third-party firmware. In response to this, Linksys came out with the WRT54GL series routers, designed specifically for hacking.

Features

The VxWorks-based firmware from Linksys does not have as many features as the third-party versions. However, they do support WPA/2-PSK and WPA/2-Enterprise, which should offer adequate protection for most home users.

Who Should Use This Firmware

This firmware is designed for the end user. It offers only a Web interface, which should suffice for most SOHO users. It contains features that lend itself to providing a wireless or wired network for the average SOHO user that may not require any advanced features.

OpenWrt

Background

OpenWrt was released in January 2004 by the newly formed OpenWrt project team in response to the sheer amount of third-party firmware available at the time. Before OpenWrt, many would take the stock Linksys Linux-based firmware and customize it for a single purpose. This led to the creation of many custom firmware distributions. The OpenWrt project designed a much better model. It would write a GNU/Linux-based core with minimal features, essentially customizing Linux to support the WRT54G processor and network interfaces. Then, a Debian-like package management system was implemented so that the end user could customize each installation to fit his needs. The result was a very slim, fast, and highly customizable embedded-device firmware operating system. The team coupled this with one of the best development environments for embedded devices, the OpenWrt software development kit (SDK).

Features

The list of individual features is too long to include here due to the sheer number of packages and extensibility of OpenWrt. Many packages are available from the default package tree, and various groups have made custom packages for OpenWrt. Some examples of packages available in the tree are Asterisk, FreeRadius, and OpenVPN. Porting packages is easy with a system called buildroot, and many open source software applications have been ported, including the Wifidog captive portal software, the BlueZ Bluetooth driver subsystem, and Snort, an open source intrusion detection system. You can find the latest, stable list of default packages at http://downloads.openwrt.org/whiterussian/packages. You can obtain a more extensive list of ported software from backports, which is located at http://downloads.openwrt.org/backports/0.9.

Installation

You can install OpenWrt via the Web GUI or via TFTP, as described earlier in this chapter. However, you must first choose the correct OpenWrt firmware image. This largely depends on which hardware you have.

NOTE

Did you know you can install OpenWrt on numerous devices other than a WRT54G? Well, you can! In fact, the list is quite long and includes devices from Belkin, D-Link, NETGEAR, and Motorola. The full list is located at http://wiki.openwrt.org/TableOfHardware?action=show.

Some of the devices in the list are only partially supported, meaning that OpenWrt will run, but it may not have driver support for the wireless card. Some are also confirmed *not* to work, and others may be a work in progress.

Use the guide in Chapter 1 to determine which WRT54G device you have. Once you have that information, you can then choose the correct OpenWrt firmware image. In all versions prior to Whiterussian RC6, OpenWrt gives you two choices for file systems: SQUASHFS and the Journaling Flash File System, version 2 (JFFS2). Although you do not have to make this decision in recent versions, it is still very important to understand the differences (in fact, one of the reasons they did away with this was that it caused confusion). For more information, see http://forum.openwrt.org/viewtopic.php?id=3474. There are some important distinctions between the different file systems, which apply to more than just OpenWrt:

- **SQUASHFS** This is the safer of the two options because it is a read–only, compressed file system. It uses a smaller JFFS2 file system to store files that need to be changed. It is a common Linux file system and it has some interesting features, such as detecting and deleting file duplicates. It is commonly found on embedded devices, and it's recommended for new users because it can help prevent a user error that would leave the device inoperable. (See http://squashfs.sourceforge.net for more information.)

- **JFFS2** This file system was designed from the ground up to run on embedded devices, and more specifically GNU licensed file systems that run natively on flash devices without using translation. This file system is not compressed, which means it takes up slightly more space on the flash. However, it is a read/write file system and it's prone to user error, which could leave your device unusable. (See http://sourceware.org/jffs2/ for more information.)

WARNING

If you chose JFFS2 in versions prior to Whiterussian RC6, you must reboot after you install OpenWrt before you can use the file system. This is especially important if you've spent time wondering why you could not change the password after the initial installation (which you should do, but after you have rebooted the device). You can do this by either unplugging the device and plugging it back in, or typing **reboot** at the command prompt and pressing **Enter**.

As of Whiterussian RC6, you no longer need to choose between file systems, because the developers made the decision to include both. Although both file systems exist, OpenWrt utilizes a third file system, *mini_fo*, acting as a proxy to the JFFS2 and SQUASHFS file systems. This means you can use JFFS2 only when writes are required.

When choosing a file system for RC6 or greater, the *<fstype>* field in Table 2.2 will always be "squashfs". In previous versions, you have a choice between the two. Regardless of file system, use Table 2.2 to choose the correct image for your hardware.

Table 2.2 OpenWrt Firmware Images for WRT54G Series Routers

Device	OpenWrt Image
Linksys WRT54G (versions 1.0, 1.1, 2.0, 2.2, 3.0, and 4.0)	
Linksys WRT54GL (versions 1.0 and 1.1)	openwrt-wrt54g-<fstype>.bin
Linksys WRT54GS (versions 1.0, 1.1, 2.0, and 3.0)	openwrt-wrt54gs-<fstype>.bin
Linksys WRT54GS (version 4.0)	openwrt-wrt54gs_v4-<fstype>.bin
Linksys WRTSL54GS (all versions as of the time of this writing)	openwrt-wrtsl54gs-<fstype>.bin

You can download OpenWrt images from http://downloads.openwrt.org. Throughout this book, we will use Whiterussian, version 0.9, which you can download from http://downloads.openwrt.org/whiterussian/0.9/default. Once you have selected and downloaded the appropriate firmware image, you can use either the Web or the TFTP method of installation. If you navigate to the Web interface, you will be prompted to change the password. Enter a password in the fields and click the **Set button**. If successful, you should see the screen display the output shown in Figure 2.6.

Figure 2.6 OpenWrt Web User Interface: Initial Password Change

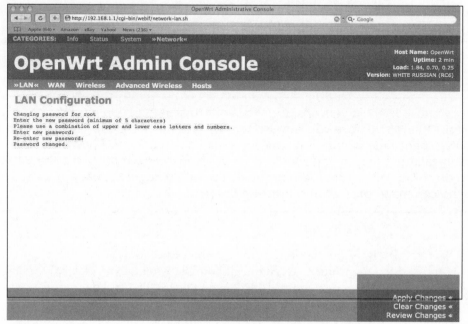

You can also change the password from the command line, as shown in Figure 2.7, and there is no time like the present to become familiar with the OpenWrt command-line interface, as we will use it extensively throughout this book. To begin using the command-line interface for the first time on a fresh OpenWrt installation you must Telnet to the router IP address. You can do this on any platform that has a Telnet client—for example, Telnet 192.168.1.1. After a new firmware upgrade, there is no Telnet password and you will be dropped directly into a root shell. The resulting screen will look like that shown in Figure 2.7.

This process was implemented by providing an invalid password for the root user in /etc/passwd by default (the password is the character "!"). SSH is enabled by default, as well as Telnet, but the telnetd daemon was run with the option *telnetd -l /bin/login*; therefore, it launches a special login script that allows you to log in without a password if no password is set yet (look at the /bin/login script details). If you try to SSH, it is not possible to log in, because there is an invalid password for root. Once you change the password, type **exit**, which will disconnect you from the router. Now you can SSH back into the router (typically the Linux/UNIX command would be *ssh root@192.168.1.1*). You cannot use Telnet to access the router anymore because /bin/login doesn't allow it. The Telnet and SSH daemons are running all the time; it is the root password that changes and makes /bin/login behave in a different way.

Figure 2.7 OpenWrt Initial Command-Line Login Screen

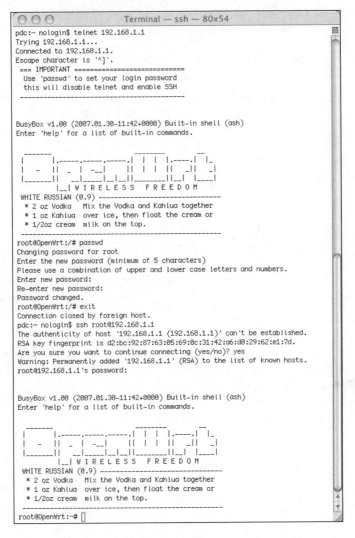

TIP

Windows does not come preinstalled with a command-line or GUI version of SSH. Although plenty of GUI SSH clients are commercially available for Windows, PuTTY is a free GUI alternative. You can find PuTTY at www.chiark.greenend.org.uk/ ~sgtatham/putty.

Are You 0wned?

Hijacked SSH Connection or Key Change?

SSH is a wonderful protocol for secure shell access, primarily on UNIX/Linux/OS X-based systems, but it also runs on Windows (see http://sshwindows.sourceforge.net). Version 2 of the SSH protocol is very secure, and it implements a number of techniques to secure your terminal sessions, one of which is host authentication using a public/private key exchange. For example, when your WRT54G router boots OpenWrt for the first time it generates a public/private key pair for the device. When your client connects to this device for the first time, you should see something similar to the following:

```
root@bud:~# ssh 192.168.1.42

The authenticity of host '192.168.1.42 (192.168.1.42)' can't be established.

RSA key fingerprint is 14:e8:3d:a5:96:27:77:8e:e3:69:19:fd:65:44:a6:53.

Are you sure you want to continue connecting (yes/no)? yes

Warning: Permanently added '192.168.1.42' (RSA) to the list of known hosts.
```

In this example, we are initiating an SSH session to the newly installed router by typing **ssh 192.168.1.42**. Our SSH client tells us that it cannot verify the authenticity of the host to which we are connecting. This is because the host's (i.e., the WRT54G) public key has not been saved to our client. It then presents us with the RSA key fingerprint. If we were very diligent, we would verify that it does, in fact, match the key fingerprint on the WRT54G. Of course, we verify the fingerprint and type **yes**, the public key is added to our $HOME/.ssh/known_hosts file, and login proceeds normally:

```
root@192.168.1.42's password:


BusyBox v1.00 (2006.11.07-01:40+0000) Built-in shell (ash)

Enter 'help' for a list of built-in commands.


  _____                           _____          __
 |       |.-----.-----.-----.|     |   |    |.-----.|  |_
 |   -   ||  _  |  -__|     ||     |   |    ||     ||   _|
 |_____||   __|_____|__|__||_____|   |    ||__|  ||____|
          |__|  W I R E L E S S   F R E E D O M
 WHITE RUSSIAN (0.9) -------------------------------------
```

Continued

```
    * 2 oz Vodka   Mix the Vodka and Kahlua together

    * 1 oz Kahlua  over ice, then float the cream or

    * 1/2oz cream  milk on the top.

    --------------------------------------------------

root@wrt-office:~#
```

Sometimes, however, we need to upgrade, install new firmware, reinstall SSH, or perform some other task that causes new keys to be generated. When this happens initiating an SSH connecting to the WRT54G produces very different results:

```
root@bud:~# ssh 192.168.1.42

@@@@@@@@@@@@@@@@@@@@@@@@@@@@@@@@@@@@@@@@@@@@@@@@@@@@@@@@@@@@@

@    WARNING: REMOTE HOST IDENTIFICATION HAS CHANGED!     @

@@@@@@@@@@@@@@@@@@@@@@@@@@@@@@@@@@@@@@@@@@@@@@@@@@@@@@@@@@@@@

IT IS POSSIBLE THAT SOMEONE IS DOING SOMETHING NASTY!

Someone could be eavesdropping on you right now (man-in-the-middle attack)!

It is also possible that the RSA host key has just been changed.

The fingerprint for the RSA key sent by the remote host is

0a:1f:86:c6:01:83:98:d5:46:e4:4e:73:05:c4:a6:f4.

Please contact your system administrator.

Add correct host key in /root/.ssh/known_hosts to get rid of this message.

Offending key in /root/.ssh/known_hosts:14

RSA host key for 192.168.1.42 has changed and you have requested strict
checking.

Host key verification failed.
```

Because the keys on the WRT54G have changed, we are presented with a new public key, which does not match the one stored in our known_hosts client file. It stops our connection attempt because if the keys do not match, someone could be trying to perform a man-in-the-middle (MITM) attack. You must once again verify the key fingerprints to ensure that it is, in fact, the WRT54G you are trying to connect to, and not some malicious hacker. To do this, go to the WRT54G command line (through some other method, such as a console connection, or directly plugged into the LAN portion of the router) and type:

```
root@wrt-office:/etc/dropbear#dropbearkey -y -f dropbear_dss_host_key

Public key portion is:

ssh-dss
AAAAB3NzaC1kc3MAAACBAIykB7kyavte792eMCTiBDFABHXWpFRyJn7Ran542xdDL/X+8f2/M1hR
uNxJdDbK7EpaVHWUiYHhmSXJh4TRe0z+6tb75YBDrwUZm1Y01A3OXbDecNoWNXoKf4uhgYgxi6wB
jUOcfm <cut>

Fingerprint: md5 e9:7a:9b:b6:df:5b:af:6a:e6:4e:81:dd:a6:8c:f3:93
```

Continued

> Once you've verified the key fingerprint, you can simply remove the original entry in your known_hosts file, which has been indicated as line 14, which states "Offending key in /root/.ssh/known_hosts:14". Then you can once again SSH to the WRT54G, verify the key fingerprint, type **yes** when prompted with the new key, and log in as usual.

Who Should Use This Firmware

This firmware is aimed at more experienced users, Linux enthusiasts, network/security engineers, and anyone who is willing to take a base Linux-embedded device and configure it for his needs. For example, a graphical Web user interface was not introduced until recent versions, and nevertheless, most of the configuration must be done via the command-line interface. However, once you become accustomed to making changes via the command line, you will find it very easy to create your own custom Linux-embedded device.

Also, if you are interested in embedded device development, this is the firmware for you. The OpenWrt project welcomes developers, and even provides us with an entire site devoted to OpenWrt development: https://dev.openwrt.org. Here you can find all the latest versions of the source code, and get access to the buildroot environment, which allows you to compile source code packages to run on OpenWrt, build your own kernels, and create your own firmware images. There is also a short tutorial on the OpenWrt forums, located at http://forum.openwrt.org/viewtopic.php?pid=31794.

DD-WRT

Background

DD-WRT was created by BrainSlayer to offer a free version of Sveasoft (see the Sveasoft write-up in the "Other Firmware Worth Mentioning" section, later in this chapter). Sveasoft was based on the original GPL versions of the WRT54G firmware from Linksys. Sveasoft decided to start charging users $20 to download the firmware for their routers. The earlier versions of DD-WRT (up to and including v22) were based on the last free version of Sveasoft, called Alchemy. It has since adopted the OpenWrt kernel base and ipkg package structure. DD-WRT sports one of the slickest Web interfaces of any WRT54G firmware solution, making it a very popular choice among computer/networking enthusiasts who want to quickly and easily take advantage of third-party firmware features.

Features

DD-WRT offers an array of interesting features that the original Linksys firmware did not offer, including:

- The ability to increase wireless radio transmit power
- Hotspot Captive Portal Support via Wifidog (http://dev.wifidog.org)

- Wireless Distribution System (WDS), bridging, or "Mesh" networking support
- Quality of Service (QoS) for both wireless (WMM, Wi-Fi MultiMedia) and LAN clients

NOTE

DD-WRT's features and software packages come built in and most are configurable via the Web GUI (see Figures 2.8 and 2.9). This is the primary difference between DD-WRT and OpenWrt. DD-WRT's GUI is very extensive and easy to use.

Installation

As with all third-party firmware, you must check to see that your hardware versions are supported, and that you download the correct firmware. The DD-WRT project supplies a comprehensive list of supported devices, very similar to OpenWrt, which should not come as a surprise because DD-WRT is based on the OpenWrt core. You can find the list of supported devices at www.dd-wrt.com/wiki/index.php/Supported_Devices.

Unlike some other projects, DD-WRT's feature availability depends on which firmware image you download and install on your router. Table 2.3 lists the available files and associated functionality.

Table 2.3 DD-WRT Features and Associated Firmware Images

Feature	Micro	Mini	Standard	Standard_nokaid	VoIP	VPN
Chillispot			X	X	X	X
HTTPS Web management			X	X	X	X
IPv6			X	X	X	X
kaid			X			
MMC/SD card support			X	X		X
NoCat			X	X	X	X
OpenVPN						X
PPTP/PPTP client		X	X	X	X	X
radvd	X	X	X	X		
RFlow			X	X	X	X
Samba client			X	X	X	X
SIPatH					X	

Continued

Table 2.3 continued DD-WRT Features and Associated Firmware Images

Feature	Micro	Mini	Standard	Standard_ nokaid	VoIP	VPN
SNMP			X	X	X	X
SSH		X	X	X	X	X
UPnP		X	X	X	X	X

You will want to be certain what you have decided to use your router for before you flash it with DD-WRT. Table 2.4 provides you with a description of each feature to help guide you in selecting an appropriate distribution.

Table 2.4 DD-WRT Features and Descriptions

Feature	Description
Chillispot	A captive portal software package that allows you to authenticate users before they can use the wireless network. Also called a *hotspot*.
HTTPS Web management	We recommend that you enable the Secure Sockets Layer (SSL) encryption on your management interface. However, some versions do not include this, such as the micro and mini DD-WRT images.
IPv6	IPv6 is the new version of IP. Most use IPv4 today; IPv6 adds more address space, security, and a host of other features to the IP stack.
kaid	This provides support for the Kai Gaming console, which lets users of many different gaming systems play online.
MMC/SD card support	Covered in Chapter 6, adding extra storage via an SD card is a useful hack, especially if you need to store data on the device, such as what we will show you in Chapter 5.
NoCat	NoCat is a captive portal, just like Chillispot.
OpenVPN	For making SSL virtual private network (VPN) connections, OpenVPN does a fantastic job. We will cover this in Chapter 3.
PPTP client	PPTP is a VPN technology, similar to OpenVPN, but not as secure and flexible.
radvd	For IPv6 users, this is a program used to send router advertisements.
RFlow	This is a remote monitoring solution for WRT54G series routers running DD-WRT.

Continued

Table 2.4 continued DD-WRT Features and Descriptions

Feature	Description
Samba client	A great way to add storage to your WRT54G is to install a Samba client, which lets you connect to shared storage on Windows and Samba servers via Server Message Block (SMB).
SIPatH	This is an open source Voice over IP (VoIP) server for embedded Linux devices, now hosted and maintained at www.milkfish.org.
SNMP	SNMP is the Simple Network Management Protocol, and you can use it to monitor devices and make configuration changes.
SSH	SecureSHell is what we recommend for command-line access to your WRT54G series router. Note: The micro and mini builds support only Telnet, not SSH.
UPnP	Universal Plug n' Play is a protocol intended to simply firewall changes by communicating to your clients and changing firewall rules accordingly. You should use it with caution because the security implications are most often not considered.

Once you have chosen the features you want to implement, you must select the appropriate firmware for your hardware. Table 2.5 lists each file and provides a description. You can replace the *<type>* value with *micro*, *mini*, *standard*, *standard_nokaid*, *voip*, or *vpn*, depending on which features you have selected.

Table 2.5 DD-WRT Firmware Image Filenames and Descriptions

Firmware Image Filename	Description
dd-wrt.v23_<type>_asus.trx	This version is for flashing Asus model routers, such as the WL-500G Deluxe. You should use it only for flashing with the Web interface.
dd-wrt.v23_<type>_generic.bin	This supports all supported devices, including all WRT54G models, except the WRT54SLGS. You should use it only when flashing with the Web interface.
dd-wrt.v23_<type>_wrt54g.bin	Supports WRT54G, versions 1.0–4.0, and WRT54GL, versions 1.0–1.1, for flashing via TFTP. Do not use this on any other model WRT54G/GS.

Continued

Table 2.5 continued DD-WRT Firmware Image Filenames and Descriptions

Firmware Image Filename	Description
dd-wrt.v23_<type>_wrt54gs.bin	Supports WRT54GS, versions 1.0–3.0, for flashing via TFTP. Do not use this on any other model WRT54G/GS.
dd-wrt.v23_<type>_wrt54gsv4.bin	Supports WRT54GS, version 4.0, for flashing via TFTP. Do not use this on any other model WRT54G/GS.
dd-wrt.v23_<type>_wrtsl54gs.bin	Supports WRTSL54GS, version 4.0, for flashing via TFTP. Do not use this on any other model WRT54G/GS.
dd-wrt.v23_<type>_moto.trx	A micro and mini version for Motorola devices only.

If you are using a model other than a WRT54G, versions 5.0–6.0, you can now follow the Web GUI or TFTP instructions, which depend on which firmware version of WRT54G you have, the features desired, and whether the images have been created for use with the Web GUI or TFTP installation. Once the installation has completed and the router has rebooted, you can browse to the device and you should see the screen shown in Figure 2.8.

Figure 2.8 DD-WRT Initial Configuration Page

Clicking on any of the tabs should prompt you for a username and password, as shown in Figure 2.9. Click on the **Administration** tab so that you can get into the device to change the default username (*root*) and the default password (*admin*).

Figure 2.9 DD-WRT Initial Login Screen

Once you have successfully logged in, you should see the colors change and more tabs become available, as shown in Figure 2.10.

Installing DD-WRT on WRT54G, Versions 5.0–6.0

DD-WRT is currently the only third-party firmware supported on WRT54G/WRT54GS, versions 5.0–6.0. As mentioned previously, these versions have only half the RAM and flash of most other models. Its micro code version has been specifically tuned to run on this platform. The installation steps are a little more involved than others; however, once installed, it will allow you to use the command-line interface and GUI just as you would for a normal DD-WRT installation. The micro code edition is greatly limited. You do not get package management support with ipkg, you must manage the router via Telnet and SSH, and there is no driver support for an additional SD card. However, many features are still available that the standard Linksys firmware does not offer. These include the ability to adjust the radio power, change virtual LANs (VLANs) on selected ports, and even participate in a WDS.

Figure 2.10 DD-WRT Administration Page

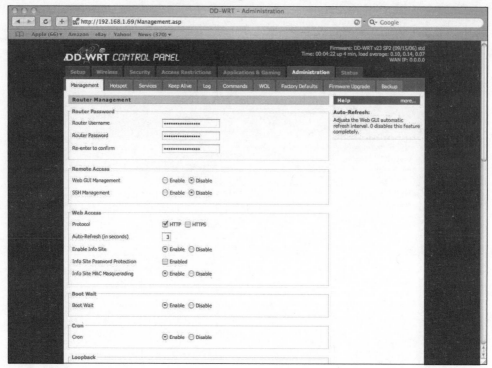

For the DD-WRT installation on the WRT54G, versions 5.0–6.0, you will need the following files:

- **www.bitsum.com/files/vxworks_prep_v03.zip** The image file contained here will overwrite the flash image, giving you a Management Mode. You should download this file and unzip it, leaving you with vxworks_prep_v03.bin.

- **www.bitsum.com/files/vxworks_killer_g_v06.zip** Once in Management Mode, upload this file to the device, which will give you a new CFE. You should download and unzip this file, leaving you with vxworks_killer_g_v06.bin.

- **www.dd-wrt.com/dd-wrtv2/down.php?path=downloads%2Fdd-wrt.v23%20SP2%2Fmicro%2F&download=dd-wrt.v23_micro_generic.bin** Finally, with the new CFE, you should upload the DD-WRT Micro, generic version, onto the flash.

Let's get started by first following the instructions in the beginning of this chapter to properly connect the WRT54G to your client computer and reset to factory defaults. Then browse to **Administration | Firmware Upgrade**, load vxworks_prep_v03.bin, and click **Upgrade**. The router will go through the normal upgrade process and reboot. Once it does, point your Web browser at 192.168.1.1. You should have a screen that looks like Figure 2.11.

Figure 2.11 Management Mode Firmware Upgrade Page

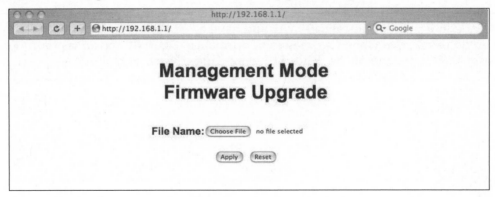

Select **Choose File**, and choose the vxworks_killer_g_v06.bin file you downloaded earlier. Click **Apply**. After waiting a minute (or two), unplug your router and plug it back in. The Power light should now be flashing, indicating that the CFE is waiting for a new firmware image via TFTP. Now, you merely need to upload one using one of the TFTP methods covered earlier in this chapter. Figure 2.12 displays an example.

Figure 2.12 TFTP DD-WRT Micro Image

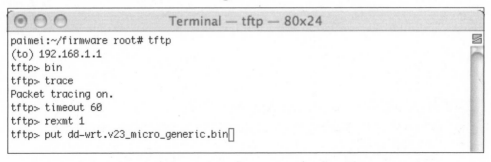

After waiting several minutes, you should have a working copy of DD-WRT micro running on your device. Browsing to the default Web page (i.e., http://192.168.1.1) should bring you to the initial configuration page shown in Figure 2.8.

Who Should Use This Firmware

Those wanting an easy-to-use, feature-rich firmware solution for their WRT54G series routers should consider DD-WRT. The major difference between DD-WRT and, say, OpenWrt, is that DD-WRT comes with all of the software already installed. It is a great firmware distribution for noncomputer geek types, as they can use the Web interface to navigate and enable/disable features. For the computer-oriented (i.e., geeks), there is a command line; however, if you find yourself on the command line in DD-WRT frequently, try OpenWrt instead as it is a full-featured command line.

> **NOTE**
>
> Although it's easy to install DD-WRT and have all of those features at your fingertips, you do pay a price when it comes to performance. DD-WRT consumes far more resources than some of the other firmware choices, such as OpenWrt.

Ewrt

Background

Erwt was originally developed by two employees of Portless Networks, named Irving Popovetsky and Brandon Psmythe, to be used in community wireless networking projects, most notably as an easy-to-use, rock-solid, self-contained wireless hotspot. Ewrt was maintained by Troy Jaqua with the continued support of Portless Networks. While we were writing this book, the project ended. The developers are currently seeking a person, or team of people, to adopt this project. You can find more information at www.portless.net. They have made all of the project files (firmware, packages, documentation, and source code) available at www.portless.net/ewrt.

Features

Ewrt is built to be a self-contained wireless hotspot. In order to accomplish this task, the Ewrt developers reused the default Linksys Web interface, as seen in Figure 2.13, and added support for configuring the additional features.

Figure 2.13 Ewrt Default Configuration Web Page

Ewrt provides a hotspot-like captive portal, similar to many that you would encounter in airports and coffee shops around the world. The user associates to an SSID and receives his IP address, gateway, and domain name system (DNS) server. All subsequent HTTP requests are then redirected to the captive portal, also known as a splash screen. Here, the user is typically presented with instructions for proceeding. In some cases, the user may be asked to agree to an acceptable usage policy and then be allowed to access the Internet, which is the default behavior of Ewrt. Hotspot configurations may vary to include payment for network access, usernames and passwords, and/or registration. In our case, the captive portal splash screen shown in Figure 2.14 will be automatically presented to all wireless clients when they begin to access network resources through their Web browsers.

Figure 2.14 Ewrt Default Captive Portal Page

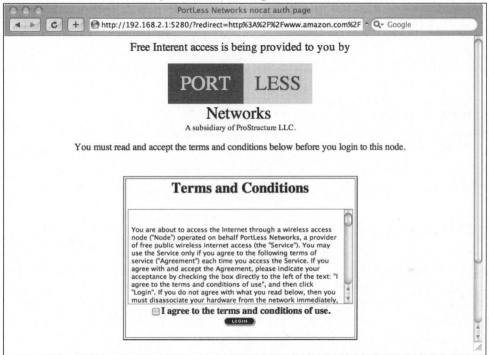

The Ewrt project based the captive portal portion of the firmware on the NoCatSplash project (http://nocat.net), which the developers have ported to the WRT54G platform. The Ewrt developers have created a writeable JFFS2 partition for customized captive portal Web pages, and have included many security and stability fixes.

The Ewrt firmware is ideally designed to be installed on a WRT54G in a remote location where physical access to the WRT54G is limited. In order to support these types of deployments, Ewrt contains some additional features over the base Linksys firmware, most notably the addition of SSH for secure command-line access and management, as shown in Figure 2.15.

Figure 2.15 Ewrt SSH Session

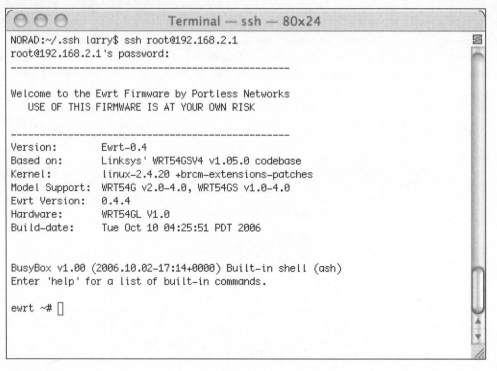

```
Terminal — ssh — 80x24
NORAD:~/.ssh larry$ ssh root@192.168.2.1
root@192.168.2.1's password:
-----------------------------------------------

Welcome to the Ewrt Firmware by Portless Networks
    USE OF THIS FIRMWARE IS AT YOUR OWN RISK


-----------------------------------------------
Version:        Ewrt-0.4
Based on:       Linksys' WRT54GSV4 v1.05.0 codebase
Kernel:         linux-2.4.20 +brcm-extensions-patches
Model Support:  WRT54G v2.0-4.0, WRT54GS v1.0-4.0
Ewrt Version:   0.4.4
Hardware:       WRT54GL V1.0
Build-date:     Tue Oct 10 04:25:51 PDT 2006


BusyBox v1.00 (2006.10.02-17:14+0000) Built-in shell (ash)
Enter 'help' for a list of built-in commands.

ewrt ~# []
```

Who Should Use This Firmware

Ewrt is clearly built for those looking to offer wireless Internet service as part of a business or social offering. Ewrt is very good at providing those solutions in an almost turnkey fashion. Ewrt is definitely recommended for these types of deployments, when you do not want to build the entire infrastructure from scratch. We will use Ewrt for two projects in this book: one in Chapter 4, where we will set up a self-contained WPA-Enterprise wireless network, and again in Chapter 6, where we will use Ewrt-based firmware to create a captive portal that logs all usernames and passwords.

Other Firmware Worth Mentioning

FairuzaWRT

Background

FairuzaWRT is based on the OpenWrt project, has been forked from the main OpenWrt project by The Hacker Pimps (www.hackerpimps.com), and has been affectionately named over the developers' obsession with the film actress, Fairuza Balk. The Hacker Pimps have developed FairuzaWRT as a proof of concept for a different attack vector for network-based security attacks. From this proof of concept, an additional version was developed to become a viable security penetration testing platform, or a platform for delivering a covert network attack. Although it does not appear that the base firmware of FairuzaWRT is under heavy development, continued support of add-on packages is available through the OpenWrt (http://downloads.openwrt.org) and FairuzaWRT (www.hacker-pimps.com/fairuzawrt) package trees.

Features

The list of individual features is too long to include here due to the sheer number of packages and extensibility of the base OpenWrt. Many packages are available from the default package tree, and various groups have made custom packages for OpenWrt, such as the FairuzaWRT branch. The FairuzaWRT branch of the package tree has some specific additions, mostly related to various net-work-based exploits and attacks. Additionally, the main focus of the firmware has been to include many tools used by a penetration tester or network-based attacker. In addition to a growing number of actual remote exploits available preinstalled, FairuzaWRT contains a number of reconnaissance and attack tools, as shown in Table 2.6.

Table 2.6 FairuzaWRT Reconnaissance and Attack Tools

Tool	Description
Arping	An ARP-based ping tool
Arpspoof	Part of the dsniff suite, used for spoofing ARP requests/replies
Dnsspoof	Part of the dsniff suite, a tool for intercepting and redirecting network DNS requests
Dsniff	Used for sniffing many clear-text usernames and passwords, including Telnet, FTP, and POP3
Fping	Ping on steroids, supporting multithreading and easily parseable output
fping6	Ping on steroids, supporting IPv6 multithreading and easily parseable output
Fprobe	A probe (stand-alone client) for NetFlow
Hexdump	A utility for dumping binary files to hexadecimal and ASCII formats
hping2	A Transmission Control Protocol/Internet Protocol (TCP/IP) packet crafting and analysis tool
hydra	A network login/password auditing tool for testing several network services, including Telnet, FTP, HTTP, HTTPS, HTTP-Proxy, SMB, SMBNT, MS-SQL, MySQL, REXEC, RSH, RLOGIN, CVS, SNMP, SMTP-AUTH, SOCKS5, VNC, POP3, IMAP, NNTP, PCNFS, ICQ, SAP/R3, LDAP2, LDAP3, Postgres, Teamspeak, Cisco auth, Cisco enable, LDAP2, and Cisco AAA

Continued

Table 2.6 continued FairuzaWRT Reconnaissance and Attack Tools

Tool	Description
mailsnarf	Part of the dsniff suite, a network sniffer for clear-text mail protocols
msgsnarf	Part of the dsniff suite, a network sniffer for clear-text Instant Messaging applications
nbtscan	A scanner for NetBIOS name servers
netcat (nc)	A utility for reading and writing data across a TCP/IP network. The unofficial "network Swiss army knife."
nmap	A port scanner and remote service identification tool
sshmitm	Part of the dsniff suite, a tool for launching SSH MITM attacks
tcpdump	A command-line network sniffer
tcpkill	Used to spoof TCP/IP network session terminations
tcpnice	A utility for controlling the speed of TCP connections via spoofing
urlsnarf	Part of the dsniff suite, a utility for gathering URLs over the network
webmitm	Part of the dsniff suite, a tool for HTTP and SSL MITM attacks

Installation

Installation of FairuzaWRT can be a very arduous task if the prerequisites have not been met. Much like the OpenWrt base, you can install FairuzaWRT via the Web GUI or TFTP, as described earlier in this chapter. However, FairuzaWRT contains a significant number of attack and penetration tools preinstalled in the firmware image, and as a result, you can install it only on WRT54G models that contain larger amounts of flash and RAM. Table 2.7 summarizes the WRT54G hardware models that FairuzaWRT supports.

Table 2.7 WRT54G Models Supported by FairuzaWRT

WRT54G Model and Version	CPU Speed	RAM	Flash
WRT54GS, version 1.0	200 MHz	32 MB	8 MB
WRT54GS, version 1.1	200 MHz	32 MB	8 MB
WRT54GS, version 2.0	200 MHz	32 MB	8 MB
WRT54GS, version 2.1	216 MHz	32 MB	8 MB
WRT54GS, version 3.0	200 MHz	32 MB	8 MB

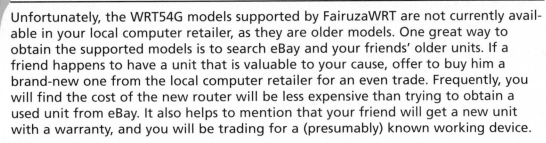

TIP

Unfortunately, the WRT54G models supported by FairuzaWRT are not currently available in your local computer retailer, as they are older models. One great way to obtain the supported models is to search eBay and your friends' older units. If a friend happens to have a unit that is valuable to your cause, offer to buy him a brand-new one from the local computer retailer for an even trade. Frequently, you will find the cost of the new router will be less expensive than trying to obtain a used unit from eBay. It also helps to mention that your friend will get a new unit with a warranty, and you will be trading for a (presumably) known working device.

Although FairuzaWRT installation is certainly possible with the GUI Web interface, it is highly recommended that you install it via TFTP, as indicated earlier in this chapter. You can download the latest image from www.hackerpimps.com/fairuzawrt/bin/fairuzawrt-02.bin. The SHA-1 sums are inside the associated README file, located at www.hackerpimps.com/fairuzawrt/bin/README.

Using FairuzaWRT

Once you have FairuzaWRT installed on your Linksys device, you must use the command line to configure its settings. The FairuzaWRT developers omitted any GUI management of the firmware for two suspected reasons: one, to save space by not installing the GUI frontend and supporting files, leaving more room for additional tools; and two, to make it more difficult to use. Given that FairuzaWRT can be a very dangerous tool when used by the wrong individuals, it makes sense that you have to pay your dues in order to use the tools contained within! FairuzaWRT does have a Web server installed and started by default, but it provides only an information splash page, as indicated in Figure 2.16.

Figure 2.16 FairuzaWRT Splash Page

In order to begin using FairuzaWRT you will need to connect to the WRT54G via Telnet the first time. Using your favorite Telnet client, connect to the WRT54G via Ethernet cable to any of the LAN ports. Upon connecting, you will be placed at the command line, as indicated in Figure 2.17.

Figure 2.17 First-Time Telnet Login to FairuzaWRT

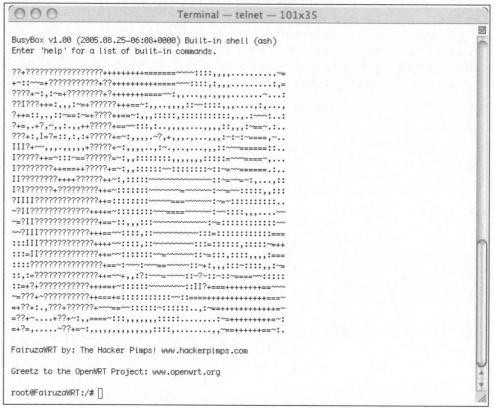

When you connect to a FairuzaWRT installation for the first time via Telnet, you should note that you are never asked for a username and password in the same manner as OpenWrt. You must follow the same process for FairuzaWRT with regard to setting the initial password. This means you must Telnet to the device, set a password using the *passwd* command, and exit.

You now must SSH with your favorite SSH client. Begin by connecting your computer via Ethernet cable to any LAN port on the WRT54G. After obtaining a DHCP address from the FairuzaWRT WRT54G, connect to the default internal IP address. For example, under most UNIX/Linux distributions and under Mac OS X, enter *ssh root@192.168.1.1* at the command prompt.

Are You 0wned?

No Password Access?

Unlike OpenWrt, FairuzaWRT, version 0.2, does not automatically shut down the *telnet* option after setting the root password. As we noted earlier in this section, connecting via Telnet requires no password by default, which could be potentially dangerous, considering that FairuzaWRT is designed to compromise networks! Unless you manually disable Telnet, it is still available to anyone who can connect to it, enabling him to gain access without a password.

In order to disable the Telnet service, you need to either delete or rename the startup script for this service. The startup script is located at /etc/init.d/S50telnet. When you rename the script to disabled_s50telnet (lowercase "s"), the init startup process will ignore the need to run the command, and it will be available to you at a later date to reenable if needed. You can rename the script by issuing the following command:

```
# mv /etc/init.d/S50telnet /etc/init.d/disabled_s50telnet
```

You can terminate the Telnet daemon with the *killall* command:

```
# killall telnetd
```

However, it is recommended that you perform a full reboot of the WRT54G in order to verify that subsequent reboots will continue to have Telnet disabled.

The FairuzaWRT Command Line

The FairuzaWRT command line is Linux/UNIX–based, and identical to that of OpenWrt. For basic configuration, please review the OpenWrt command-line section, earlier in this chapter. Instead of repeating the information contained there, here we'll outline some of the more specialized tools preinstalled with FairuzaWRT.

The Main Menu

FairuzaWRT has a menu system available to simplify basic configuration and use of some of the default tools. To start the menu while connected to the WRT54G, issue the following command:

```
# sh /usr/bin/fairuzaus.sh
```

The menu will be displayed as shown in Figure 2.18.

Figure 2.18 The FairuzaWRT Main Menu

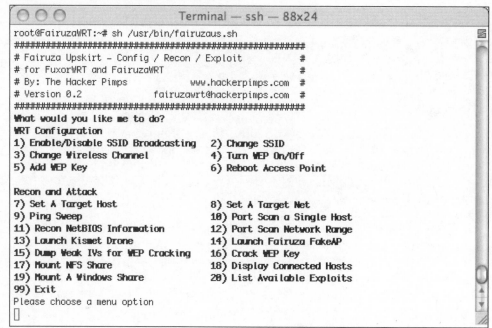

The menu is composed of two main sections: WRT54G Configuration, and Recon and Attack. Table 2.8 lists the menu items.

Table 2.8 WRT54G Configuration Menu

Menu Item	Description
Enable/Disable SSID Broadcasting	Enables or disables the wireless Service Set Identifier (SSID) broadcast. A setting of 0 sets the broadcast to on; 1 sets the broadcast to off (setting a "cloaked" network).
Change SSID	Sets the wireless SSID to that of your choosing
Change Wireless Channel	Sets the wireless channel. Valid options are the numbers 1–11 (U.S. 802.11 channel range).
Turn WEP On/Off	Enables or disables WEP. A setting of 0 turns off WEP, and 1 turns it on.
Add WEP Key	Defines the active WEP key. A 64-bit or 128-bit encryption is determined automatically by the length of the key. Five to 10 characters will enable 64-bit encryption and 13 to 26 characters will enable 128-bit encryption. This option is ignored if WEP is disabled.
Reboot Access Point	Reboots the WRT54G

As an alternative to the menu commands, the same functionality is available from the command line as a series of NVRAM commands. For additional information on NVRAM commands, see Chapter 3. Table 2.9 lists the Recon and Attack menu.

Table 2.9 Recon and Attack Menu

Menu Item	Description
Set a Target Host	Defines a single host for additional actions by IP address
Set a Target Net	Defines a network range for further actions by IP range
Ping Sweep	Performs a ping of all IP addresses defined by "Set a Target Net" using Nmap. This command will be ignored if no target network is defined.
Port Scan a Single Host	Performs a port scan of a single IP address defined by "Set a Target Host" using Nmap. This command will be ignored if no target host is defined.
Recon NetBIOS Information	Displays all available NetBIOS information obtained from the target network using nbtscan. This command will be ignored if no target network is defined.
Port Scan Network Range	Performs a port scan of an IP address range defined by "Set a Target Network" using Nmap. This command will be ignored if no target network is defined.
Launch Kismet Drone	Starts Kismet Drone, a wireless recon tool. This command will fail if Kismet Drone is not installed. You can install Kismet Drone with *ipkg install kismet-drone* at the command line.
Launch Fairuza FakeAP	Starts FairuzaWRT FakeAP, but it is not supported in the current build
Dump Weak IVs for WEP Cracking	Utilizes airodump to capture weak WEP traffic to begin the WEP key cracking process. Requires installation of Aircrack, described later in this section.
Crack WEP Key	Performs WEP key cracking against data collected from "Dump Weak IVs for WEP Cracking." Requires installation of Aircrack.
Mount NFS Share	Mounts a Network File System (NFS) share from an IP address. Requires an existing valid mount point, such as /tmp/nfs.
Display Connected Hosts	Lists the hosts that have been successfully exploited

Continued

Table 2.9 continued Recon and Attack Menu

Menu Item	Description
Mount a Windows Share	Mounts a Windows share from a universal naming convention (UNC) path. Requires an existing valid Windows share, such as \\host\share.
List Available Exploits	Lists some of the available exploits located in /usr/bin. Executing the exploits is not currently supported by the menu.
Exit	Exits the menu and returns to the command line

Several of the commands in the menu are nonfunctional, as they have not been fully developed. However, all of the tools listed in the menu, and many more, are located under /usr/bin and /usr/sbin. Aircrack, one tool that we will cover in this section, does work with the menu but requires a few steps beforehand to install it.

Installing Software under FairuzaWRT

FairuzaWRT comes with a robust package management system used for installing, removing, and updating software. The package management system, called ipkg, is identical to that of OpenWrt. Setting up ipkg under FairuzaWRT is subtly different from ipkg OpenWrt setup. FairuzaWRT is configured to utilize the FairuzaWRT package repository as the default place to look for and obtain packages. Although the FairuzaWRT package repository is very similar to that of OpenWrt, the FairuzaWRT repository may not be up-to-date with the latest OpenWrt packages, or provide many older or additional packages offered by OpenWrt. As FairuzaWRT is based on the OpenWrt project, the packages are interchangeable.

Installing Aircrack-ng with FairuzaWRT

We are using Aircrack-ng as an example in this section because it is one of the most popular wireless networking auditing tools. It has the capability to sniff wireless traffic and crack WEP keys. It is an essential tool for wireless audits and penetration testing, and when you combine it with a small, embedded device you can use it for mobile deployments. For example, if you have gained physical access to an organization and wish to leave something behind for auditing the wireless network further, a WRT54G with Aircrack-ng is a useful device for this purpose.

In order to install Aircrack-ng with FairuzaWRT, you need to modify the default ipkg repositories. Unfortunately, The Hacker Pimps do not include Aircrack in the base install, nor do they include it in the online package repositories. Fortunately, OpenWrt does provide an Aircrack-ng package in its repository. As you may recall, The Hacker Pimps have modified the configuration to use their own package repository. As a result, you need to add an additional package repository to the configuration.

In order to add the additional package repository to the configuration, you need to modify the ipkg.conf file located in the /etc directory. If you perform a directory listing, you will note that the ipkg.conf file is a symbolic link to /rom/etc/ipkg.conf:

```
lrwxrwxrwx    1 root      root        18 Jan  1  2000 ipkg.conf -> /rom/etc/ipkg.conf
```

The destination of the symbolic link points to a location that has been made read-only, as indicated by the initial /rom path (ROM stands for Read Only Memory). In order to edit this file, you need to create a writeable version in /etc. With the following commands you can create a backup of the original symbolic link, and copy a version of the file that you are able to edit:

```
# mv /etc/ipkg.conf  /etc/ipkg-backup.conf
# cp /rom/etc/ipkg.conf /etc/ipkg.conf
```

You now need to edit the new ipkg.conf to add the additional repository. You can use a common text editor, such as vi, to edit this file.

You will now add a third package repository that contains the Aircrack-ng package by inserting the package repository from the OpenWrt project for Whiterussian 0.9 backports located at http://downloads.openwrt.org/backports/0.9. Add another source ("src") directive and provide a descriptive name for the repository:

```
src openwrt-wr-09-backports http://downloads.openwrt.org/backports/0.9
```

Now save the file and exit vi to update your configuration.

TIP

You can find the vi text editor on just about every POSIX-based operating system on the planet, and as a result, it is extremely valuable to know how to use it. Although vi may be very Spartan in its appearance, it is in fact a very powerful text editor. For more information on using vi, visit http://docs.freebsd.org/44doc/usd/12.vi/paper.html.

In order to have your configuration take effect, you need to have ipkg update its repositories from the configuration, by issuing the following command:

```
# ipkg update
```

Now that you have updated the package listing from all three package repositories, you can successfully install Aircrack from your new repository. To install Aircrack-ng, you need to issue the following command:

```
# ipkg install aircrack-ng
```

Once Aircrack-ng has been installed, you need to modify the menu to make it function with Aircrack-ng, as The Hacker Pimps have only included the functionality for the discontinued version of Aircrack (non-ng). You need to modify lines 206 and 207 of the menu script, /usr/bin/fairuzaus.sh, with vi. The original lines read as follows:

```
if [ -n "$ffactor" ] && [ -f "/usr/sbin/aircrack"] && [ -n "ivLoc"]; then
          aircrack $ffactor -f $ivLoc
```

You need to modify them so that they read as shown here, effectively replacing *aircrack* with *aircrack-ng*:

```
if [ -n "$ffactor" ] && [ -f "/usr/sbin/aircrack-ng"] && [ -n "ivLoc"]; then
            aircrack-ng $ffactor -f $ivLoc
```

After you save your modifications to the menu, Aircrack-ng should be fully functional under the menu. You can find more information on using Aircrack-ng manually at www.aircrack-ng.org.

Tools & Traps...

Aircrack versus Aircrack-ng

Although Aircrack is the tool primarily used for the FairuzaWRT menu, Aircrack-ng is a better alternative which we have instructed you how to install.

Aircrack-ng is the updated version of the discontinued Aircrack, and it contains new features and some speed improvements. Given that the WRT54G is a small, embedded system with a processor that is significantly less powerful than modern desktop systems, we need all the speed that we can get.

Additionally, Aircrack-ng provides a significant upgrade over Aircrack. Although Aircrack was only able to crack WEP, Aircrack-ng has added the capability to crack WPA-PSK with the addition of a wordlist. Chances are that the wordlist you will want to use will be significantly larger than the space available on the WRT54G, so you'll need to resort to other options. You can increase the storage capacity of the WRT54G (see Chapter 7), or mount the wordlist over the network using a remote file system. You can mount remote file systems over the network with either the FairuzaWRT menu, or via the command line using either the *mount* command for NFS shares or the *mount.cifs* command for Windows shares.

To make matters more confusing, a new tool based on Aircrack is available, called Aircrack-ptw (www.cdc.informatik.tu-darmstadt.de/aircrack-ptw), which (through even more intense math and by taking advantage of newly discovered WEP vulnerabilities) can crack a 128-bit (also known as a 104-bit) WEP key in less than 60 seconds. This tool has not been ported to the WRT54G as of this writing.

Who Should Use This Firmware

The FairuzaWRT firmware is certainly not intended to be used as the firmware on the router you use every day, and the FairuzaWRT authors reiterate those sentiments. This firmware is geared toward the professional penetration tester, computer security professional, or someone looking to gain access to networks for nefarious purposes. This firmware is certainly best suited for someone interested in computer security, both good and bad.

Although FairuzaWRT is poorly documented, it is based on many tools that are widely documented across the Internet, which will make it easy to learn. It would also be very easy to take the concepts and software learned with FairuzaWRT to use OpenWrt and build your own penetration testing WRT54G suitable to your needs.

Sveasoft

Background

Sveasoft was one of the first third-party firmware packages available for the WRT54G platform. In the beginning, it was free. Sveasoft now requires a commercial license ($20 per year) which includes support through user forums (www.sveasoft.com/modules/phpBB2/index.php). The newer versions also offer a redesigned Web interface. The software is locked to five MAC addresses (due to licensing restrictions), so you will need to purchase one for every five routers you install it on. Sveasoft is now based on the OpenWrt packages and offers multiple firmware versions tailored to different uses: Basic, Micro, VPN, Hotspot, Mesh, VoIP, and OEM. There has been some recent news from the OpenWrt team with Sveasoft. Apparently, OpenWrt has rescinded Sveasoft's right to redistribute under the GPL, as Sveasoft is apparently not releasing the modifications as required by the OpenWrt license.

Sveasoft has released a number of different firmware lines since the beginning of the project. Although the Talisman version is the currently supported version, it does require the paid license. The free versions, Alchemy (v1), Satori (v4), and Samadhi (v2), are available from Sveasoft (www.sveasoft.com/modules/phpBB2/dlman.php?func=select_folder&folder_id=10); however, it appears that they are no longer maintained and support through the forums is nonexistent. Also, the firmware will not work on newer hardware revisions of the WRT54G. It is not recommended that you use the free versions from the Sveasoft project.

From the Talisman branch of firmware, several sub-builds are customized to a specific task, as indicated in Table 2.10.

Table 2.10 Sveasoft Tailored Builds

Build	Description
Talisman Basic	This is the core of the Talisman branch. It contains all of the basic features one would expect from a WRT54G, plus a few enhancements, including those to the Web interface and wireless transmit power.
Talisman Micro	The micro build of Talisman reduces the firmware size so that it is suitable for installation on hardware that contains only 2 MB of flash memory. In order to appropriately reduce the size, the functionality of PPoE, PPTP, and DHCP was sacrificed.

Continued

Table 2.10 continued Sveasoft Tailored Builds

Build	Description
Talisman VPN	Talisman VPN adds IPSec and PPTP servers to the basic branch feature set. This firmware is dedicated to creating a VPN endpoint.
Talisman Hotspot	The Hotspot version of the firmware is ideal for creating a wireless hotspot, much like Ewrt. In addition to the Ewrt captive portal, Talisman Hotspot features its own internal Remote Authentication Dial-in User Service (RADIUS) and SQL servers. External RADIUS server support is also included.
Talisman Mesh	Talisman Mesh is ideally suited to those looking to create a wireless mesh network, such as a wireless Internet service provider (ISP) or community-based wireless network.
Talisman VOIP	This version turns the base installation into a Session Initiation Protocol (SIP) gateway. You can use this firmware to locally terminate SIP connections, or forward them to an outside VoIP/SIP provider.

Although Sveasoft Talisman has a number of tailored builds, it is not very extensible beyond those aims. Talisman does not fully support OpenWrt packages, as Sveasoft maintains its own packaging system, spkg. At the time of this writing, four packages were listed in the Sveasoft repository, located at www.sveasoft.com/modules/phpBB2/dlman.php?func=select_folder&folder_id=23.

NOTE

You can install Sveasoft Talisman with the standard Web and TFTP methods described earlier in this book. Upon installation, you can access it via the Web interface with the default username of *root* and password of *admin*.

Features

The first feature we will notice in Sveasoft Talisman is the redesigned, very comprehensive Web interface shown in Figure 2.19.

The Web interface within Sveasoft will allow you to accomplish every modification you can think of. The only reason you may want to Telnet or SSH to the Sveasoft firmware would be to install additional software. However, package installation and command-line commands can be issued through the Web interface as well.

Figure 2.19 Talisman Basic Web Interface

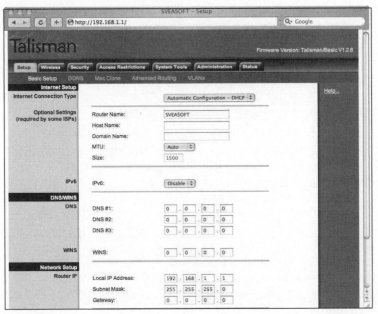

For those wanting to increase the transmit power of the wireless radio, SveaSoft Talisman Basic may be for you. This firmware upgrade allows for the highest output power of all of the firmware currently available, at a whopping 1000mW on some devices! However, the 1000mW output appears to function only on hardware from Buffalo. Sveasoft Talisman will set the maximum power possible on the WRT54G if you're using the 1000mW setting. Typically, the WRT54G will use the maximum possible setting when set at the 1000mW setting, which is usually 251mW. You can find the option for transmit power settings, called TX Power, under **Wireless | Advanced Settings**, as shown in Figure 2.20.

Figure 2.20 Sveasoft Transmit Power Increase

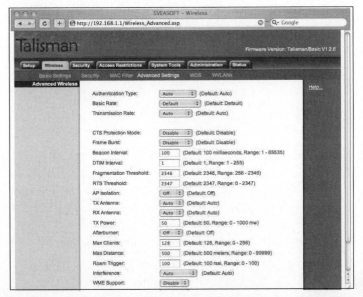

Notes from the Underground...

Increasing Radio Power: Avoid a Fire

One nice feature of third-party firmware for the WRT54G platform is the ability to change the radio transmit power (TX Power). The default setting for Sveasoft is 50 mW, and the default Linksys firmware does not allow you to change this. As a function of the wireless card, the TX power is 89mW.

Using one of the firmware add-ons discussed in this book you can increase it all the way to 251 mW, the hardware maximum for all WRT54G models, including the WRT54GS, WRT54GL, and WRTSL54GS. The Sveasoft firmware indicates that you can increase the power level to 1000 mW; however, the wireless chipset will not output more than 251 mW. This artificially increased setting with Sveasoft is so that it can support additional devices other than Linksys hardware.

CAUTION: Increasing your radio power beyond 89mW could cause overheating, and potentially melt your WRT54G, and even cause a fire.

For more information about signal strength and antennas, please refer to Chapter 7.

Who Should Use This Firmware

Sveasoft's Talisman Basic is a great firmware solution for those who have a fear of the command line, and want to use GUI management through a Web browser for all manner of configuration. You will pay the price for GUI management, in the form of $20 for licensing and support fees per year. Additionally, the other flavors of the firmware are equally as robust with GUI management, and are also recommended for those with a fear of the command line and specific requirements.

Please note the ongoing issues surrounding Sveasoft and OpenWrt regarding GPL licensing, and Sveasoft's alleged violation. If you choose to utilize Sveasoft, it may be beneficial to keep a watchful eye on the situation, as it may directly affect Sveasoft's business model.

HyperWRT

Background

HyperWRT's original goal was to add some limited features to the base Linksys firmware, maintaining a very similar look and feel to the stock Linksys firmware. Initially, HyperWRT's claim to fame was the ability to increase the wireless transmit power, but it has now added other functionality.

Timothy Jans created the original HyperWRT firmware in 2004, and stopped development in 2005, when a developer named Rupan adopted the project. Later in 2005 two developers, Thibor and tofu, took over HyperWRT development, thus creating two separate forks of the project. As a result of these forks, many differences were evident in the separate versions. Although both Thibor and tofu worked together and shared many features, there were plenty of gaps and confusion. Most notable was the support for the newer WRT54GL models in tofu, whereas Thibor did not support it.

In early 2006, tofu elected to stop development on his fork of the HyperWRT firmware, and provided the fork's code to Thibor. Shortly thereafter, Thibor was able to incorporate all of the features from tofu previously missing in Thibor into the Thibor fork. As a result, there is now only one official HyperWRT port. This single, official version has reduced confusion regarding what firmware needs to be used for each device. Thibor has been able to support the WRT54GL with the integration of the tofu codebase.

NOTE

The Web site for the original HyperWRT project still exists at www.hyperwrt.org, even though development on this original firmware has ceased. You can find the currently supported HyperWRT release, HyperWRT Thibor, at www.thibor.co.uk.

NOTE

You can install HyperWRT with the standard Web and TFTP methods described earlier in this book. Upon installation, you can access it via the Web interface with a blank username and a password of *admin*.

Features

HyperWRT looks almost identical to the original Linksys GUI Web management console, as shown in Figure 2.21.
This interface keeps much of what makes the Linksys interface very comfortable to many home users.

HyperWRT has included many features that have been missing from much of the stock Linksys firmware, including the ability to adjust wireless transmit power, without the cost of the Sveasoft firmware. You can find the wireless transmit power under the Web management menu, under **Wireless | Advanced Wireless**, as shown in Figure 2.22.

Figure 2.21 HyperWRT's Linksys Web Management Interface

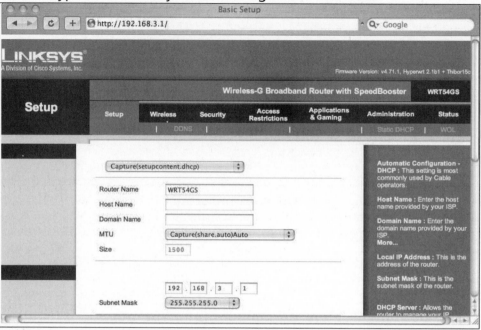

Figure 2.22 Increasing Wireless Transmit Power with HyperWRT

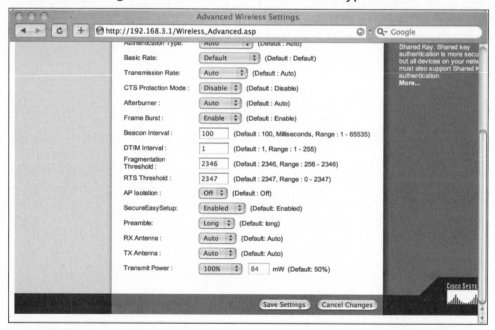

HyperWRT offers the ability to set the wireless transmit power based on a percentage of the suggested maximum range. HyperWRT's 100 percent setting equates to 84 mW, which is in an

acceptable operating range of the wireless chipset. It is possible to provide a manual setting for the transmit power by selecting **Manual** from the drop-down box, and defining the desired transmit power value in the provided field. The maximum manual setting acceptable to the firmware is 251mW, and the Web management interface will reject any value over that.

In addition to adjusting the transmit power, HyperWRT allows the use of all 14 available wireless channels, including 1–11 for the United States, the addition of channels of 12 and 13 for Europe, and channel 14 for Japan, as we indicate in Chapter 6. .

WARNING

HyperWRT does not restrict which channels you can use in a particular region. Be aware that in certain locations, it may be against country, government, or federal regulations to use certain channels. For example, in the United States it is against FCC regulations to use channels 12, 13, and 14. HyperWRT unlocks these additional channels, so please be mindful which channels are legal for use in your area.

In addition to the previous adjustments, HyperWRT provides a significant upgrade to the default Linksys port forwarding and game definition settings of the firewall, by providing several more line items for available settings. Additionally, HyperWRT provides more robust QoS for many predefined applications, and allows for custom definitions. QoS is important to time-sensitive applications, such as online games, and voice applications such as Skype and VoIP. QoS can allow for this type of application to be identified, and can ensure that particular network traffic receives priority over any other network traffic.

One other unusual feature that is included in HyperWRT and is useful for remote management is Wake On Lan (WOL) capabilities, as shown in Figure 2.23.

Figure 2.23 HyperWRT Wake On Lan Settings

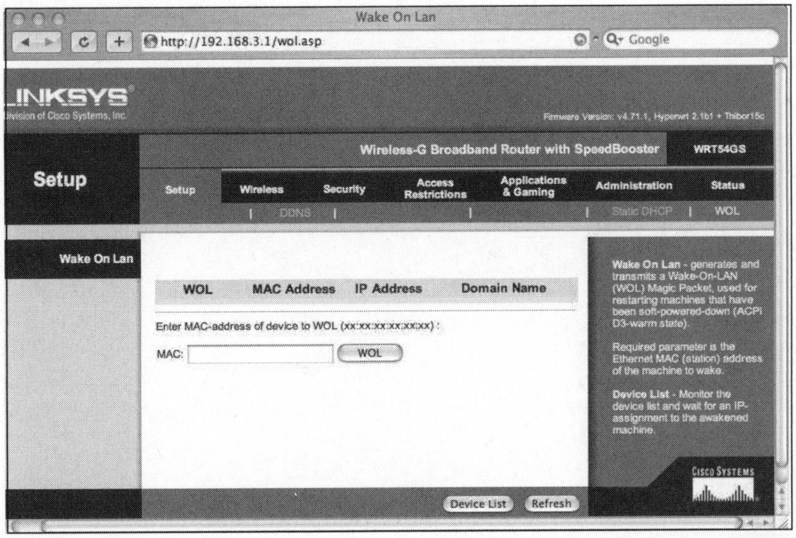

HyperWRT will act as a Wake On Lan client, generate a WOL Magic Packet, and send it on the LAN for the specified MAC address. If the computer is properly configured, this Magic Packet will turn on the destination computer, when in the powered-off state. This is extremely helpful if you need to provide remote support to computers attached to the WRT54G with HyperWRT, allowing you to potentially turn on computers from a remote location.

Who Should Use This Firmware

HyperWRT is an awesome, free upgrade for a home user who wants additional appropriate functionality on his WRT54G router without the hassle of learning the command line. This firmware would also be ideal for a small-business network due to the additional firewall configurations and Internet filtering capabilities, which could help to secure company commuters. These same features may be useful for the average home user as well.

Summary

It is extremely important to read and understand the installation procedures outlined in the beginning of this chapter and test them in your own environment on nonproduction equipment, if possible. They will prepare you for implementing the WRT54G hacks and projects that follow in the remainder of this book. We covered the TFTP method of installation extensively, and provided a short step-by-step guide for easy reference. We then went on to cover the individual third-party firmware distributions that are available, and how to select the appropriate image and install it.

It would be next to impossible for us to cover every third-party firmware distribution in great detail. We have highlighted some, and outlined their strengths and weaknesses. These include distributions that cost money (Sveasoft), and freely available firmware such as HyperWRT and FairuzaWRT. The remainder of this book will focus on using OpenWrt, DD-WRT, and Ewrt exclusively. Although it may seem as though we're focusing on OpenWrt throughout this book, be aware that both DD-WRT and Ewrt are OpenWrt-based firmware distributions; therefore, becoming familiar with OpenWrt will help provide the foundation for understanding many other firmware distributions.

Solutions Fast Track

Installing Third-Party Firmware on Your WRT54G

☑ Installing third-party firmware voids the warranty on your WRT54G.

☑ Installing third-party firmware via the Web interface is by far the easiest and most convenient method.

☑ TFTP installations can be very reliable, albeit more difficult. TFTP is a great way to install firmware when you have gotten yourself into a jam.

Introduction to Firmware Used in This Book

☑ OpenWrt is the basis for most of the third-party firmware covered in this book. It uses a Debian-like package structure called ipkg. Most configuration changes are completed through the command-line interface.

☑ DD-WRT is a great firmware for the novice user. It comes with many features in the default installation. The GUI is quite extensive, allowing you to configure just about anything within the operating system. DD-WRT also provides a command-line interface for when you are ready to get down and dirty.

☑ Most projects and configurations will rely heavily on knowledge of OpenWrt throughout the rest of this book, as it is the basis of many of our projects.

Other Firmware Worth Mentioning

☑ Many third-party firmware options are available. Some offer commercial support, such as Sveasoft. Others are provided for a specific purpose, such as Ewrt, which allows you to create a captive portal. Some different flavors also include HyperWRT, whose purpose is to provide an easy way for you to access some of the advanced features, such as increasing your radio power.

☑ Many third-party firmware installations reuse and add to the already familiar Linksys stock interfaces.

☑ FairuzaWRT is a penetration testing platform that runs on a WRT54GS only. It includes popular tools such as Nmap and dsniff, and some wireless auditing tools. The FairuzaWRT project offers its own package distribution tree.

Links to Sites

http://wiki.openwrt.org/OpenWrtDocs/Configuration The OpenWrt Basic Configuration page, which includes documentation on the basic configuration for OpenWrt, including networking, NVRAM, WDS, iptables, and NTP.

http://wiki.openwrt.org/OpenWrtDocs/Installing This is the OpenWrt guide to installing the firmware. It contains many useful tips, hints, and tricks on installation, as well as additional information pertaining to upgrading, backing up, and restoring OpenWrt.

www.dd-wrt.com/wiki/index.php?title=Installation This is the DD-WRT guide to installing the firmware. It also contains many useful tips, hints, and tricks on installation, as well as additional information pertaining to troubleshooting and installation on different hardware platforms.

ftp://ftp.linksys.com/pub/network/ If you need to find a specific version of the Linksys firmware, this is the place for you. You may want to test the Ping Hack just to see how it works, and this is the place to acquire the vulnerable versions.

http://downloads.openwrt.org/people/mbm/openwrt.html This page, written by Mike Baker, provides some insight into the inner workings of the WRT54G hardware and kernel, including a nice write-up of the Ping Hack.

www.linux-mtd.infradead.org/faq/general.html A general Frequently Asked Questions repository of information on MTD, referred to throughout the book as *flash*. This site also includes a nice discussion on JFFS2.

www.linux-mips.org/ A fantastic reference for information about Linux running on MIPS processors, including discussions on PMON, CFE, Linux kernels for MIPS processors, and MIPS emulators.

http://wiki.openwrt.org/OpenWrtDocs/Customizing/Firmware/CFE The OpenWrt project's description of CFE, including how make changes with a JTAG cable. Use with extreme caution.

www.broadcom.com/products/communications_processors_downloads.php Information and downloads for the CFE associated with Broadcom processors, including the CFE source code for those interested.

www.hackerpimps.com/projects.html Home page for FairuzaWRT, including links to documentation and the software repository.

www.bitsum.com/openwiking/owbase/ow.asp?WRT54G5%5FCFE The original guide to installing DD-WRT on a WRT54G, versions 5.0–6.0.

Frequently Asked Questions

The following Frequently Asked Questions, answered by the authors of this book, are designed to both measure your understanding of the concepts presented in this chapter and to assist you with real-life implementation of these concepts. To have your questions about this chapter answered by the author, browse to **www. syngress.com/solutions** and click on the **"Ask the Author"** form.

Q: Should I use the Web or TFTP method of installation?

A: Most users will feel more comfortable using the Web method of installation. It allows you to easily select the new firmware from within the Web GUI and install it onto the flash.

Q: When I install third-party firmware using the TFTP method I get the error "Code pattern is incorrect." What does that mean?

A: That means you are trying to install a firmware image that was created for a different model router. Be certain that the image file you've downloaded corresponds to the router model you are trying to reimage. For more information on the different router models refer to Chapter 1.

Q: I installed OpenWrt and when it first booted it asked me to change the password. When I tried to change it, I got an error. Why?

A: If you chose JFFS as your file system, you need to reboot after the initial installation. The file system will not be writeable until you reboot; thus, you are not able to change the password (which requires writing to /etc/shadow).

Q: When I install third-party firmware using the TFTP method I get the error "Invalid Password." What does that mean?

A: That means your router has booted past the PMON/CFE TFTP server and into the operating system. The TFTP server you are accessing is in the operating system. Try putting a bug in between your TFTP client and the router, increasing the wait time using *wait_time=<seconds>*, and/or statically assigning the MAC address of your router to 192.168.1.1 in the ARP table on the TFTP client.

Q: In what version of OpenWrt was a Web GUI introduced?

A: The Web GUI was introduced in OpenWrt Whiterussian RC1, the initial release of Whiterussian.

Q: OpenWrt supports two different filesystems: SQUASHFS and JFFS2. Which one should I use?

A: SQUASHFS is a read-only file system, whereas JFFS2 is read-write. With regard to OpenWrt, the architecture has changed so that this decision is not necessary anymore.

Q: What is the difference between OpenWrt and DD-WRT?

A: OpenWrt is a full-featured operating system for the WRT54G platform (and many other devices). Its goal is to create a stable and extensible operating system for embedded devices that allows developers to easily create and modify code. DD-WRT uses OpenWrt as its foundation, with a heavy focus on providing the user with the best, most full-featured, graphical interface.

Q: What is the name of the penetration testing firmware and why would I want to use it?

A: FairuzaWRT is the penetration testing software for the WRT54GS routers, versions 1.0–3.0. You can use this as a platform to perform penetration testing and wireless assessments. However, it's best served as an example of just how extensible the OpenWrt development platform is, including creating your own package repository.

Q: What if I just want to increase the radio transmit power of my WRT54G; which firmware should I choose?

A: The HyperWRT firmware advertises itself as being developed specifically to allow users to increase the radio transmit power. However, if you are going to go through the trouble of putting third-party software on your router, use OpenWrt as you will then be able to take advantage of all the features and receive frequent software updates in addition to always being able to access the software repository.

## Chapter 3

Using Third-Party Firmware

Solutions in this chapter:

- **Configuring and Using OpenWrt**
- **Configuring and Using DD-WRT**
- **Securing Your Firmware**

☑ **Summary**

☑ **Solutions Fast Track**

☑ **Frequently Asked Questions**

Introduction

Configuring and Using OpenWrt

Once you have OpenWrt installed on your Linksys device, you can use either the GUI or the command line to configure its settings. We strongly recommend that you use the command line to configure OpenWrt. It is very powerful and allows you to very easily implement advanced configurations. The GUI, covered briefly in Chapter 2, allows you to access only a small subset of functionality and configure only basic settings. This was not intentional; OpenWrt was intended primarily for developers in the beginning and is still working on becoming more "user friendly" with respect to a Web interface. This chapter will also cover X-Wrt, a Web interface that is full-featured and mirrors the functionality of the command line. The sections that follow will show you how to use the OpenWrt command-line interface and implement numerous configuration changes to perform various tasks such as enabling the Universal Serial Bus (USB), Syslog, Samba, and more!

NOTE

The version of OpenWrt used throughout this book is Whiterussian version 0.9 (which uses BusyBox v1.00), based on a Linux 2.4 kernel (2.4.30). The version of DD-WRT used throughout the book is DD-WRT V23 SP2.

The OpenWrt Command Line

The OpenWrt command line is Linux/UNIX-based, so readers who are familiar with those platforms should be very comfortable. For those just getting started with the Linux/UNIX command line, remember one thing: Don't be afraid of it. Think of the command line as merely a different way to configure the device. Instead of clicking your way around, you need to know which commands to enter. The following sections offer a good introduction to the command line, for even the most novice user.

TIP

The command line in OpenWrt is handled by BusyBox (www.busybox.net). BusyBox is a small, single executable that combines many Linux/UNIX commands. It has a small footprint and is extremely modular, allowing you to add or remove components to suit your needs. For complete documentation on all of its commands, see www.busybox.net/downloads/BusyBox.html. Please note that not all of these commands may be built into OpenWrt.

Configuring OpenWrt Using nvram

The *nvram* command allows you to manipulate the configuration settings contained within the reserved 64KB of flash memory known as NVRAM. Issuing the *nvram show* command will display a list of the configuration variables and their value. The *nvram get <variable>* command will show you this variable's value, and *nvram set <variable>=<value>* is the command to change the variable's value. Here is an example of how to change the device SSID (or wireless network name):

```
# nvram get wl0_ssid
OpenWrt
# nvram set wl0_ssid="GetPwn3dHere"
# nvram get wl0_ssid
GetPwn3dHere
# nvram commit
```

First, we issue the *nvram get wl0_ssid* command command to retrieve the current SSID assigned to the access point. Next, we change the default SSID (always a good idea) using the *nvram set* command from *"OpenWrt"* to *"GetPwn3dHere"*. We must always remember to write the changes from memory (RAM) to the NVRAM partition on the flash by executing the command *nvram commit*. Although changing NVRAM and committing to flash stores the variable and value, you may need to run other scripts or programs (or even reboot the device) to really apply those values. In the examples that follow, we will specify the actions that need to be taken in order for your changes to take effect. For the preceding changes to take effect, you will need to run the command */sbin/wifi*, which applies the current wireless configuration.

Tools & Traps…

Fear of nvram commit-ment?

Throughout this book, we recommend that at the end of NVRAM modifications using the *nvram set* command, that you completed the commands with an *nvram commit*. The final *nvram commit* will copy the *nvram* contents from memory (RAM), and will save a copy to flash, allowing it to survive a reboot.

However, for testing purposes, you may wish to omit the *nvram commit*, and make the changes active with the appropriate commands (such as */sbin/wifi* in the case of wireless changes). This will allow you to perform a reboot, and revert to the previous NVRAM settings should something go wrong, or if the settings are not desirable.

NOTE

Although many of the examples will show you how to set or change a variable's value, sometimes you may want to clear the contents of a variable. You can do this by issuing the command *nvram set <variable>=""*. This is different from leaving a variable undefined through the *nvram unset <variable>* command. Depending on the variable, the end result can be the same using both methods, or not.

Changing the IP Address

So, let's assume you've just installed OpenWrt on your WRT54G and you plan to use it for purposes other than your firewall/router/access point to the Internet. It might be best to do this on a test router first, in order to become familiar with the operating system and how it works before using it as your primary firewall. Also, many projects in this book are written with the assumption that the device is not your primary router/firewall.

Once you've installed the new firmware on the router, you should change the Internet Protocol (IP) address of the device before plugging it into your network and SSH to it for the first time. This ensures that there are no IP address conflicts, especially ones involving the default gateway, as many times you may have a default gateway of 192.168.1.1. Given that we recommend that you restore to factory defaults, which sets the router to a default IP address of 192.168.1.1, before applying firmware, changing the IP address is usually the first step. You will need to make certain that your username is *root*; otherwise, you will not be able to log in to the router. OpenWrt does not have the concept of multiple users, so all logins are done with the *root* username.

```
pdc:~ nologin$ssh root 192.168.1.1
The authenticity of host '192.168.1.1 (192.168.1.1)' can't be established.
RSA key fingerprint is a0:88:ee:8b:10:13:1f:7f:5d:cc:9c:53:1b:c4:20:d8.
Are you sure you want to continue connecting (yes/no)? yes
Warning: Permanently added '192.168.1.85' (RSA) to the list of known hosts.
root@192.168.1.85's password:
```

You will notice that the SSH client asks you to accept the key, which is normal because this is the first time you are connecting to the device through SSH. In Chapter 2, we explained how to establish the initial Telnet or Web connection to change the default password. To change the IP address that is accessible from the local area network (LAN) assigned ports, use the following commands:

```
# nvram set lan_ipaddr="192.168.1.85"
# nvram set lan_gateway="192.168.1.1"
# nvram set lan_dns="192.168.1.10"
# nvram commit
```

The settings that control the actual IP address of your device all begin with *lan_*. Using the *nvram* command, make the appropriate changes for the new IP address (*lan_ipaddr*), default gateway (*lan_gateway*), and local domain name system (DNS) server (*lan_dns*). By default, these settings are changed only in RAM, so you need to run the *nvram commit* command to commit them from RAM to the NVRAM partition on the flash memory. You then need to tell the system to begin using these new values. To tell OpenWrt to reread and apply the network settings for the LAN interface run the following command:

```
# ifup lan
```

You will then lose your network connection to the device. Using SSH you can quickly reestablish your terminal session using the new IP address, and accept the new SSH key entry (as the IP address has changed and will place a new entry in the client SSH known_hosts file).

```
pdc:~ nologin$ ssh 192.168.1.85
The authenticity of host '192.168.1.85 (192.168.1.85)' can't be established.
RSA key fingerprint is a0:88:ee:8b:10:13:1f:7f:5d:cc:9c:53:1b:c4:20:d8.
Are you sure you want to continue connecting (yes/no)? yes
Warning: Permanently added '192.168.1.85' (RSA) to the list of known hosts.
root@192.168.1.85's password:


BusyBox v1.00 (2007.01.30-11:42+0000) Built-in shell (ash)
Enter 'help' for a list of built-in commands.
```

```
 _____                  _____     __
|       |.-----.-----.-----.|  |  |  |.-----.|  |_
|   -   ||  _  |  -__|     ||  |  |  ||  _  ||   _|
|_____||   __|_____|__|__||_____||___|  |____|
         |__| W I R E L E S S   F R E E D O M
WHITE RUSSIAN (0.9) -------------------------------
 * 2 oz Vodka   Mix the Vodka and Kahlua together
 * 1 oz Kahlua  over ice, then float the cream or
 * 1/2oz cream  milk on the top.
 ---------------------------------------------------
root@OpenWrt:~#
```

TIP

To better manage your SSH connections from your Linux client it is advisable to set up the $HOME/.ssh/config file to automatically set certain parameters when you log in to devices. You can do this by adding the following lines to your config file:

host wrt-hacker
    hostname 192.168.1.85
    user root

Now, when you type **ssh wrt-hacker**, your SSH client will know to use *root* as the username and 192.168.1.85 as the IP address.

In this case, you changed the IP address and will have to reconnect using its new IP address. Next, you may want to disable the wireless interface until you are ready to use it. This will prevent someone from associating to your router and attacking it or the rest of your network while you are in the process of configuring it:

```
# nvram set wl0_radio="0"
# nvram set wl0_akm="none"
# nvram commit
```

The *wl0_radio* NVRAM variable sends a command to the driver to disable the wireless interface. (For more information, run the command *wl radio*. Installation instructions for the *wl* command will follow.) The command *wl0_akm* specifies the wireless authentication and encryption mode— Wi-Fi Protected Access (WPA), Wi-Fi Protected Access 2 (WPA2), WPA-PSK, and so on—which is good to disable along with the radio. As with the LAN interface settings, you need to tell OpenWrt to reread and apply the NVRAM variables before the changes will take effect. You can do this by issuing the following command:

```
# /sbin/wifi
```

Before you get too far down the hacking path, you will want to turn on *boot_wait*:

```
# nvram set boot_wait="on"
# nvram commit
```

The *boot_wait* setting will allow you to easily upgrade or change firmware using the Trivial File Transfer Protocol (TFTP) method described in Chapter 2. Finally, you should set a proper hostname (*wan_hostname*) and commit your changes:

```
# nvram set wan_hostname="wrt-hacker"
# nvram commit
# reboot
```

Once your router has finished rebooting, you can SSH to it again and see that the prompt now displays your new hostname as:

```
root@wrt-hacker:~#
```

Installing Software with Ipkg

OpenWrt comes with a robust package management system used for installing, removing, and updating software, called ipkg. Those familiar with the Debian "apt" (Advanced Packaging Tool) structure should be very comfortable using ipkg, as ipkg very closely resembles the Debian project's package management system. In order to take advantage of the package management system, you must have a working Internet connection and a network configuration on the router (covered in the preceding section).

The first task you will want to perform on your OpenWrt installation is a complete package update. This will update your system with the current list of available packages, and you do it by issuing the command *ipkg update*:

```
# ipkg update
Downloading http://downloads.openwrt.org/whiterussian/packages/Packages
Updated list of available packages in /usr/lib/ipkg/lists/whiterussian
Downloading http://downloads.openwrt.org/whiterussian/packages/non-free/Packages
Updated list of available packages in /usr/lib/ipkg/lists/non-free
Successfully terminated.
```

WARNING

It is very important that you back up your router before applying a package upgrade. The package upgrade process could break any changes that you have made, or even brick your router. Be certain to follow the backup procedures covered in this chapter. Also, when the upgrade is complete, reboot your router to be certain that it will come back. If it does, you will need to telnet to the router's IP address and reset your password, just as you did the first time you installed OpenWrt.

Once you have the latest list of packages, you are now ready to begin installing software. The first step is to make certain that you have all of the latest versions of the previously installed packages. You do this by issuing the command *ipkg upgrade*:

```
# ipkg upgrade
Nothing to be done
Successfully terminated.
```

The *ipkg* command is good about telling you what it did, and the results of your commands. The preceding code is the message displayed when all your packages are up-to-date. These first two steps are vital to ensuring that subsequent packages are installed properly.

NOTE

During the writing of this book, there was a new release of OpenWrt which ended the Whiterussian development branch as of RC6 (version 0.9). RC6 (or Release Candidate 6) was the last major release, which made some fairly major changes (such as implementing the mini_ro file system). A minor release was made, 0.9, which contains minor bug fixes and you can apply it by running *ipkg update* and *ipkg upgrade* commands, as shown earlier.

When installing software, a good first step is to list the available packages in the OpenWrt package tree. You do this by issuing the *ipkg list* command. There are many to choose from, and each includes a short description. Here are some examples:

```
tcpdump - 3.8.3-1 - A tool for network monitoring and data acquisition.
tor - 0.1.0.17-1 - An anonymous Internet communication system
vsftpd - 2.0.4-1 - a fast and secure FTP server
wpa-supplicant - 0.4.7-1 - WPA Supplicant with support for WPA and WPA2
```

To list only the installed components you can run *ipkg list_installed*. Here is the complete installed package listing for OpenWrt from a newly installed system, representing the base packages that would be installed, for example, on a WRT54GL:

```
# ipkg list_installed
base-files - 8 - OpenWrt filesystem structure and scripts
base-files-brcm - 2 - Board/architecture specific files
bridge - 1.0.6-1 - Ethernet bridging tools
busybox - 1.00-4 - Core utilities for embedded Linux systems
dnsmasq - 2.33-1 - A lightweight DNS and DHCP server
dropbear - 0.48.1-1 - a small SSH 2 server/client designed for small memory
environments.
haserl - 0.8.0-1 - a CGI wrapper to embed shell scripts in HTML documents
ipkg - 0.99.149-2 - lightweight package management system
iptables - 1.3.3-2 - The netfilter firewalling software for IPv4
iwlib - 28.pre7-1 - Library for setting up WiFi cards using the Wireless Extension
kernel - 2.4.30-brcm-4 -
kmod-brcm-wl - 2.4.30-brcm-4 - Proprietary driver for Broadcom Wireless chipsets
kmod-diag - 2.4.30-brcm-5 - Kernel modules for LEDs and buttons
kmod-switch - 2.4.30-brcm-1 - switch driver for robo/admtek switch
kmod-wlcompat - 2.4.30-brcm-4 - Compatibility module for using the Wireless
Extension with broadcom's wl
mtd - 4 - Tool for modifying the flash chip
nvram - 1 - NVRAM utility and libraries for Broadcom hardware
uclibc - 0.9.27-8 - Standard C library for embedded Linux systems
webif - 0.2-1 - A modular, extensible web interface for OpenWrt.
wificonf - 6 - Replacement utility for wlconf
wireless-tools - 28.pre7-1 - Tools for setting up WiFi cards using the Wireless
Extension
```

Installing Packages

Installing software packages using OpenWrt is a straightforward process and you can do it using the *ipkg install <pkgname>* command. For this example, we will install tcpdump, an extremely useful tool for traffic sniffing and network troubleshooting. To install tcpdump, execute the command *ipkg install tcpdump*:

```
# ipkg install tcpdump
Installing tcpdump (3.8.3-1) to root...
Downloading http://downloads.openwrt.org/whiterussian/packages/tcpdump_3.8.3-
1_mipsel.ipk
Installing libpcap (0.9.4-1) to root...
Downloading http://downloads.openwrt.org/whiterussian/packages/libpcap_0.9.4-
1_mipsel.ipk
Configuring libpcap
Configuring tcpdump
Successfully terminated.
```

As you can see, the package *tcpdump_3.8.3-1_mipsel.ipk* was downloaded and installed, in addition to *libpcap_0.9.4-1_mispel.ipk*. But wait, we didn't tell it to install *libpcap*! This is one of the powerful features of ipkg. It automatically recognizes and installs dependencies. In this example, we told it that we wanted to install tcpdump. The package management system knows that in order for tcpdump to work properly (or work at all, for that matter) it needs libpcap, so it happily installs it for you. You will also notice the two lines that read *Configuring libpcap* and *Configuring tcpdump*. This is yet another nice feature of ipkg. It will configure your OpenWrt installation properly to allow the installed packages to run (environment variables, scripts, etc.).

Working with VLANs

Now that you have gone through the process of getting your newly "hacked" WRT54G configured on your network, you may want to change the network ports configuration. Unlike the default Linksys firmware, OpenWrt allows you to be more flexible when it comes to how the WRT54G functions on the network, and reassign ports and virtual LANs (VLANs) just as you would one any other enterprise switch. Figure 3.1 displays the default port layout.

Figure 3.1 WRT54G 546L Default Port Assignments

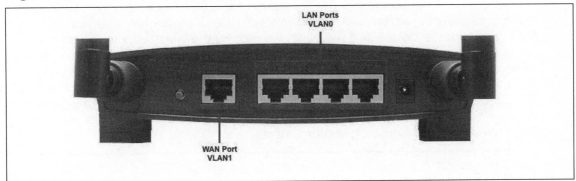

It is important to understand that the LAN port assignments in Figure 3.1 on the outside of the WRT54G above the LAN ports are there only to correspond to the lights on the front of the device. They have no meaning when referring to them using OpenWrt, as the LAN ports are assigned numbers 0–3, and the wide area network (WAN) port is assigned to port 4 on the internal switch. You can view and change which VLAN is assigned to a particular port by manipulating NVRAM variables:

```
vlan0hwname="et0"
vlan1hwname="et0"
vlan0ports="3 2 1 0 5*"
vlan1ports="4 5"
```

The *vlanXhwname* variables refer to the physical interface associated with the switching hardware—that is, the internal built-in switch represented by *et0*. The WRT54G and WRT54GL have only a single internal switch (*et0*); other routers may have more than one. The *et0* interface is associated to one or multiple VLANs, with one or more ports assigned to each VLAN. The *vlanXports* variables contain the switch ports assigned to that particular VLAN, indicated by number (*X*). Port numbers 0–3 are the physical LAN ports (labeled on the back of the WRT54G as 1–4). Port 4 is the WAN (or Internet) port, and port 5* is reserved for the VLAN tagging interlace.

TIP

Need an extra LAN port? Did you know that you can change the function of the WAN port (the one labeled "Internet" on the back) to act like a LAN port? This gives you one extra switch port in cases where you just want to use your WRT54G as a wireless access point or switch and not use it as a router. Here are the NVRAM settings required to convert port 4 (the default port number for the WAN interface) from the WAN VLAN (*vlan1*) to the LAN VLAN (*vlan0*):

```
# nvram set vlan0ports="0 1 2 3 4 5*"
# nvram set vlan1ports="5"
# nvram set wan_proto=static
# nvram commit
# reboot
```

The first command modifies the *vlan0ports* variable to include port 0, which changes the WAN interface VLAN assignment to *vlan0*; remember, port number 0 corresponds to the WAN interface. Next, we modify the *vlan1ports* variable to remove port 0 from *vlan1*, leaving just the virtual port 5 in case we ever want to reuse this VLAN (port 5 is the virtual tagging port that must exist in every VLAN). Then, we set the *wan_proto* variable from the default setting of *dhcp* to *static*. This will disable the Dynamic Host Configuration Protocol (DHCP) client for that interface because it is no longer necessary. All that is left is to commit the changes and reboot. Once completed, enjoy the extra switch port!

Setting the Wireless Radio Transmit Power

One of the most common features sought after by WRT54G hackers is the ability to adjust the wireless radio transmit power (TX power). Entire firmware distributions are dedicated to this ability (for instance, HyperWRT, covered in Chapter 2). There are a few items to note that we covered briefly up until now, but that we believe require more explanation. The actual transmit power limit of the WRT54G hardware and associated driver is 251mW. As stated in Chapter 2, this will cause overheating. In addition to melting, cranking up the power this high to achieve more gain will actually have the reverse effect. Due to the noise created by such a high output power, the signal actually bleeds into other channels and becomes less efficient (see http://explorer.cyberstreet.com/wrt54g/WRT54g-spectraloutput.html). The optimum output power, meaning one that will increase gain and not introduce noise, is documented as 89mW. This setting will also not overheat the router; however, we do recommend that you provide adequate ventilation for your WRT54G routers (e.g., do not put them in your desk drawer).

You can easily change the transmit power using OpenWrt from the command line. First, let's take a look at the default wireless transmission power value in OpenWrt (Whiterussian 0.9). To do this we will need to install the wl command-line program. This is a small, proprietary, binary program from Broadcom that allows you to view and change the settings of the wireless driver.

```
# ipkg install wl
Installing wl (3.90.37-1) to root...
Downloading http://downloads.openwrt.org/whiterussian/packages/non-free/wl_3.90.37-1_mipsel.ipk
Configuring wl
Successfully terminated.
```

WARNING

During the course of writing this book, the authors uncovered a bug in the *wl* command. If you execute this command (with any parameter) while the radio is disabled (*nvram set wl0_radio="0"; nvram commit ; /sbin/wifi*) you will receive an error, as show here:

> # wl txpwrlimit
> *Segmentation fault*

Once this command has executed and generated the preceding error, any subsequent attempt to access the wireless subsystem will result in the command hanging and not responding. These commands include *wl*, *wifi*, and even *reboot*. You will still be able to connect to the router via SSH from the LAN or WAN ports; however, to fix the wireless problem you need to power-cycle the device. It is a good idea to be certain that your wireless radio/interface is enabled before executing commands that access it (*nvram get wl0_radio*). The authors are in the process of contacting the vendor (because the wl binary comes from Broadcom) and reporting this bug. Check www.wrt54ghacks.com for updates.

Once you have downloaded and installed the wl program, you can use it to query the driver for the transmit power setting:

```
# wl txpwrlimit
Current TX Power Limit:              89 mW ( 19.50 dBm)
```

The default setting, once you install OpenWrt, depends on the default driver setting, which in most cases will be 89mW (19.5 dBm), the optimum power output for the radio on the WRT54G. TX power is often expressed in dBm, a measure of absolute power. For reference, you can read http://en.wikipedia.org/wiki/DBm. However, suppose you want to decrease the radio transmit power? This could help to limit the range and save power consumption (especially if you are implementing one of the battery hacks in Chapter 7). To change the transmit power do the following:

```
# nvram set wl0_txpwr="56"
# nvram commit
# wifi
# wl txpwrlimit
Current TX Power Limit:              25 mW ( 14.00 dBM)
```

In the first command, we set the NVRAM variable *wl0_txpwr* to *56*. This variable is expressed as *qdBm*, which means that it is four times (one-quarter) the value of dBm. The default value is 78 qdBm. A setting of 56 means that we should have a dBm of 14 (56 / 4 = 14). We then commit the changes to the NVRAM partition and reload the wireless settings using the *wifi* command. To verify that the settings have taken effect, we can again use the *wl txpwrlimit* command, which returns 14 dBm as our output power.

The *wl txpwr1* provides even more comprehensive and accurate information by displaying the current TX power in all the different measurement units already described:

```
# wl txpwr1
TxPower is 56 qdbm,  14.00 dbm, 25 mW  Override is Off
```

You can also double-check that this value was set properly by using the *iwconfig* command:

```
# iwconfig
lo        no wireless extensions.


eth0      no wireless extensions.


eth1      IEEE 802.11-DS  ESSID:"OpenWrt"
          Mode:Master  Frequency:2.437 GHz  Access Point: 00:18:F8:D8:09:22
          Tx-Power:14 dBm
          RTS thr=2347 B    Fragment thr=2346 B
          Encryption key:off
          Link Noise level:-12 dBm
          Rx invalid nwid:0  Rx invalid crypt:0  Rx invalid frag:0
          Tx excessive retries:1284  Invalid misc:0   Missed beacon:0
```

In the preceding example, you can see that the *iwconfig* command output indicates a transmit power of 14dBm. Chapter 7 provides full coverage of wireless power measurements, radio transmit power, and adding antennas for increasing signal gain.

NOTE

For reference, most WRT54G model routers come from the factory with the radio power set to 89mW, which is approximately 19.5 dBm. It is left up to the operating system on the router to interact with the driver to change this setting.

WARNING

Please be certain that when adjusting power, and adding antennas, as covered in Chapter 7, you are abiding by the regulations in your associated jurisdiction. The following resources are helpful in determining these limits, which are set to 1 watt (indoors) by the FCC in the United States and 100mW by the ETSI in the EU:

United States "Understanding the FCC Part 15 Regulations for Low Power, Non-Licensed Transmitters"; www.fcc.gov/Bureaus/Engineering_Technology/

Documents/bulletins/oet63/oet63rev.pdf (Pages 20 & 21)

Europe "Electromagnetic compatibility and Radio Spectrum Matters (ERM); Wideband transmission systems; Data transmission equipment operating in the 2.4 GHz ISM band and using spread spectrum modulation techniques; Harmonized EN covering essential requirements under article 3.2 of the R&TTE Directive"; http://webapp.etsi.org/action/OP/OP20060922/en_300328v010701o.pdf (pages 10 and 11)

Configuring the DNS and DHCP Server Using dnsmasq

DNS and DHCP are two of the most fundamental protocols in use on the Internet today. Whereas DHCP provides hosts with dynamic IP addresses, DNS is used to resolve hostnames to IP addresses and vice versa. Your WRT54G running OpenWrt (and DD-WRT, for that matter) uses an open source DNS/DHCP server called dnsmasq. Dnsmasq is a lightweight server that provides functionality for both DNS and DHCP, in addition to some useful features which we will cover shortly. If you do not plan to use your WRT54G as a DNS or DHCP server, refer to the last section in this chapter, "Securing Your Firmware," as it details how to disable this service.

Configuring a Caching-Only DNS Server

A caching-only DNS server is a great way to control your local DNS lookups. Instead of having to connect to your Internet service provider's (ISP's) DNS servers, you can set up your own server to answer queries from the local network, which then are forwarded to the ISP's servers. For each lookup that you do, the local DNS server will cache the lookup so that each subsequent lookup will come directly from the local DNS server. The other advantage this has is the ability to "blackhole" certain domains. For example, there is a list of domains that are commonly used to provide banner ads, and others that are commonly used to distribute malware. By adding entries for these domains to resolve to 127.0.0.1, you can effectively prevent yourself from seeing the banner ads or potentially downloading malware. For example, Web sites use banner ad companies to not only display annoying animated images, but also possibly collect personal information about you. Using cookies, a company such as DoubleClick could log your IP address, Web browser type and version, and operating system, and even your name! These same images could be used to distribute malware, either through directly exploiting your computer with the images (see the Microsoft advisory MS06-001, www.microsoft.com/technet/security/Bulletin/MS06-001.mspx) or by enticing you to click on a link which will take you to a Web site that will attempt to exploit your Web browser software and/or operating system.

The first step in the process is to disable the default startup script for dnsmasq, which is the program that controls DNS and DHCP for OpenWrt:

```
# cd /etc/init.d
# mv S60dnsmasq disabled_s60dnsmasq
# chmod -x disabled_s60dnsmasq
```

Next, you need to create a replacement file. The new S60dnsmasq startup script should look as follows:

```
#!/bin/sh
dnsmasq -C /etc/dnsmasq.conf
```

This startup script requires execute permissions to run. You can set these using the following command:

```
# chmod 755 /etc/init.d/S60dnsmasq
```

Next, you need to remove the default /etc/resolv.conf file and replace it with your own:

```
# rm /etc/resolv.conf
# cat > /etc/resolv.conf
nameserver isp.dns.srv.ip1
nameserver isp.dns.srv.ip2
<CTRL-D>
```

Be certain to replace *isp.dns.srv.ip1* and *isp.dns.srv.ip2* with the IP addresses of your ISP-provided DNS servers. Next, you need to update the DNS resolution file option in /etc/dnsmasq.conf, which you should change to the following value:

```
resolv-file=/etc/resolv.conf
```

Finally, reboot the device so that your changes will take effect and you can verify that your startup script changes were successful.

```
# reboot
```

Once the system has rebooted, you can go to any other host and use the *nslookup* command to test your new DNS server. The *nslookup* examples in this section are from a Linux client:

```
paulda@bud:~$ nslookup
> server 192.168.1.85
Default server: 192.168.1.85
Address: 192.168.1.85#53
> pauldotcom.com
Server:          192.168.1.85
Address:         192.168.1.85#53


Non-authoritative answer:
Name:    pauldotcom.com
Address: 67.15.62.53
>
```

In the preceding example, we are on another host on our local network, called *bud*. When we type **nslookup**, it gives us the standard tool prompt in the form of the ">" symbol. By typing **server 192.168.1.85**, we tell nslookup to use that IP address as the DNS server, instead of the one in the local /etc/resolv.conf file. When we look up a hostname, nslookup comes back and tells us that using 192.168.1.85 as the DNS server, it is able to resolve the hostname given—in this case, *pauldotcom.com*.

Once you have the configuration working, you can then add the list of domains that you want to blackhole. Add the following lines to /etc/dnsmasq.conf:

```
# Blackhole ad domains

address=/adcentriconline.com/127.0.0.1
address=/addynamix.com/127.0.0.1
address=/adelphia.com/127.0.0.1
address=/adelphia.net/127.0.0.1
address=/adlegend.com/127.0.0.1
address=/adserver.com/127.0.0.1
address=/adware.com/127.0.0.1
address=/allfreethings.com/127.0.0.1
address=/bluestreak.com/127.0.0.1
address=/centrport.com/127.0.0.1
address=/chicagowebs.com/127.0.0.1
address=/clickaffiliate.com/127.0.0.1
address=/clickagents.com/127.0.0.1
```

```
address=/clickfire.com/127.0.0.1
address=/cossette.com/127.0.0.1
address=/deepmetrix.com/127.0.0.1
address=/digitalriver.com/127.0.0.1
address=/dmpi.net/127.0.0.1
address=/doubleclick.com/127.0.0.1
address=/doubleclick.net/127.0.0.1
address=/eboz.com/127.0.0.1
address=/eyeblaster.com/127.0.0.1
address=/fastclick.com/127.0.0.1
address=/imrworldwide.com/127.0.0.1
address=/insightexpress.com/127.0.0.1
address=/interpolls.com/127.0.0.1
address=/klipmart.com/127.0.0.1
address=/kliptracker.com/127.0.0.1
address=/linkbuddies.com/127.0.0.1
address=/nextag.com/127.0.0.1
address=/nielsen-netratings.com/127.0.0.1
address=/overture.com/127.0.0.1
address=/planninggroup.com/127.0.0.1
address=/pointroll.com/127.0.0.1
address=/questionmarket.com/127.0.0.1
address=/redsheriff.com/127.0.0.1
address=/serving-sys.com/127.0.0.1
address=/streamexchange.com/127.0.0.1
address=/topdownloads.com/127.0.0.1
address=/trueffect.com/127.0.0.1
address=/unicast.com/127.0.0.1
address=/valueclick.com/127.0.0.1
address=/videobanner.com/127.0.0.1
```

NOTE

You can download this file directly to the WRT54G by using the command *wget http://www.wrt54ghacks.com/whiterussian/BlackholeAdDomains* and copying to the appropriate filename and location.

Now, restart the dnsmasq server:

```
# killall dnsmasq
# /etc/init.d/S60dnsmasq
```

Again, you can test this by going to any other host and using the *nslookup* command:

```
paulda@bud:~$ nslookup
> server 192.168.1.85
Default server: 192.168.1.85
Address: 192.168.1.85#53
> doubleclick.net
Server:        192.168.1.85
Address:       192.168.1.85#53


Name:    doubleclick.net
Address: 127.0.0.1
>
```

Now that you have a working configuration, you are ready to use your new DNS server for local client lookups. You can do this in the various operating systems in the network interface configuration. Each time the client performs a lookup for a host in the blackhole list, the DNS server will return **127.0.0.1**. Typically, there is no Web server on the client performing the Web browsing, so the Web browser will quickly return an error in place of an annoying banner ad. In the next section, we will show you how to configure the DHCP server so that it will distribute your new DNS server address automatically.

Configuring a Custom DHCP Server

Dnsmasq also provides a DHCP server which you can customize for your own use. First, we will show you how to set up a standard DHCP server that will provide clients with an IP address, DNS server, and default gateway. Then, we will show you how to assign fixed IP addresses based on Media Access Control (MAC) addresses so that specific computers will always receive the same IP address. To enable the DHCP server, edit the /etc/dnsmasq.conf file and be certain that it contains the following directives:

```
# enable dhcp (start,end,netmask,leasetime)
dhcp-authoritative
dhcp-range=192.168.1.100,192.168.1.150,255.255.255.0,12h
dhcp-leasefile=/tmp/dhcp.leases


# other useful options:


# Default Gateway
dhcp-option=3,192.168.1.1
```

```
# DNS Servers
dhcp-option=6,192.168.1.85
```

The first three lines tell the DHCP server to be authoritative (i.e., it will act as though it is the only DHCP server on the network), specifies the range of IP addresses that it will be handing out to clients (from .100 to .150), and provides the lease file location where it will store DHCP leases. The *dhcp-option* parameter allows you to specify individual DHCP options by number (for a complete listing, see www.iana.org/assignments/bootp-dhcp-parameters). Now, stop and restart dnsmasq:

```
# killall dnsmasq
# /etc/init.d/S60dnsmasq
```

To test the DHCP server you can use any client that supports DHCP. Windows systems work well to identify the DHCP server settings. Simply put a Windows server on the same subnet as your router and configure the network interface for DHCP. Then start a command prompt (go to **Start | Run**, type **cmd.exe**, and click **OK**) and enter **ipconfig /all**. Review the results and be certain that your machine received the appropriate IP address, subnet mask, default gateway, and DNS server.

If all that looks good, you are ready to move on to the next step, assigning a fixed IP address via DHCP. To enable this feature, add the following lines to your /etc/dnsmasq.conf file:

```
# use /etc/ethers for static hosts; same format as --dhcp-host
# <hwaddr> <ipaddr>
read-ethers
```

The preceding directive tells dnsmasq to read the static MAC address to IP address mappings from a file. Save and exit this file, and create a new file that contains the mappings:

```
# cat > /etc/ethers
00:04:75:F7:B0:BE 192.168.1.45
<CTRL-D>
```

This tells dnsmasq that every time a device with a MAC address of 00:04:75:F7:B0:BE makes a request for an IP address, give it the 192.168.1.45 IP address. To enable your change you must once again stop and restart dnsmasq, as you did earlier:

```
# killall dnsmasq
# /etc/init.d/S60dnsmasq
```

Now you are ready to start using the enhanced DNS and DHCP server configuration. It would be best to have at least two DNSs on your network in case one fails. You can do this easily using the earlier configuration examples.

NOTE

You could also run two DHCP servers on your subnet for redundancy. You would want to remove the *dhcp-authoritative* directive and make certain that the dynamic DHCP ranges are different on each one. Your client would use whichever DHCP server responded first, which would be fine for a home or small-office environment.

SSH Server Security

Although SSH is already a very secure protocol, there are a few minor enhancements you can make to be certain that you are using it properly. SSH supports public key cryptography for authentication and encryption, meaning that you have a public/private key pair, and your router has a public/private key pair. Let's create this for accessing our routers.

First, create a public key on the host from which you will be managing your router:

```
paulda@bud:~$ ssh-keygen -t dsa
Generating public/private dsa key pair.
Enter file in which to save the key (/home/paulda/.ssh/id_dsa):
Enter passphrase (empty for no passphrase):
Enter same passphrase again:
Your identification has been saved in /home/paulda/.ssh/id_dsa.
Your public key has been saved in /home/paulda/.ssh/id_dsa.pub.
The key fingerprint is:
60:99:71:df:d3:b2:6e:52:32:bc:cd:80:46:b6:ed:90 paulda@bud
```

Copy the public key to the router:

```
paulda@bud:~$ scp ~/.ssh/id_dsa.pub wrt-hacker:/tmp/
root@192.168.1.85's password:
id_dsa.pub                        100%  597     0.6KB/s   00:00
```

Create the authorized keys file on the router:

```
# cd /etc/dropbear/
# cat /tmp/id*.pub >> authorized_keys
# chmod 0600 authorized_keys
```

Now when you SSH to the router, instead of asking you for your password, it will ask you for the passphrase protecting your private key:

```
paulda@bud:~$ ssh wrt-hacker
Enter passphrase for key '/home/paulda/.ssh/id_dsa':

BusyBox v1.00 (2006.11.07-01:40+0000) Built-in shell (ash)
```

```
Enter 'help' for a list of built-in commands.


 _____               _____     __
|       |.-----.-----.-----.|  |  |  |.-----.| |_
|   -   ||  _  |  -__||  |  |  ||  _||  _|
|_____||   __|_____|__|__||_____||__|  |____|
         |__|  W I R E L E S S   F R E E D O M
WHITE RUSSIAN (0.9) -------------------------------
  * 2 oz Vodka   Mix the Vodka and Kahlua together
  * 1 oz Kahlua  over ice, then float the cream or
  * 1/2oz cream  milk on the top.
 ---------------------------------------------------
root@wrt-hacker:~#
```

Reprogramming the SES Button As a WiFi Toggle

Let's face it; if you've made it this far in the WRT54G hacking process, you probably don't care too much about the SecureEasySetup (SES) feature that came with your router. In fact, if you've applied third-party firmware, it is most likely already broken. Because it's there, we want to do something useful with it, such as turn the wireless radio on and off. This is a useful feature, especially if you want to have an open access point only for a certain period. With the script that follows, disabling and enabling the radio is as easy as pressing a button!

The diag kernel module controls the communications with the LED lights, and the Reset and SES buttons. The diag kernel module, among many other things, controls the lights by looking for scripts in a particular directory. You must first create the directory for the SES button:

```
# mkdir /etc/hotplug.d/button
```

In this directory, place the following file and call it "01-wifitoggle", which is a shell script:

```
#!/bin/sh


#
# If the Cisco SES button was pressed and released
#
if [ $BUTTON = "ses" -a $ACTION = "released" ]
then
        # Make SES button flash white when pressed
        echo "f" > /proc/diag/led/ses_white

        # If the Wifi is disabled when button pushed
        if [ "$(nvram get wl0_radio)" = "0" ]
        then
```

```
        # Enable the Wifi and set light to orange
        logger -t wifi "Activating wi-fi"
        echo "1" > /proc/diag/led/ses_orange
        nvram set wl0_radio=1
        wifi
    else
        # If Wifi was already enabled, disable it
        # then turn off the light
        logger -t wifi "De-Activating wi-fi"
        nvram set wl0_radio=0
        echo "0" > /proc/diag/led/ses_orange
        wifi
    fi
    sleep 1
    echo "0" > /proc/diag/led/ses_white
fi
```

> **NOTE**
>
> You can download this file directly to the WRT54G using the command *wget http://www.wrt54ghacks.com/whiterussian/wifi-toggle.sh* and copying to the appropriate filename and location.

Now when you press the SES button, you should see the light flash white, and then turn solid orange. This means WiFi is enabled. If you press the button again, you should see the button flash white and then go off. This means WiFi is disabled. You can verify that the script is running and writing to the logs by issuing the *logread* command. In the output, you should see the following:

```
Jan  1 08:02:26 (none) user.notice wifi: Activating wi-fi
Jan  1 08:04:16 (none) user.notice wifi: De-Activating wi-fi
```

Configuring NTP Time Synchronization

You will want to be certain that your WRT54G is keeping the correct time. This becomes important when analyzing logs for troubleshooting or investigating security incidents. Configuring time in OpenWrt requires installation of the ntpclient package and some minor configuration.

First, you must download and install ntpclient:

```
ipkg install ntpclient
```

The most difficult part of this process is determining the best time server. When in doubt, refer to your ISP's documentation to find out if they are maintaining a time server, as that would be the best one to use. For a complete listing and NTP-related documentation, refer to http://ntp.isc.org. Once you have found the appropriate NTP server, you can then add the following script to /etc/init.d/S65ntpclient:

```
#!/bin/sh

NTPSERVER=time.nist.gov

#
# kill any existing ntpclient processes
#
/usr/bin/killall ntpclient

#
# Sync the system clock to time server
#
/usr/sbin/ntpclient -l -h $NTPSERVER -c 1 -s &
```

> **NOTE**
>
> You can download this file directly to the WRT54G using the command *wget http://www.wrt54ghacks.com/whiterussian/ntpclient.sh* and copying to the appropriate filename and location.

You should replace *time.nist.gov* with your local NTP server. This will synchronize your clock each time you reboot your router.

This startup script requires execute permissions to run. You can set these using the following command:

```
# chmod 755 /etc/init.d/S65ntpclient
```

You will also want to synchronize time at a regular interval. To synchronize the system time every 30 minutes, you can add a cron job as follows:

```
crontab -e
```

Running this command will allow you to edit the root user's cron jobs. Simply add the following lines:

```
# Sync system time every 30 minutes
*/30 * * * * /etc/init.d/S65ntpclient
```

The final task is to set the time zone. By default, OpenWrt sets the time zone to UTC. To specify the time zone you will need to first select which time zone you are in by using the reference located in section "5.8 Timezone" in the OpenWrt configuration guide (http://wiki.openwrt.org/OpenWrtDocs/Configuration).

```
echo "EST5EDT" > /etc/TZ
```

This will set the time zone to U.S. Eastern Standard Time (EST).

Storage Using USB

NOTE

You will need a WRTSL54GS model router for this section.

One of the fundamental challenges we face when working with a small embedded device such as the WRT54G is limited storage capacity. Even the routers with the most available flash contain only 16MB of storage space. To make the most out of your routers with USB ports, such as the WRTSL54GS, adding USB support and attaching a large drive is handy. The first step is to add USB 1.1/2.0 support by installing the following packages:

```
ipkg install kmod-usb-uhci   # Kernel driver for UHCI USB controllers
ipkg install kmod-usb-core   # Kernel Support for USB
ipkg install kmod-usb-ohci   # Kernel driver for OHCI USB controllers
ipkg install kmod-usb-storage     # Kernel modules for USB storage support
ipkg install kmod-usb2            # USB 2.0 Support
```

Next, check the *dmesg* output and be certain that OpenWrt has found your USB controller:

```
usb.c: registered new driver usbdevfs
usb.c: registered new driver hub
PCI: Setting latency timer of device 00:03.0 to 64
usb-ohci.c: USB OHCI at membase 0xb8003000, IRQ 6
usb-ohci.c: usb-00:03.0, PCI device 14e4:4715
usb.c: new USB bus registered, assigned bus number 1
hub.c: USB hub found
hub.c: 2 ports detected
PCI: Enabling device 01:02.0 (0000 -> 0002)
PCI: Setting latency timer of device 01:02.0 to 64
usb-ohci.c: USB OHCI at membase 0xc018b000, IRQ 2
usb-ohci.c: usb-01:02.0, PCI device 1033:0035
usb.c: new USB bus registered, assigned bus number 2
hub.c: USB hub found
hub.c: 3 ports detected
```

```
PCI: Enabling device 01:02.1 (0000 -> 0002)
PCI: Setting latency timer of device 01:02.1 to 64
usb-ohci.c: USB OHCI at membase 0xc018d000, IRQ 2
usb-ohci.c: usb-01:02.1, PCI device 1033:0035
usb.c: new USB bus registered, assigned bus number 3
hub.c: USB hub found
hub.c: 2 ports detected
SCSI subsystem driver Revision: 1.00
Initializing USB Mass Storage driver...
usb.c: registered new driver usb-storage
USB Mass Storage support registered.
hub.c: new USB device 01:02.0-1, assigned address 2
PCI: Enabling device 01:02.2 (0000 -> 0002)
ehci_hcd 01:02.2: PCI device 1033:00e0
ehci_hcd 01:02.2: irq 2, pci mem c01c0000
usb.c: new USB bus registered, assigned bus number 4
ehci_hcd 01:02.2: USB 2.0 enabled, EHCI 1.00, driver 2003-Dec-29/2.4
hub.c: USB hub found
hub.c: 5 ports detected
usb.c: USB device not responding, giving up (error=-145)
hub.c: new USB device 01:02.2-1, assigned address 2
```

Now connect the drive you want to use to the USB port and verify that you can see it by entering the command *df –h*:

```
# df -h
Filesystem                Size      Used Available Use% Mounted on
/dev/root                896.0k    896.0k         0 100% /rom
none                      14.9M     28.0k     14.9M   0% /tmp
/dev/mtdblock/4            6.3M      1.9M      4.4M  30% /jffs
/jffs                    896.0k    896.0k         0 100% /
/dev/scsi/host0/bus0/target0/lun0/part1    465.6G     32.0k     465.6G    0%
/mnt/disc0_1
```

You can see in the preceding code snippet that the 500GB drive is now available as *mnt/disc0_1*. You also have the option of repartitioning and/or reformatting the drive to suit your needs. You can do this by plugging the drive into another device, or if you want to use OpenWrt, you must install the fdisk package (*ipkg install fdisk*).

Storage with Samba

Again, trying to overcome the limited storage on a WRT54G is challenging, and even more so if you do not have a USB port. For most WRT54G models, the best way to add more storage, without making hardware modifications, is to install Samba support. Samba will allow your routers to attach to Windows networking shares, sometimes referred to as SMB shares, CIFS, or NetBIOS shares. Your WRT54G can be either a Samba client, or Samba server sharing out files to the rest of your network (which works best with the USB configuration mentioned earlier).

The first step is to configure OpenWrt to look at the Backports package tree. Backports is a collection of useful software that has been made available from the development branches of OpenWrt. These packages are not all fully supported and, as such, should be installed with caution.

WARNING

Be certain that you have enough free space on your flash device before installing packages. When installing large packages (Python, for example), you can very easily run out of flash space. The Linux command *df –h* will list the currently mounted partitions approximately and how much available space is left on each.

To use Backports you must tell ipkg to look at the Backports package tree by adding the following line to /etc/ipkg.conf:

```
src backports http://downloads.openwrt.org/backports/0.9
```

Then run an *ipkg update* and you should see the following in the output:

```
Downloading http://downloads.openwrt.org/backports/0.9/Packages
Updated list of available packages in /usr/lib/ipkg/lists/backports
```

Configuring a Samba Server

NOTE

Although you can install a Samba server and have it share what is on the default flash chip, it is not so useful, as there is only a limited amount of storage. This section will use the WRTSL54GS model router to share the USB storage device on the network using Samba.

To complement our USB storage, let's share out the attached USB drive so that it is accessible via Samba to the rest of the network. The first step is to install file system support for some common file systems you might want to use, such as ext2, ext3, and vfat, which allows you to mount FAT file system partitions:

```
# ipkg install samba-server kmod-vfat kmod-ext2 kmod-ext3
```

Once you've installed Samba, you need to first modify your /etc/hosts file so that your router has an appropriate entry, such as:

```
127.0.0.1 localhost
192.168.1.70 wrtsl54gs
```

where *192.168.1.70* is the IP address of your router, and *wrtsl54gs* is your router's hostname (*nvram set wan_hostname=wrtsl54gs*).

Next, you need to edit /etc/samba/smb.conf. Here is an example:

```
[global]
 syslog = 0
 syslog only = yes
 workgroup = OpenWrt
 server string = OpenWrt Samba Server
 security = share
 encrypt passwords = yes
# guest account = nobody
 guest account = root
 local master = yes
 name resolve order = lmhosts hosts bcast


[tmp]
 comment = /tmp
 path = /tmp
 browseable = yes
 public = yes
 writeable = no


[MyBackupDrive]
 comment = /mnt/disc0_1
 path = /mnt/disc0_1
 browseable = yes
 public = yes
 writeable = yes
```

There are a few notable items in the preceding configuration. We have commented out the line *guest account = nobody*, and replaced it with *guest account = root*. This allows remote Samba users to write files to the Samba shares. We are also sharing out /tmp, which is typically the JFFS2 writable partition. The backup drive, called *MyBackupDrive*, has the writable flag set, which means that with the current configuration, anyone can connect to this share and write files to the disk. There are many aspects of Samba security, and they go beyond the scope of this book. The preceding configuration is merely an example, so please take the time to properly secure your network and systems if you plan to use it. For an extra layer of security, consider configuring the device's iptables firewall to limit which hosts on your network can access the Samba shares.

Next, we need to set Samba so that it starts automatically on boot:

```
# mv /etc/init.d/samba /etc/init.d/S75samba
```

The final step is to reboot the router and then connect to the share with any compatible Samba client, including the native clients in Windows and Mac OS X.

Configuring a Samba Client

The easiest way to get extra storage on WRT54G series routers is to use the CIFS file system, which allows you to act as a CIFS client and mount Samba shares. This is an excellent way to get storage on WRT54G series routers that do not have a USB port. First, you need to install the CIFS kernel module and the cifsmount package, which will allow you to mount remote Samba or Windows Server Message Block (SMB) shares:

```
ipkg install cifsmount kmod-cifs
```

Once the installation has completed, you need to add CIFS file system support into the kernel with the following command:

```
# insmod cifs
Using /lib/modules/2.4.30/cifs.o
```

Next, you will create a directory to which to mount your remote file share:

```
# mkdir /mnt/smblog/
```

And finally, mount the remote share:

```
# mount.cifs //192.168.1.208/wrt54g /mnt/smblog
Password: <enter your password here>
```

To verify that the share was mounted successfully, issue the *mount* command. You should see a line that looks as follows:

```
//192.168.1.208/wrt54g on /mnt/smblog type cifs
(rw,mand,nodiratime,unc=\\192.168.1.208\wrt54g,username=root,domain=,rsize=4100,wsi
ze=4100)
```

Backing Up and Restoring

Now that you can add local storage with USB and even mount remote file shares, let's put together a backup strategy for your WRT54G. The following script will automate backing up the router's firmware image (kernel, packages, and JFFS2 partition), in addition to the NVRAM partition which holds all of your settings:

```
#! /bin/sh

DATE=`date +%m%d%Y`
```

```
HOSTNAME=`nvram get wan_hostname`
BACKUP_FILE=$HOSTNAME.$DATE
SMBSHARE=/mnt/smblog


#
# Check for the existance of the SMB Share
# and that we can write to it
#
touch $SMBSHARE/.backup

if [ -f $SMBSHARE/.backup ]; then

        #
        # The following command will create a backup of the
        # firmware image (kernel, packages, and JFFS2)
        #
        dd if=/dev/mtdblock/1 of=/$SMBSHARE/$BACKUP_FILE.trx

        if [ -s $SMBSHARE/$BACKUP_FILE.trx ]; then
                logger -s "Firmware Backed Up Successfully"
        else
                logger -s "Firmware backup did not complete"
        fi


        #
        # The following will backup the NVRAM parition
        #
        dd if=/dev/mtdblock/3 > /$SMBSHARE/$BACKUP_FILE.bin

        if [ -s $SMBSHARE/$BACKUP_FILE.bin ]; then
                logger -s "NVRAM Backed Up Successfully"
        else
                logger -s "NVRAM backup did not complete"
        fi

else

        logger -s "SMB Share $SMBSHARE not available. Exiting..."
        exit 1

fi
```

> **NOTE**
>
> You can download this file directly to the WRT54G by using the command *wget http://www.wrt54ghacks.com/whiterussian/backup.sh* and copying to the appropriate filename and location.

The preceding script requires that an SMB share be made available. However, you could easily modify the script to save the configuration to a USB share or, with slightly more modifications, use SSH to send your backups to any SSH server. Of course, no backup strategy is complete without the ability to restore your configuration. To restore the firmware and/or NVRAM partition, use the following commands:

```
# Restore NVRAM
dd if=/tmp/nvram-backup.bin of=/dev/mtdblock/3


# Restore Firmware
mount -o remount,ro /dev/mtdblock/4 /
mtd -r write /tmp/firmware-backup.trx linux
```

Replace the nvram-backup.bin and firmware-backup.trx files with the appropriate NVRAM and firmware backup files from the backup script shown earlier.

In this section, you learned how to take the default installation of OpenWrt and customize it to suit your needs, preparing it for further hacking. You locked it down by configuring security protocols and disabling the ones you do not need. More configuration settings were tweaked, such that your routers keep the right time and get backed up on a regular basis. You then learned how to create DNS and DHCP servers and Samba servers with your WRT54Gs as well.

Installing and Using
X-Wrt: A Web GUI for OpenWrt

X-Wrt is a full-featured, robust Web interface for OpenWrt. The project has greatly expanded upon the simple Web interface that comes with OpenWrt, and includes features such as QoS configuration, an interface for creating iptables firewall rules, easy updating via the Web interface, and more. X-Wrt is perfect for those just getting started with OpenWrt, primarily because, just as with OpenWrt, as you make changes in the GUI you can click the **Review Changes** link in the lower right-hand corner and see the equivalent command-line statements to all actions in the Web interface.

There are three ways to install X-Wrt:

- Install it as a firmware upgrade, replacing the firmware you currently have installed.
- Install it from the Web-based installer on the X-Wrt Web site.
- Manually install the X-Wrt packages from the command line.

We will cover the third option, installing X-Wrt from the command line. You must have OpenWrt already installed to use this option (Whiterussian RC5, RC6, and 0.9 were supported at the time of this writing, with Kamikaze support on the way). To install the latest, versio, issue the following command:

```
# ipkg install http://ftp.berlios.de/pub/xwrt/webif_latest_stable.ipk
Downloading http://ftp.berlios.de/pub/xwrt/webif_latest_stable.ipk
Upgrading webif on root from 0.2-1 to 0.3-6...
Configuring webif
Downloading http://downloads.openwrt.org/backports/rc6/Packages
Updated list of available packages in /usr/lib/ipkg/lists/rc6-backports
Downloading http://download2.berlios.de/pub/xwrt/packages/Packages
Updated list of available packages in /usr/lib/ipkg/lists/X-Wrt
Downloading http://downloads.openwrt.org/whiterussian/packages/Packages
Updated list of available packages in /usr/lib/ipkg/lists/whiterussian
Downloading http://downloads.openwrt.org/whiterussian/packages/non-free/Packages
Updated list of available packages in /usr/lib/ipkg/lists/non-free
Downloading http://downloads.openwrt.org/backports/0.9/Packages
Updated list of available packages in /usr/lib/ipkg/lists/backports
Successfully terminated.
Device: Linksys WRT54G/GS/GL
Committing new device id ...
Committing new firmware id ...
SUCCESS! Webif^2 installation appears OK. Welcome to X-Wrt!
You may need to do a hard REFRESH to clear old CSS style from your browser.
Reinitializing httpd ...
I'm sorry, but I must reboot your router. This is a ONE time thing and
 future upgrades of the webif will NOT require a reboot.
Please wait about one minute for your router to reboot ...
Successfully terminated.
```

Your router will then reboot, allowing you to browse to the router's default Web page to begin using X-Wrt, as shown in Figure 3.2.

Figure 3.2 X-Wrt Initial Configuration Screen

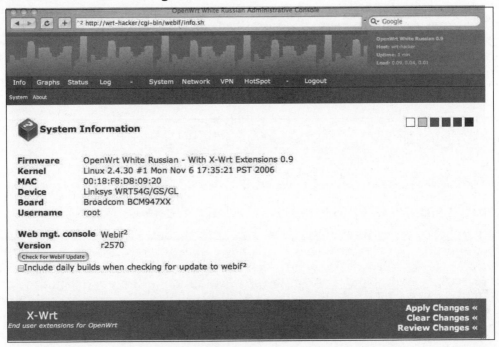

As you can see, X-Wrt closely resembles the OpenWrt Web interface, except you have far more options and configuration screens to choose from. For example, changing VLANs is very easy. Go to **Network | VLAN**. You will see the screen depicted in Figure 3.3.

Figure 3.3 X-Wrt VLAN Configuration Screen

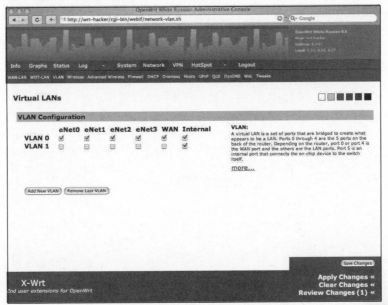

Now, switching the WAN port to be on the LAN VLAN is as easy as unchecking the box in the **WAN** column in the **VLAN 1** row, and checking the box in the **WAN** column in the **VLAN 0** row. Once you've done that, you can click **Save Changes**, and then **Apply Changes**.

X–Wrt is a very promising project that is certain to grow into a stable, easy-to-use platform that will enable many to take advantage of the OpenWrt firmware, without having to be a command-line expert.

Tools & Traps…

Switching among Firmware Distributions

During the course of this book, you may want to try out different firmware distributions until you find the one you like. You may even want to experiment with different versions of a particular firmware, such as OpenWrt Kamikaze or DD-WRT beta releases. Before installing a new firmware distribution, it is a good idea to wipe the NVRAM partition, which clears out any settings from previous installations. There are two ways to do this. The following command is the not-so-safe way:

```
mtd -r nvram erase
```

Use caution with this command, as it will force a reboot and, depending on your model/firmware, will have to reinstall a new image. Also, this does not work for all WRT54G series routers. Refer to the following table before running this command:

WRT54G Version	mtd –r nvram erase Is…
WRT54G v 1.*x*	Not safe
WRT54G v 2.*x*	Safe
WRT54G v 3.*x*	Safe
WRT54G v 4.0	Safe
WRT54GL 1.*x*	Safe
WRTSL54GS	Safe

However, if you are planning to install a new image anyway, it's a good way to wipe out the previous firmware's settings. A safe way to revert back to the defaults contained specifically within the OpenWrt firmware is to follow these commands:

```
cd /tmp
wget http://downloads.openwrt.org/people/kaloz/nvram-clean.sh
chmod a+x /tmp/nvram-clean.sh
/tmp/nvram-clean.sh
```

Continued

Then you can enter *nvram commit* and enjoy your cleaned-up NVRAM variable listing. This method is best for when you've installed OpenWrt and want to clean out variables from other firmware you may have installed.

Configuring and Using DD-WRT

Your primary interface to DD-WRT will be the Web interface. It allows you to configure many of the useful features offered by DD-WRT and is more enhanced than its OpenWrt counterpart. For this reason, many novice users will prefer DD-WRT. In addition to the Web interface, you can still use the command line to make changes; however, be certain to read the documentation as the command-line interface for DD-WRT is not as full-featured or well documented as the OpenWrt command line. We provide a few examples of DD-WRT configuration so that you can get a feel for the interface. This will enable you to configure other options by exploring the Web interface and DD-WRT documentation (located at www.dd-wrt.com).

Setting the Wireless Radio Transmit Power

Not only does DD-WRT allow you to change the transmit power of the radio, but it also offers the ability to graphically view and change these settings (see Figure 3.4).

Figure 3.4 DD-WRT Advanced Wireless Settings

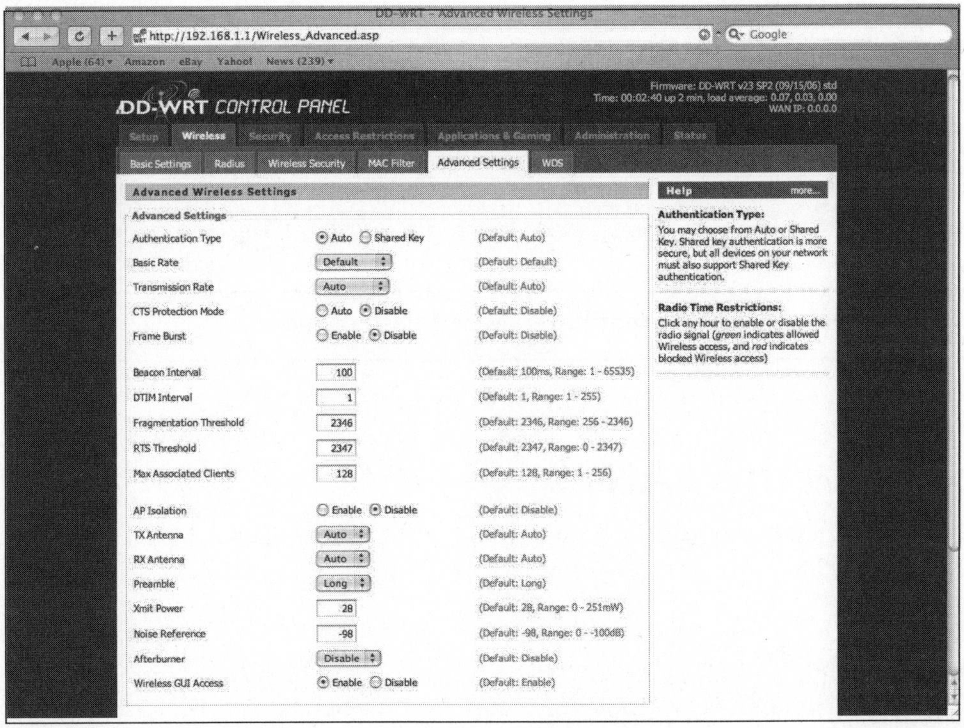

The setting most users are typically interested in is about one-third of the way down, and labeled "Xmit Power", which corresponds to the transmit power of the radio measured in milliwatts (mW).

You might be looking at the screen in Figure 3.4 and wondering what Afterburner is. No, we are not talking about the video game, but about wireless chipset manufacturers attempt to get more throughput using 802.11g. Broadcom's attempt was marketed to device manufacturers as "Afterburner" and rebranded by Linksys as "SpeedBooster". It uses a combination of reduced signal overhead and combining packets to provide more throughput. Of course, this does nothing to improve distance and the client card must also support this technology to see any performance improvements (in fact, using it with cards that do not support it can decrease performance!). Linksys originally intended that the WRT54GS models would only support SpeedBooster; however, third-party firmware can enable this on even WRT54G models because the same chipsets are used. See www.dd-wrt.com/wiki/index.php/Afterburner for more information.

Making the File System Writable

DD-WRT, by default, comes with the SQUASHFS file system enabled, so, unlike old versions of OpenWRT, you do not have to choose a file system at installation time. You can enable the writable JFFS2 file system by going to the command line and changing the NVRAM variables. You can get to the command line on DD-WRT by using Telnet. Later, we will show you how to enable SSH. To enable JFFS2, do the following:

```
# nvram set jffs_mounted=1
# nvram set enable_jffs2=1
# nvram set sys_enable_jffs2=1
# nvram set clean_jffs2=1
# nvram set sys_clean_jffs2=1
# nvram commit
# reboot
```

NOTE

This works only on devices that have 4MB of flash or more.

Working with VLANs

DD-WRT provides a nice interface for changing VLANs on selected ports, and even creating new VLANs (see Figure 3.5).

Figure 3.5 DD-WRT VLAN Configuration

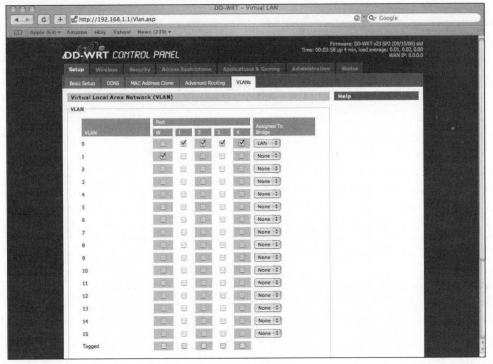

As you can see in Figure 3.5, the five ports on the WRT54G are represented in the column headings (LAN ports 1–4, and the "W" for the WAN port). Ports 1–4 are assigned to VLAN 0, and the WAN port is assigned to VLAN 1. By checking and unchecking the radio buttons, you can enable or disable selected ports, and change the VLAN assignment of each port.

Securing Your Firmware

Many distributions come with services enabled by default in order to provide a better user experience. However, usability and security are typically mutually exclusive, and one must trade usability for security. What follows is a guide to securing the default installations, sometimes called "hardening," of both OpenWrt and DD-WRT. The services offered by both are identical. How you secure them is very different in each distribution.

Securing OpenWrt

The first step when trying to secure a network device is to execute a portscan of the device while it is on the network to see what services it is offering. Each service could potentially be a security risk, so your strategy is to enable only those services that you absolutely need. A great tool for discovering the services running on your WRT54G is Nmap (www.insecure.org/nmap). It runs on Linux, Windows, and Mac OS X and does a fantastic job of describing to which services are available on the WRT54G:

```
nologin@pdc:~# nmap -O -sS -T4 -p1-65535 wrt-hacker

Starting Nmap 4.20 ( http://insecure.org ) at 2007-02-16 18:20 EST
Interesting ports on 192.168.1.85:
Not shown: 65531 closed ports
PORT    STATE SERVICE
22/tcp open   ssh
23/tcp open   telnet
53/tcp open   domain
80/tcp open   http
MAC Address: 00:18:F8:D8:09:20 (Cisco-Linksys)
Device type: broadband router
Running: Linksys embedded
OS details: Linksys WRT54GS v4 running OpenWrt w/Linux kernel 2.4.30
Network Distance: 1 hop

OS detection performed. Please report any incorrect results at
http://insecure.org/nmap/submit/ .
Nmap finished: 1 IP address (1 host up) scanned in 35.242 seconds
```

The command *nmap −O −sS -T4 −p 1-65535 wrt-hacker* attempts to connect to every Transmission Control Protocol (TCP) port on the WRT54G to determine whether it is listening. The switch *−p 1-65535* denotes the ports that we want to test, and the *−sS* tells Nmap to try to determine which TCP ports are opened using a SYN scan. The *−O* switch provides us with operating system fingerprinting information. The *−T4* tells Nmap to scan the device quickly using "aggressive" timing.

Notes from the Underground…

UDP Ports and Embedded Devices

UDP is a different protocol than TCP, as it is connectionless and unreliable, and does little to verify the packets once they are sent to the network. As such, scanning a WRT54G running either OpenWrt or DD-WRT for open UDP ports takes more than 16 hours, even when adjusting the timeout values that determine how long the scanner should wait for a port to respond. Getting a list of UDP ports is easy using the built-in *netstat* command:

```
# netstat -anu
Active Internet connections (servers and established)
```

Continued

```
Proto Recv-Q Send-Q Local Address        Foreign Address        State

udp      0      0 0.0.0.0:1024           0.0.0.0:*

udp      0      0 0.0.0.0:53             0.0.0.0:*
```

The –a command-line switch tells netstat to display all sockets, even those that are connected; the –n flag indicates that it should not attempt to resolve names; and the –u flag will show only UDP ports. This does not show you which process is responsible for the listening process. Unfortunately, there is not a version for the Linux/UNIX lsof command for OpenWrt or DD-WRT. In the preceding output, we know that the dnsmasq process is responsible for port 53 UDP, as that is the standard port for DNS. However, we need to identify which process is responsible for UDP port 1024. Researching the documentation for dnsmasq reveals that the dnsmasq process will listen on this port for incoming DNS replies. It is not a security hole, per se, because it will only accept replies. You can find more information on the dnsmasq FAQ (http://ftp.axis.com/pub/users/cii/floppyfw-2.9.x/dnsmasq-1.18/FAQ).

In the default installation, these are the only two listening UDP services and both are associated with dnsmasq. Refer to the sections earlier in this chapter for more information on configuring dnsmasq.

Disabling Telnet

Because you will be using SSH to log in to the router, you do not need Telnet, even though it is not configured to accept login requests, as shown here:

```
pdc:~ nologin$ telnet wrt-hacker
Trying 192.168.1.85...
Connected to wrt-hacker
Escape character is '^]'.
Login failed.
Connection closed by foreign host.
```

The preceding code could still be an attack vector if an attacker were to uncover a remote buffer overflow in the Telnet service (besides, if you are using this in an environment that ever has succumbed to an IT audit, having Telnet enabled with not help you make friends with your local auditor). To disable it altogether, do the following:

```
# cd /etc/init.d
# mv S50telnet disabled_s50telnet
# chmod -x disabled_s50telnet
```

Now reboot your router and verify that Telnet is disabled by going to any other host command line and entering **telnet <router-ip-address>**. Enabling SSH is not required because it comes enabled by default once the router password is initially changed. The only SSH version provided by the OpenWrt SSH server is version 2.

Disabling HTTP and Enabling HTTPS

As with Telnet, HTTP will transmit your usernames, passwords, and all data in clear text across the network. This means that anyone on the same subnet on either the client or the server networks could intercept the traffic and steal your credentials. Using packages from Backports, you can install an HTTPS-only Web server:

```
# ipkg install mini-httpd-openssl
Installing mini-httpd-openssl (1.19-1) to root...
Downloading http://downloads.openwrt.org/backports/0.9/mini-httpd-openssl_1.19-1_mipsel.ipk
Installing libopenssl (0.9.8d-1) to root...
Downloading http://downloads.openwrt.org/whiterussian/packages/libopenssl_0.9.8d-1_mipsel.ipk
Configuring libopenssl
Configuring mini-httpd-openssl
Successfully terminated.
```

The mini-httpd-openssl package works even if you have installed the advanced X-Wrt Web-based interface covered in this chapter. Verify that this works by going to https://<router-ip-address>. You will receive a certificate error upon visiting this Web site because the Web server uses a self-signed Secure Sockets Layer (SSL) local certificate.

TIP

To solve the problem of the certificate error you can make a secure connection to the device via SSH and extract the certificate from the cert.pem file:

```
# cd /etc
# cat mini_httpd.pem
-------BEGIN RSA PRIVATE KEY-----
<Private key removed from output>
-----END RSA PRIVATE KEY-----
-----BEGIN CERTIFICATE-----
MIICOTCCAaKgAwIBAgIJANRuTbnzy8ObMA0GCSqGSIb3DQEBBAUAMFMxCzAJBgNV
BAYTAkZSMQ4wDAYDVQQIEwVQYXJpczEOMAwGA1UEBxMFUGFyaXMxEDAOBgNVBAoT
B015IEhvbWUxEjAQBgNVBAMTCU15IFJvdXRlcjAeFw0wNTAxMTQwMjQzMjdaFw0w
NjAxMTQwMjQzMjdaMFMxCzAJBgNVBAYTAkZSMQ4wDAYDVQQIEwVQYXJpczEOMAwG
A1UEBxMFUGFyaXMxEDAOBgNVBAoTB015IEhvbWUxEjAQBgNVBAMTCU15IFJvdXRl
cjCBnzANBgkqhkiG9w0BAQEFAAOBjQAwgYkCgYEAuaxSTkGpMDJhfWqFZwF2kCzj
j6GDhJNff5bPVWbdWan80Lk2xhhq4DCA3JQdJBzBb0m83olYzJ60nUEzXtYDkABr
R4R4qroKy6h/Zt8Kjnq23/2Iq4YnPVOl/UWlgugczYHGFNULT59bA7WzDRQAeo8x
d1u+hCJRxKG4DLX6rccCAwEAAaMVMBMwEQYJYIZIAYb4QgEBBAQDAgZAMA0GCSqG
SIb3DQEBBAUAA4GBAErl3QmcZVzjxKcoPTO3z8cRJV87SVFp0qbIjbYCBDUWB1QY
/bMkQPr2zJyfJmUYLEs4iKgHrmlaUCMHy9NZKOg9ZxrW42BtQ5QnOtDm3UifwzJW
oCFC3uPWfTYsZn/FrUXlErds+xXXT63VJzBe6DdXwHcdcdxzl05olyL9JIzl
     -----END CERTIFICATE-----
```

A pem file consists of the private key (which has been removed for privacy and brevity) and the certificate information. Because you need only the certificate information, copy the text starting with -----*BEGIN CERTIFICATE*----- all the way down to where it says -----*END CERTIFICATE*-----. Now create a new file on whatever operating system you are using on your client system, and paste in the contents. Depending on which operating system you are using, the instructions for importing this new certificate will vary. Here are some resources to assist you with importing your new certificate and trusting it:

Windows XP www.microsoft.com/resources/documentation/windows/ xp/all/proddocs/en-us/sag_cmprocsimport.msp

Mac OS X http://docs.info.apple.com/article.html?path=Mac/ 10.4/en/mh1779.html

Once you have verified that it works, you can disable the HTTP Web server using the following commands:

```
# cd /etc/init.d
# mv S50httpd disabled_s50httpd
# chmod -x disabled_s50httpd
# mv mini_httpd S50httpd
# chmod +x S50httpd
```

Alternatively, you could skip the preceding step that installs mini-httpd-openssl and disable the Web interface entirely using the following commands:

```
# mv S50httpd disabled_s50httpd
# chmod -x disabled_s50httpd
# killall httpd
```

The first two commands will disable the startup script, and the *killall httpd* command stops the running HTTP server on the router. Now you can remove the packages that you no longer require:

```
ipkg remove haserl webif
```

which in JFFS2 and OpenWrt version 0.9 or later will actually free up some space on your JFFS2 partition. At this point, you should be able to reboot and browse to https://<router-ip-address>—for example, https://192.168.1.85/.

Disabling DNS and DHCP Servers

If you have chosen not to use your WRT54G as a DNS or DHCP server, you can disable them both using the following commands:

```
# mv S60dnsmasq disabled_s60dnsmasq
# chmod -x disabled_s60dnsmasq
# reboot
```

These commands will tell the system not to start dnsmasq upon startup, disabling all of the DNS and DHCP server functionality (you will still be able to act as a DHCP client, using the udhcpc program).

Verifying the Results

When you are finished, it is crucial to verify the results:

```
pdc:~ root# nmap -O -sS -T4 -p1-65535 wrt-hacker


Starting Nmap 4.20 ( http://insecure.org ) at 2007-02-18 12:07 EST
Interesting ports on wrt-hacker (192.168.1.85):
Not shown: 65533 closed ports
PORT     STATE SERVICE
22/tcp   open  ssh
443/tcp  open  https
MAC Address: 00:18:F8:D8:09:20 (Cisco-Linksys)
Device type: broadband router
Running: Linksys embedded
OS details: Linksys WRT54GS v4 running OpenWrt w/Linux kernel 2.4.30
Network Distance: 1 hop


OS detection performed. Please report any incorrect results at
http://insecure.org/nmap/submit/ .
Nmap finished: 1 IP address (1 host up) scanned in 104.279 seconds
```

Another way to check is to locally issue the *netstat* command:

```
# netstat -ant
Active Internet connections (servers and established)
Proto Recv-Q Send-Q Local Address          Foreign Address         State
tcp       0      0 0.0.0.0:22             0.0.0.0:*               LISTEN
tcp       0      0 0.0.0.0:443            0.0.0.0:*               LISTEN
```

The netstat command is great for listing the ports that are open and actively listening. The *−a* tells *netstat* to list all listening and nonlistening sockets, the *-t* will list only TCP ports, and the *−n* tells *netstat* not to attempt any DNS lookups.

Securing DD-WRT

This is the same exercise as before; however, we will apply the security settings in DD-WRT using the Web interface. When you Nmap a router running DD-WRT, the services available are identical to those that come enabled by default in OpenWrt, except for the SSH daemon and the OS finger-printing results:

```
pdc:~ root# nmap -O -sS -T4 -p1-65535 ddwrt

Starting Nmap 4.20 ( http://insecure.org ) at 2007-02-18 12:26 EST
Interesting ports on ddwrt (192.168.1.35):
Not shown: 65532 closed ports
PORT    STATE SERVICE
23/tcp open  telnet
53/tcp open  domain
80/tcp open  http
MAC Address: 00:18:F8:D8:08:90 (Cisco-Linksys)
Device type: WAP|general purpose
Running: Linux 2.4.X
OS details: Linksys Linux 2.4.30 (X86), or Linksys WRT54G WAP running DD-WRT Linux
kernel 2.4.34-pre2
Uptime: 3.142 days (since Thu Feb 15 09:03:09 2007)
Network Distance: 1 hop

OS detection performed. Please report any incorrect results at
http://insecure.org/nmap/submit/ .
Nmap finished: 1 IP address (1 host up) scanned in 46.838 seconds
```

Disabling HTTP and Enabling HTTPS

Once you have completed the installation, you will want to enable the secure management protocols. By default, the access methods are Telnet and HTTP. What follows are instructions on how to enable SSH (the next section) and HTTPS to replace Telnet and HTTP, respectively.

To enable HTTPS in the Web interface go to **Administration | Management | Web Access**, and click the **HTTPS checkbox**, and uncheck the **HTTP checkbox**, as shown in Figure 3.6.

Figure 3.6 DD-WRT Enabling HTTPS

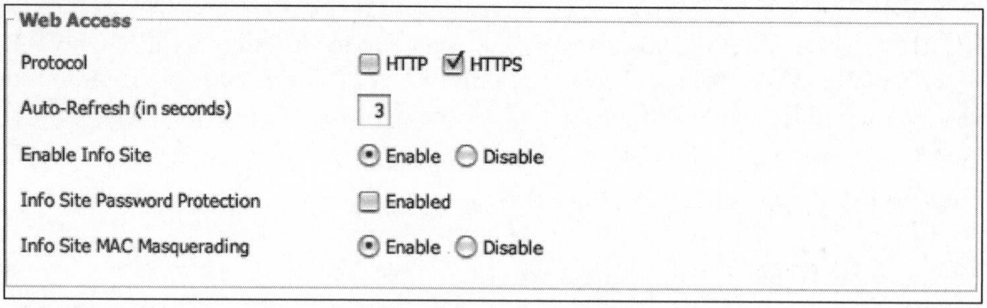

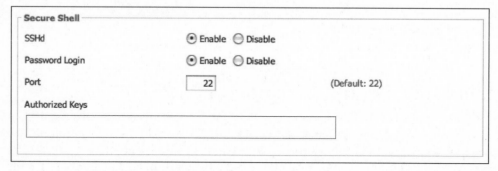

Go to the bottom of the page and click **Save Settings**. When the page comes back, click **Reboot Router**. After a minute, your router will come back and you will be able to browse to https://<router-ip-address>. You will get a certificate error when connecting because it uses an SSL self-signed local certificate. See the previous OpenWrt tip for instructions on extracting the certificate (in DD-WRT, the certificate is located in /etc/cert.pem).

Disabling Telnet and Enabling SSH

The next step is to disable Telnet and enable SSH. To do so you will first enable SSH and test it, and then disable Telnet. This will allow you access to the router in case anything goes wrong with your SSH server when you enable it. To turn on the SSH server go to **Administration | Services | Secure Shell** and set SSHd to **Enable**, as shown in Figure 3.7.

Figure 3.7 DD-WRT Enabling SSH

You must click **Save Settings** and then **Restart Router** before your changes will take effect.

At this point, using any SSH client, you should be able to SSH to your router, as shown in previous examples. Once verified, you can disable Telnet by going to the DD-WRT Web interface, navigating to **Administration | Services | TELNET**, and choosing **Disable**, as shown in Figure 3.8.

Figure 3.8 DD-WRT Disabling Telnet

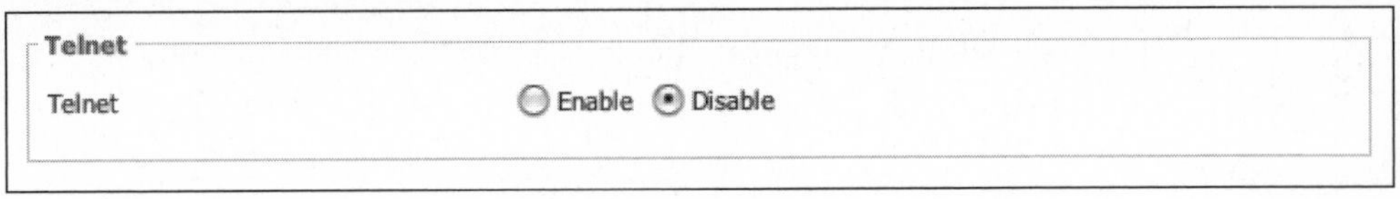

Disabling DHCP and DNS Servers

To disable both DNS and DHCP in DD-WRT, go to **Administration | Services | DNSMasq** and click **Disable**, as shown in Figure 3.9.

Figure 3.9 DD-WRT Disabling DNS and DHCP

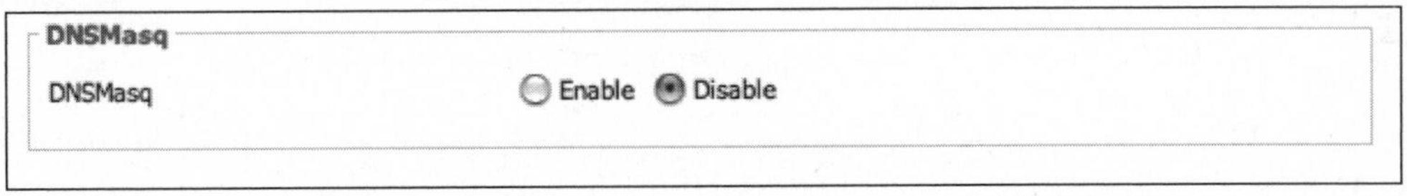

You must click **Save Settings** and then **Restart Router** before your changes will take effect. You can verify the results the same way you did with OpenWrt, using a combination of *nmap* and *netstat*.

Keeping Up-to-Date

You must keep security up-to-date. This means that each time you upgrade, you should follow the same steps as we outlined earlier, making certain that an upgrade did not enable any services that you do not need. However, how do you know whether your router needs an update? You could constantly monitor the Web site and look for updates; however, you could easily miss the announcement (and anyway, this is not terribly efficient). With the script that follows, your router will check for updated software nightly. If your packages are out-of-date, it will send you an e-mail telling you it's time to update. We tested the following script with OpenWrt Whiterussian 0.9:

```
#!/bin/ash


HOSTNAME=`nvram get wan_hostname`
EMAIL="you@yourmaildomain.com"
SMTP_RELAY=your.isp.relay.net


#
# Make sure we have mini-sendmail installed
#
if [ -z "$(ipkg list_installed | grep sendmail)" ]; then
        echo -e "ERROR: You must have the mini-sendmail package installed from
backports to use this script \n"
```

```
        echo -e "Add backports to /etc/ipkg.conf, then ipkg install mini-sendmail
\n"
        echo -e "Reference: http://wiki.openwrt.org/rsync-usb-sambaHowTo \n"
        exit 1
fi


logger "Updating Package Tree..."
ipkg update > /dev/null 2>&1

if [ ! -z "$(ipkg -test upgrade | grep "Upgrading")" ]; then

        BODY=`ipkg -test upgrade | grep "Upgrading"`
        SUBJECT="$HOSTNAME - Packages are out of date"

        # Send Email notification with a list of packages to be upgraded
        (echo "To: <${EMAIL}>"
        echo "From: <${HOSTNAME}> $HOSTNAME"
        echo "Subject: $SUBJECT"
        echo
        echo $BODY
        echo "<eom>"
        ) | mini_sendmail -f"${HOSTNAME}" -s"${SMTP_RELAY}" $EMAIL

else
        logger "Packages are up-to-date"
fi
```

NOTE

You can download this file directly to the WRT54G using the command *wget http://www.wrt54ghacks.com/whiterussian/update-alert.sh* and copying to the appropriate filename and location.

Change the variables in the preceding script to suit your environment, which includes your local Simple Mail Transfer Protocol (SMTP) server and e-mail address that will receive the notifications. Make certain that you set this script to run on a cron job nightly, as follows, by typing:

```
crontab -e
```

and then adding the following lines:

```
# Check for package updates
30 3 * * * /mnt/update-alert.sh > /dev/null 2>&1
```

Summary

OpenWrt and DD-WRT are two of the firmware distributions which we will use as examples throughout this book, and they seem to be the most popular of all firmware distributions. OpenWrt's primary interface is the command line; however, an ambitious project called X-Wrt is aimed at providing a full-featured Web interface. The DD-WRT primary management interface is its full-featured and easy-to-use Web server.

You can make many small configuration enhancements to improve the maintainability and usability of your firmware, which include Samba, USB, NTP, and using the SES button as a WiFi toggle.

Security is important to every network device, and WRT54G series routers are no exception. Following best practices standards is the desire approach. This means disabling services that are not in use or required, and using encrypted protocols in favor of clear-text protocols.

Resources

- **http://wiki.openwrt.org/DropbearPublicKeyAuthenticationHowto** OpenWrt Wiki entry that covers how to set up public key authentication, and includes detailed instructions on how to configure clients, such as putty, an SSH client for Windows.

- **www.linuxdevices.com/articles/AT4802795572.html** An animated BusyBox mini-tutorial that covers what BusyBox is, pros and cons, and how to customize your own instance.

- **www.dd-wrt.com/wiki/index.php/Ipkg** A tutorial on the *ipkg* command from the DD-WRT project, including alternative sources for packages, and other DD-WRT-specific configuration examples.

- **www.tcpdump.org/tcpdump_man.html** The complete *tcpdump* command reference (man page), which includes details on all *tcpdump* command-line switches. For example, to capture all packets in their entirety and disable service and name resolution, use *tcpdump −X −s0 −nn −i <interface>*.

- **www.daleholley.com/linksys/linksys.htm** A WRT54G "cooling hack," which details how one person modified a WRT54G, version 2.0, using PC chipset coolers and heat syncs. Use at your own risk!

- **http://thekelleys.org.uk/dnsmasq/doc.html** The main site for dnsmasq, including FAQs and command documentation in the form of an online man page.

- **http://matt.ucc.asn.au/dropbear/dropbear.html** The project home page for dropbear, the SSH server used in many firmware distributions for the WRT54G, such as OpenWrt. It includes a complete list of other projects using dropbear.

- **www.bleedingsnort.com/blackhole-dns/** An excellent article from bleedingsnort.com that explains how to use DNS blackholes for malware prevention, including links to a few different DNS blackhole lists.

- **www.securityfocus.com/infocus/1806** A great article on SSH host keys, the security they provide, generating keys, and verifying the integrity of SSH host keys.

- **http://ntp.isc.org/bin/view/Servers/WebHome** General information about NTP servers, including a searchable list of public NTP servers.

Solutions Fast Track

Configuring and Using OpenWrt

☑ OpenWrt relies on the command-line interface to manipulate its settings. It uses a stripped-down Linux shell called BusyBox to provide a Linux/UNIX interface. Configuration data stored in NVRAM is easily changed using the nvram command.

☑ Ipkg is a package management system similar to the Debian Linux "apt" project. It provides for package updates, easy software installation, and dependency handling. You can point ipkg at a few different package repositories, including backports, a collection of ported software not in the main OpenWrt package tree.

☑ Using OpenWrt, you can customize your DNS and DHCP environments, including domain filtering and fixed address assignment by MAC address.

☑ Adding USB support and/or configuring Samba will provide your router with access to more disk space. If you have disk space attached to the router itself, you can share this with the rest of your network using Samba too.

Configuring and Using DD-WRT

☑ DD-WRT relies on the Web interface for configuration. It is one of the most complete Web interfaces, allowing you to change and configure all aspects of your WRT54G.

☑ Changing VLANs and adjusting radio transmit power is easy in the various configuration screens. Changing the VLAN assignment of a port is as easy as manipulating checkboxes in the Web interface.

☑ The command-line interface to DD-WRT is somewhat limited; however, for certain tasks (such as enabling the JFFS file system), you will need to use the command line.

Securing Your Firmware

☑ The first step to securing your firmware is to use Nmap to detect the services available from the network (open ports).

☑ Whenever possible, disable insecure plain-text management services such as HTTP and Telnet and replace them with their more secure, encrypted equivalents such as HTTPS and SSH. Disable any unused services that listen on a network interface.

☑ Disabling Telnet and HTTP in favor of SSH and HTTPS greatly improves the security of your router when managing it. Both firmware distributions, OpenWrt and DD-WRT, allow you to do this without too much trouble.

☑ If you are not using the DNS and DHCP server components, it's best to turn them off. Not only will this help to secure the device, but it can improve performance as well.

Frequently Asked Questions

The following Frequently Asked Questions, answered by the authors of this book, are designed to both measure your understanding of the concepts presented in this chapter and to assist you with real-life implementation of these concepts. To have your questions about this chapter answered by the author, browse to **www.syngress.com/solutions** and click on the **"Ask the Author"** form.

Q: How do I keep my software up-to-date once I flash my WRT54G with OpenWrt?

A: OpenWrt uses ipkg to keep everything up-to-date. Issuing *ipkg update* and then *ipkg upgrade* will bring you to the latest package level for that release. If you are upgrading releases (for example, Whiterussian RC5 to Whiterussian RC6), it is recommended that you reflash.

Q: I've always used Telnet and HTTP to manage my WRT54G routers. Why should I change?

A: Your usernames and passwords could be sniffed if an attacker where to be on the client or server subnet, or any network between the client and the server. One method for doing this in a switched environment is through ARP cache poisoning to achieve a man-in-the-middle attack. Using secure protocols such as SSH and HTTPS helps to defend against these attacks.

Q: I've made configuration changes and now my router will not boot. What do I do?

A: To reset your NVRAM configuration type **mtd –r erase nvram**. This will erase the NVRAM partition on the flash, causing the CFE to reset to defaults upon reboot. Use caution, as this does not work on all routers.

Q: My ISP does not provide me with an NTP server. Where can I find one?

A: http://ntp.isc.org/bin/view/Servers/WebHome contains a list of public NTP servers. To find the closest NTP server with the best response time, consider using the Linux/UNIX command *ntp-sweep*.

Q: Which router do I need if I want to get USB support?

A: You will need a WRTSL54GS model router to gain support for USB. Additionally, the Asus WL-500G Premium has a very similar processor architecture and has two USB 2.0 ports.

Q: What is the best way to provide additional storage on a WRT54G?

A: Samba, and specifically the CIFS file system, works well to mount remote Samba/Windows file shares to provide additional storage.

Q: I really like OpenWrt, but I am not familiar with the command line and the GUI that comes by default is limited. What are my options?

A: X-Wrt, although still in beta, is an excellent choice for a Web interface until you can become comfortable with the command line. Each task you perform in the GUI is translated to the command-line equivalent and displayed to you on the screen while you are committing the changes.

Q: How do I see how much space is left on the flash device?

A: Issuing the command *df −h* will list each mounted volume, the available disk space, the used disk space, and the total disk space for each in human-readable format.

Chapter 4

WRT54G
Fun Projects

Solutions in this chapter:

- **Wardriving-in-a-Box**
- **Setting Up a Wireless Media Adapter**
- **Captive Portal-in-a-Box**
- **Asterisk for VoIP**

☑ **Summary**

☑ **Solutions Fast Track**

☑ **Frequently Asked Questions**

Introduction

Up to this point, we have laid the foundation by explaining the differences and similarities among all of the WRT54G series routers, showed how to hack them with third-party firmware, and discussed how to configure some common parameters on your newly hacked WRT54G. In this chapter, we want to showcase some of the fun and interesting things you can do, such as build a wardriving kit that lives entirely on a WRT54G, use your WRT54G as a Voice over IP (VoIP) private branch exchange (PBX), create wireless bridges for your favorite video gaming system, and set up a captive portal on a WRT54G to impress all of your geek friends when they visit. We tend to live by the expression "All work and no play make Jack a dull boy," so don't be afraid to tackle some, or all, of the projects in this chapter because, well, you can!

Wardriving-in-a-Box

A wardriving-in-a-box unit is a helpful tool for wireless aficionados as well as penetration testers performing a wireless audit. **Wardriving** is a method of finding wireless networks by utilizing some software to interface with the wireless radio, to monitor all wireless channels and examine them for traffic. As the name may indicate (with the "drive" base), there is a concept of movement of the monitoring station, which makes noting location important, and is typically done by GPS.

Typically, a wardriving setup would require software, a laptop, a power source, antenna(s), a GPS receiver, and an appropriate wireless card. With a WRT54G, you can deliver all of this in a much smaller form factor, with reduced power requirements. With the WRT54G's reduced size, you can put it on the dashboard, or hide it inside a small bag or other camouflaging device.

Prerequisites for This Hack

In order to complete this hack, you need to have a few things in place before you can begin, as building a self-contained wardriving WRT54G is quite involved. In short, you need:

- A working and writable MMC/SD card mod, as described in Chapter 7. We'll assume in this example that your SD card is mounted under /mnt/mmc, as configured in Chapter 7. It is possible to complete this hack without the MMC/SD card, but due to the large quantity of data that you can capture, it would be very limited in its uses.

- A working, configured serial port on /dev/ttyS1, as described in Chapter 7.

- A third-party serial GPS receiver that can output NMEA (National Marine Electronics Association) data. In this example, we will be using a Garmin eTrex Basic with a serial cable.

Once you have met these prerequisites, you can begin to build your self-contained wardriving WRT54G.

Kismet

Kismet is an open source 802.11 Layer 2 wireless network detector, sniffer, and intrusion detection system, developed by Mike Kershaw. Kismet will work with any wireless card that supports raw monitoring (RFMON) mode, and it can sniff 802.11b, 802.11a, and 802.11g traffic. Kismet identifies networks by passively collecting packets and detecting standard named networks, detecting (and, given time, decloaking) hidden networks, and inferring the presence of nonbeaconing networks via data traffic.

Kismet works a bit differently than most other wireless network discovery tools, in that it is completely passive; it only listens for wireless traffic. Most other tools actively send out requests for wireless networks. By just listening, we gain several advantages: It is unlikely that Kismet will be detected, as it does not generate any traffic to be seen by another; and by listening, we can determine information that other tools cannot.

> **NOTE**
>
> Kismet is under constant development and is well supported through user forums. For more information and assistance with Kismet, visit the project Web site at www.kismetwireless.net.

Fortunately for this hack, Kismet has already been ported to the WRT54G; however, there are some issues with the ipkg installation. Most notably, the OpenWrt package repositories have the appropriate GPS interface code removed. Because you will likely be wardriving on the move, GPS data becomes very valuable when analyzing the data in order to determine where individual access points are located. You can acquire working Kismet code elsewhere, as shown in our instructions. In order to install Kismet, you only need to install *kismet-server* on your WRT54G. In order to start this multistep process, you need to obtain and extract the precompiled Kismet binaries:

```
# cd /tmp
# wget http://wrt54ghacks.com/whiterussian/kismet-2006-04-R1-wrt54.tar.gz
# tar -zxvf kismet-2006-04-R1-wrt54.tar.gz
```

Now copy your precompiled binaries and configuration files to some useable locations:

```
# cd /tmp/kismet-2006-04-R1-wrt54
# cp kismet_server /usr/bin/kismet_server
# cp conf/* /etc/kismet/
```

In order for Kismet to function properly, you also need to install libpcap to support network packet capture. You can install libpcap from the default OpenWrt repository with:

```
# ipkg install libpcap
```

For the third step, you need to edit your Kismet configuration file in /etc/kismet/kismet.conf for your environment. The following lines should replace the existing lines in the current /etc/kismet/kismet.conf:

```
source=wrt54g,prism0,wrt54g
suiduser=root
channelhop=false
```

```
logtypes=csv,gps
gps=true
```

These changes to your configuration file define your capture source for your WRT54G and set the user to operate as. You are also disabling channel hopping, as the WRT54G wireless card driver implementations do not support channel hopping. Additionally, you are defining some log types, significantly reduced compared to what is considered standard, and you are enabling GPS data collection.

> ### NOTE
>
> We elected to reduce our logging types for two reasons. One is to cut down on space by removing unused information. The other removes the *dump* option, which captures all data packets that Kismet collects over the wireless connection. In some jurisdictions, it may be considered against the law to capture network traffic from networks that you do not have permission to intercept. As we will likely encounter these types of networks during a wardrive, it is better to be safe than sorry!

After installation is complete, you can test Kismet by specifying the path to your configuration file:

```
# kismet_server -f /etc/kismet/kismet.conf
```

After starting Kismet, you should be presented with some console output, the end of which, including a wireless discovery, is shown here:

```
Kismet 2006.04.R1 (Kismet)
GPSD cannot connect: Connection refused
Listening on port 2501.
Allowing connections from 127.0.0.1/255.255.255.255
Registering builtin client/server protocols...
Registering requested alerts...
Registering builtin timer events...
Gathering packets...
Sat Jan  1 00:23:20 2000 Found new network "linksys" bssid 00:12:17:BA:14:04 Crypt
Y Ch 6 @ 54.00 mbit
```

At this stage of the Kismet installation, although it technically works, you need to ensure that a number of things work properly in order to be truly effective and to stay within your legal limits. We will complete those steps next.

Tools & Traps…

My WRT54G Doesn't Work under Kismet

Due to the significant wireless differences in the WRT54G versions, as discussed in Chapter 1, Kismet may not function as installed. The instructions in this chapter should support most versions of the WRT54G, WRT54GS, WRT54GL, and WRTSL54GS, but you can make the other versions work with a few minor changes.

Kismet's configuration files instruct the software as to which capture source, or wireless card, to use while operating. As shown earlier, we defined a capture source for our WRT54GL v1.1 in /etc/kismet/kismet.conf as *source=wrt54g,prism0,wrt54g*. Here are the other combinations for some earlier WRT54G models:

WRT54G, versions 1.0 and 1.1:

```
source=wrt54g,eth2,wrt54g
```

WRT54G, version 2.0:

```
source=wrt54g,eth1,wrt54g
```

WRT54G, version 3.0:

```
source=wrt54g,eth1:prism0,wrt54g
```

And the default, as instructed earlier:

```
source=wrt54g,prism0,wrt54g
```

Although Kismet does support channel hopping by default, it utilizes the channel hopping capability in the particular wireless driver. As indicated earlier, we disabled channel-hop capability. When channel hopping is disabled, Kismet will begin operating on the last configured channel, typically channel 6, and will stay fixed on this channel. Channel hopping is a method in which you set the wireless radio to cycle through all available channels in the WiFi spectrum. Unfortunately, the proprietary closed source driver provided by Broadcom for wireless radios does not support channel hopping! The lack of supported channel hopping will seriously hinder your wardriving operations, as wireless access points can be configured to be on a number of channels, and if your Kismet installation is fixed to only one channel, much of the wireless environment will essentially be invisible to you!

You can fix this problem by creating a shell script that will manually cycle the radio channels in the background while Kismet is running. Before you create the channel-hopping script, you need to install the wl package to support setting the channel. You can do this by entering the following at the command prompt:

```
# ipkg update
# ipkg install wl
```

As this is intended to be a single-purpose WRT54G, solely for wardriving, you are going to set a channel-hopping shell script to be executed at startup. The contents of the channel-hopping script that you will create as /usr/bin/chanhop.sh will allow you to set the channel of the wireless chipset using the *wl* command every second:

> **NOTE**
>
> You can download the following script using wget on the WRT54G with the command *wget http://wrt54ghacks.com/whiterussian/chanhop.sh* and then copy the file to the appropriate location, as shown in these instructions.

```
#!/bin/ash
# Channel hopping shell script
# GPLv2
# Portions of code graciously taken from Bill Stearns defragfile
# http://www.stearns.org/defragfile/
#
# jwright@hasborg.com
#
# 02/28/2006 - paul@pauldotcom.com
# Ported to OpenWrt
# - Added the "-p" option to specify platform
# - Made appropriate changes to run with busy box
# - Currently only supports whiterussian (tested on 0.9)
#
# NOTE: To enable all channels in OpenWrt do "nvram set wl0_country_code=All"

# Defaults
BANDS="IEEE80211B"
DWELLTIME=".25"

CHANB="1 6 11 2 7 3 8 4 9 5 10"
CHANBJP="1 13 6 11 2 12 7 3 8 14 4 9 5 10"
CHANBINTL="1 13 6 11 2 12 7 3 8 4 9 5 10"
CHANA="36 40 44 48 52 56 60 149 153 157 161"

requireutil () {
```

```
        while [ -n "$1" ]; do
                if ! type -path "$1" >/dev/null 2>/dev/null ; then
                        echo Missing utility "$1". Please install it. >&2
                        return 1        #False, app is not available.
                fi
                shift
        done
        return 0        #True, app is there.
} #End of requireutil


fail () {
        while [ -n "$1" ]; do
                echo "$1" >&2
                shift
        done
        echo "Exiting." >&2
        echo
        exit 1
} #End of fail


usage () {
        fail 'chanhop.sh: Usage:' \
         "$0 [-i|--interface] [-b|--band] [-d|--dwelltime]" \
         '-i or --interface specifies the interface name to hop on [mandatory]' \
         '-b or --band specifies the bands to use for channel hopping, one of' \
         '       IEEE80211B       Channels 1-11 [default]' \
         '       IEEE80211BINTL  Channels 1-13' \
         '       IEEE80211BJP    Channels 1-14' \
         '       IEEE80211A      Channels 36-161' \
         '    Use multiple -b arguments for multiple channels' \
         "-d or --dwelltime amount of time to spend on each channel [default
$DWELLTIME seconds]" \
         '-p or --platform specifies the operating system, use openwrt for wrt54g
usage ' \
         ' ' \
         "e.x. $0 -i ath0 -b IEEE80211BINTL -b IEEE80211A -d .10"
  } #End of usage


# main


while [ -n "$1" ]; do
```

```
        case "$1" in
        -i|--interface)
                INTERFACE="$2"
                shift
                ;;
        -b|--band)
                ARG_BANDS="$2 $ARG_BANDS"
                shift
                ;;
        -d|--dwelltime)
                ARG_DWELLTIME="$2"
                shift
                ;;
        -p|--platform)
                ARG_PLATFORM="$2"
                shift
                ;;
        *)
                echo "Unsupported argument \"$1\"."
                usage
                fail
                ;;
        esac
        shift
done


if [ $ARG_PLATFORM = "openwrt" ]; then
        if [ -z "$(ipkg list_installed | grep 'wl \- 3.90')" ]; then
                echo -e "ERROR: You must have the wl package installed \n"
            exit 1
        fi

        CHANGECHANNEL="wl channel"
        # busybox sleep does not take anything < 1 second
        DWELLTIME="1"
else
        requireutil sleep whoami iwconfig || exit 1
        CHANGECHANNEL="iwconfig $INTERFACE channel"

        if [ `whoami` != root ]; then
```

```
                echo "You must run this script as root, or under \"sudo\"."
                usage
                fail
        fi
fi


if [ -z "$INTERFACE" ]; then
        usage;
        exit 1
fi


# Test the sleep duration value
if [ ! -z "$ARG_DWELLTIME" ] ; then
        sleep $ARG_DWELLTIME 2>/dev/null
        if [ $? -ne 0 ] ; then
                fail "Invalid dwell time specified: \"$ARG_DWELLTIME\"."
        fi
        DWELLTIME=$ARG_DWELLTIME
fi


# If the user specified the -b argument, we use that instead of default
if [ ! -z "$ARG_BANDS" ] ; then
        BANDS=$ARG_BANDS
fi


# Expand specified bands into a list of channels
for BAND in $BANDS ; do
        case "$BAND" in
        IEEE80211B|IEEE80211b|ieee80211b)
                CHANNELS="$CHANNELS $CHANB"
                ;;
        IEEE80211BJP|IEEE80211bjp|ieee80211bjp)
                CHANNELS="$CHANNELS $CHANBJP"
                ;;
        IEEE80211BINTL|IEEE80211bintl|ieee80211bintl)
                CHANNELS="$CHANNELS $CHANBINTL"
                ;;
        IEEE80211A|IEEE80211a|ieee80211a)
                CHANNELS="$CHANNELS $CHANA"
                ;;
```

```
        *)
                        fail "Unsupported band specified \"$BAND\"."
                        ;;
        esac
done


echo "Starting channel hopping, press CTRL/C to exit."
while true; do
        for CHANNEL in $CHANNELS ; do
                #iwconfig $INTERFACE channel $CHANNEL
                $CHANGECHANNEL $CHANNEL
                if [ $? -ne 0 ] ; then
                        fail "iwconfig returned an error when setting channel
$CHANNEL"
                fi
                sleep $DWELLTIME
        done
done
```

You also need to create a startup script to start the channel hopping at boot. You'll create the startup script in /etc/init.d and call it *S95chanhop*. The contents of our S95chanhop startup script are as follows:

```
#!/bin/sh
/usr/bin/chanhop.sh -b IEEE80211B -p openwrt &
```

This starts the channel-hopping script, and scans channels 1 through 11 (as defined with the *–b* switch), as well as specifies the platform as OpenWrt (as specified by the *–p* switch). You also need to change the permissions to the script and startup script to be executable at boot with:

```
# chmod 755 /usr/bin/chanhop.sh
# chmod 755 /etc/init.d/S95chanhop
```

NOTE

This script was originally created by Joshua Wright after performing some hard-core math to determine the appropriate channel-hopping order for the best performance. Joshua's research indicated that the script contains the best channel-hopping order, as opposed to performing the hopping in numerical order. Paul used Josh's latest work and configured it to work on OpenWrt.

After your next reboot, Kismet will be able to monitor all 11 channels. Alternatively, you can start the script immediately by executing */usr/bin/chanhop &*.

Are You 0wned?

Missing Wireless Channels?

As an astute reader, you may notice that the channel-hopping script is missing channels 12 through 14, which are available in locations outside the United States. Certainly we need to be able to detect a wireless network on at least the first 11 channels (1 through 11), as a nefarious individual can certainly use those channels anywhere in the world. However, it is possible for another party to violate any FCC (or equivalent regulatory agency) regulations in order to avoid detection. Remember, a determined attacker (whom you may be trying to detect) will not always obey federal regulations while potentially breaking other laws!

We can resolve the missing-channels problem by enabling them with an NVRAM setting to allow channels 12 through 14. Please note that the authors do not condone violating any government regulations! With that said, we can enable the additional channels with:

```
# nvram set wl0_country_code=All
# nvram commit
```

We also need to update the startup script to reference the additional channels already included in the script. We can do this by modifying the /etc/init.d/S95chanhop script and replacing the –*b* switch option to use the channels 1 through 14, which are authorized for use in Japan:

```
#!/bin/sh
/usr/bin/chanhop.sh -b IEEE80211JP -p openwrt &
```

We will need to reboot to reload the NVRAM variables before wl can take full use of the additional channels.

The Finishing Touches

We have only a few more steps to perform before our wardriving-in-a-box WRT54G is complete! As we mentioned in the beginning of this hack, we need to be able to measure our physical location with a GPS receiver, which is approaching one of the final steps that we need to perform.

With our GPS receiver powered on, locked on to our satellites ,and attached to the serial port on our router, we need to configure the GPS software to acquire location data, and be able to provide the coordinates to Kismet. In order to interface with the GPS, we need to use the GPSd package.

WARNING

Not all versions of GPSd are created equal! After GPSd, version 2.10, code was introduced that does not work well with Kismet, or on embedded devices. Do not install the GPSd package from the default OpenWrt package tree; be sure to use the 2.10 version indicated in these instructions.

You can obtain version 2.10 of the GPSd package from www.wrt54ghacks.com/whiterussian/gpsd_2.10_mipsel.ipk.

You can install GPSd, version 2.10, by obtaining it from an alternative location with the following command:

```
# ipkg install http://wrt54ghacks.com/whiterussian/gpsd_2.10_mipsel.ipk
```

Once you've installed it, create a startup script, called S92gpsd in /etc/init.d, with the following contents:

```
#!/bin/sh
/usr/bin/gpsd -p /dev/tts/1 &
```

This script starts GPSd and, by using the *−p* flag, defines the port for the GPS receiver. In our case, it is connected to the serial port named /dev/tts/1. You also need to remember to set this startup script as an executable with:

```
# chmod 755 /etc/init.d/S92gpsd
```

In addition, you need to be sure that you are logging all of your Kismet data somewhere other than the internal flash memory. Depending on the fruitfulness of your impending wardrive, you may fill up the flash chip quite quickly! It would also be helpful for you to be able to gain access to the data after your wardrive is complete, without having to repower or remove the device from its location (possibly in a vehicle). Enter the SD card mod! With your SD card mod mounted on /tmp/mmc, as described in Chapter 7, you can quite readily accomplish those goals.

In order to write your log files to the SD card, you need to modify /etc/kismet/kismet.conf, and replace the existing *logtemplate* definition with:

```
logtemplate=/mnt/mmc/%n-%d-%i.%l
```

This new *logtemplate* directive is essentially a copy of the existing directive, except we have prepended /mnt/mmc to the filename variables in order to always define an absolute path for our log files to be saved on the SD card.

NOTE

For more information on log file naming variables and conventions, consult the *logtemplates* section of kismet.conf, or the Kismet documentation page at www.kismetwireless.net/documentation.shtml.

WARNING

!

Currently, a freshly booted WRT54G does not retain current date information. You could set the date at boot by installing and configuring the ntpclient package, but that requires an active Internet connection to function properly. In most cases, with a dedicated wardriving WRT54G, the active Internet connection will not be available, rendering ntpclient useless. The default date that a WRT54G will boot with is Sat Jan 1 00:00:00 UTC 2000, and the Kismet log files with the current configuration will reflect this date.

The final step to our wardriving-in-a-box WRT54G is to set Kismet to start at every boot. Kismet will need to start after the serial ports have been set, but before channel hopping occurs. To accomplish this, we will create a S93kismet_server startup script in /etc/init.d with the following contents:

```
#! /bin/sh
/sbin/ifconfig eth1 up
/usr/sbin/wl ap 0
/usr/sbin/wl passive 1
/usr/sbin/wl promisc 1
/usr/sbin/wl monitor 1
/usr/bin/kismet_server -f /etc/kismet/kismet.conf > /dev/null 2>&1 &
sleep 3
echo "kismet_server now running"
```

This script performs a number of steps to ensure that Kismet will start properly:

- It uses *ifconfig* to set the *eth1* interface up, or to an active state, in preparation for capture. This is just a precaution, as the interface should already be active.

- The *wl ap* command sets the AP mode to be that of a client, instead of acting as an access point.

- Passive mode is set with *wl passive* to prevent the transmission of any network or wireless packets during our Kismet use to prevent it from contacting unauthorized networks.

- *wl promisc* sets the wireless card in promiscuous mode, allowing all network traffic (at Layer 2) to be captured, regardless of source or destination Media Access Control (MAC) addresses.

- Monitor mode is enabled through the *wl monitor* command to capture all wireless traffic (at Layer 2), including management, control, and data 802.11 frames.

- Kismet is started utilizing our custom configuration in /etc/kismet.conf, and sends the unused console output to /dev/null (nowhere).

Don't forget to set *S93kismet_server* to be executable with

```
# chmod 755 S93kismet_server
```

You should now have a setup that looks something like the one in Figure 4.1.

Figure 4.1 Complete Wardriving-in-a-Box Setup

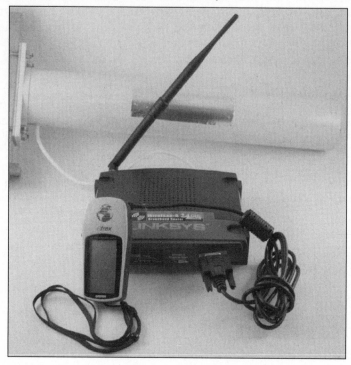

With all of these steps complete, you should be able to obtain your wardriving information off the SD card. After your wardrive, you should power off your wardriving-in-a-box WRT54G before removing the SD card from the router so that you do not corrupt the data or damage the SD card itself.

! WARNING

Currently, kismet.conf is set to write collected data to disk every 300 seconds. This means you could potentially lose data that has not been written to disk in the past 300 seconds when powering down the WRT54G. You can change the *writeinterval* directive in kismet.conf to a lower figure, such as 60 seconds, to minimize losses. Any lower settings could impact performance, so be certain to test your settings before going out on an actual wardrive.

Setting Up a Wireless Media Adapter

All modern console game systems on the market today use an Internet connection; in fact, some require it. This can present some interesting challenges for the average gamer, parents of an avid gamer, and even someone who may have networking experience. Running cables through your house is, well, not fun. We've done it with mixed degrees of success (after you've put that first hole through your hardwood floor, it's not so bad). A much better way is to purchase a wireless gaming adapter. Linksys even makes a separate device for this purpose: the Linksys WGA54G Wireless-G Gaming Adapter, which retailed for approximately $90 at the time of this writing. The WGA54G has the following "features" that are much better reproduced on the WRT54G platform:

- No Wi-Fi Protected Access (WPA) support (only Wireless Encryption Protocol [WEP] support)

- Only one wired Ethernet port

- No easy way to upgrade the external antenna

As we mentioned earlier, WPA/WPA2 is the standard for wireless security and you should use it wherever possible. If you have an existing wireless network and then want to add a WGA54G or similar product, and it supports only WEP, you have to convert your entire network to WEP. With more and more devices in your entertainment center requiring an Internet connection, installing a device that has only one Ethernet port would seem to be shortsighted. For example, the concepts that follow will work for providing access to your TiVo as well. A gaming system may not be confined to the living room; typical households may have one in the basement on a spare TV, or in a child's bedroom. These alternative locations may not get a strong signal on your wireless network, so the option for a wireless antenna is key to solving this problem. What follows are two practical examples of how you can use a WRT54G as a wireless gaming adapter, complete with WPA support, five available Ethernet ports, and two easily upgradeable external antennas.

Creating a Wireless Ethernet Bridge (WET)

WET, which stands for Wireless Ethernet Bridge, will allow clients connected to the Ethernet ports (or local area network [LAN] ports) to communicate with networks that may be reachable only via wireless. Consider the example network shown in Figure 4.2.

In Figure 4.2, we plug the game system, such as an Xbox, into a WRT54G called "wrt-bridge". Wrt-bridge is made to be a wireless client (instead of an access point). As a client, wrt-bridge associates to another access point called "wrt-livingrm". In order for our communications to be secure, we will set up WPA-PSK, using the original version of WPA (sometimes called WPA1 or WPA, version 1) as the encryption protocol. Wrt-livingrm is connected to the rest of the network via wired links and Ethernet cables. The network also has a local domain name system (DNS) server.

Figure 4.2 Wireless Ethernet Bridge Setup

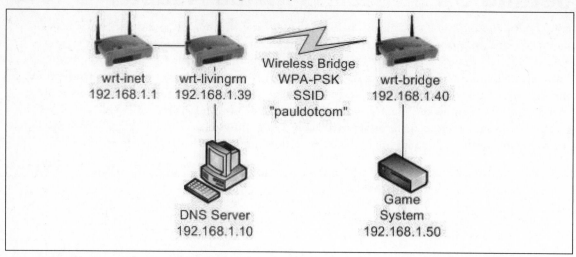

Configuring the Bridge

The first thing you need to do is give the wrt-bridge access point a proper Internet Protocol (IP) address that will be reachable from your network—in this case, 192.168.1.40:

```
# nvram set lan_ipaddr="192.168.1.40"
# nvram set lan_gateway="192.168.1.1"
# nvram set lan_dns="192.168.1.10"
# nvram commit
# ifup lan
```

Notice that we have also added a default gateway and DNS server. This is required so that, among other things, you can use the *ipkg* command to keep the box up-to-date with packages and install software. Next, we will enable the bridge and disable the Dynamic Host Configuration Protocol (DHCP):

```
# nvram set wl0_mode="wet"        # bridged client
# nvram commit
# wifi
# cd /etc/init.d
# mv S50dnsmasq disabled_s50dnsmasq
# chmod -x s50dnsmasq
# killall dnsmasq
```

The nas package is required for WPA, while the wl package is not, it will allow you to do some cool things, such as look at all of the surrounding wireless networks and their encryption types:

```
# ipkg install nas wl
```

Notes from the Underground...

Reinstall NAS Package after Upgrading

The NAS package in OpenWrt is the proprietary binary tool that allows you to set up WPA/WEP encryption for your wireless connections. While setting up the WET bridge, we ran into problems and realized that an upgrade from RC5 to RC6 was the cause. The fix was to reinstall the NAS package as follows:

```
# ipkg remove nas
# ipkg install nas
```

We found this tip in the OpenWrt forums, which we highly recommend that you sign up for and read on a regular basis. They are very useful for troubleshooting problems with OpenWrt. The following forum posting is what led us to the afore-mentioned solution: **http://forum.openwrt.org/viewtopic.php?pid=38430**. The forum handle "mbm," mentioned in this post, is Mike Baker, OpenWrt project cofounder and lead developer. For more information about NAS, see **http://wiki.openwrt.org/OpenWrtDocs/nas.**

Next, issue the following command to scan for other wireless networks to which to connect:

```
# wl scan ; sleep 1 ; wl scanresults
```

In our example, we see a wireless network called *pauldotcom* that is running WPA:

```
SSID: "pauldotcom"
Mode: Managed   RSSI: -23 dBm   noise: -92 dBm   Channel: 6
BSSID: 00:18:39:5B:81:11          Capability: ESS WEP ShortSlot
Supported Rates: [ 1(b) 2(b) 5.5(b) 11(b) 18 24 36 54 6 9 12 48 ]
WPA:
        multicast cipher: TKIP
        unicast ciphers(1): TKIP
        AKM Suites(1): WPA-PSK
        WPA Capabilities(0x0): Pairwise, 1 PTK Replay Ctr(s)
```

The *wl* command provides us with useful information about surrounding wireless networks. It displays the SSID as *pauldotcom*, shows that the key management protocol is *TKIP*, and shows that the protocol in use is WPA. Next, we will configure wrt-bridge as a wireless client for the WPA-PSK network called *pauldotcom*:

```
# nvram set wl0_akm="psk"
# nvram set wl0_channel="6"
```

```
# nvram set wl0_wpa_psk="hacknaked"
# nvram set wl0_ssid="pauldotcom"
# nvram set wl0_crypto="tkip"
# nvram commit
```

> **NOTE**
>
> WPA2, or more appropriately called 802.11i, is not supported by OpenWrt in WET mode. It is our understanding that this is a limitation of the wireless driver. Refer to the following posting on the OpenWrt forum for more information: **http://forum.openwrt.org/viewtopic.php?pid=24280**.

Reload the wireless network settings:

```
# /sbin/wifi
```

Run the *iwconfig* command to be certain that the changes have taken effect:

```
# iwconfig
lo          no wireless extensions.


eth0        no wireless extensions.


eth1        IEEE 802.11-DS  ESSID:"pauldotcom"
            Mode:Repeater  Frequency:2.412 GHz  Access Point: 00:18:39:5B:81:02
            Tx-Power:19 dBm
            RTS thr=2347 B   Fragment thr=2346 B
            Encryption key:0847-8043-6AC6-7211-4CD9-CBB2-6FE8-F80D-0000-0000-0000-
0000-3B89-5F01-F869-09C0 [2]
            Link Noise level:-93 dBm
            Rx invalid nwid:0  Rx invalid crypt:0  Rx invalid frag:0
            Tx excessive retries:169304  Invalid misc:0   Missed beacon:0
```

The preceding output contains a field labeled "Encryption Key": If this field in your output has a value similar to what is displayed in this code, you are in good shape and are ready to test your client connectivity. If it has a value of *off*, check your configuration settings.

> **TIP**
>
> You may find yourself needing to review many of the same variables repeatedly. For example, in the preceding configuration, it is very important that the WPA parameters match on the client (in this case, wrt-bridge) and on the AP (in this case, wrt-liv-

ingrm). To quickly check these configuration settings you can issue the following command:

> # *nvram show | egrep '(crypto|akm|wpa)'*
> *size: 1623 bytes (31145 left)*
> *wl0_akm=psk*
> *wl0_wpa_psk=hacknaked*
> *wl0_crypto=tkip*
> In the preceding output, the NVRAM settings for *wl0_crypto, wl0_akm* and *wl0_wpa_psk* should be displayed.

Setting Up a Routed Bridge

A routed bridge is configured differently than a WET. In this example, we will put the WRT54G wireless radio into "STA" mode, which is short for *station*, referring to its capability to become a wireless client. Consider the example network in Figure 4.3.

Figure 4.3 Wireless Routed Bridge Setup

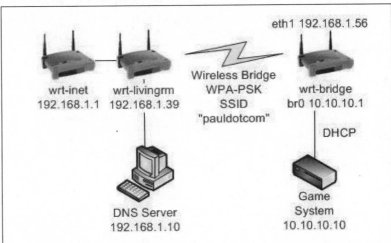

In Figure 4.3, we have wrt-bridge behaving more like a router, and less like a bridge. We use two virtual LANs (VLANs) on the device to separate the two subnets into what is referred to as "routed bridge mode." Let's take a look at this configuration. We first have to break the default bridge that connects the wireless interface to the wired LAN ports:

```
# nvram set lan_ifnames="vlan0"
# nvram set wan_ifname="eth1"          # the wireless interface
```

The first command sets the *lan_ifnames* variable to only be *vlan0*. By default, on a WRT54GL, it would also include *eth1*, the wireless interface. Because we want the wireless interface to appear as a wide area network (WAN) port, we run the next command and set *eth1* to be the *wan_ifname*, which tells the networking subsystem to treat this interface as the WAN port, saving us the trouble of having to reconfigure the firewall rules.

> ### WARNING
>
> Before you change the VLAN assignment on your WRT54G, be certain that you reference the VLANs that correspond to your router model! For full reference, refer to the following guide:
>
> http://wiki.openwrt.org/OpenWrtDocs/Configuration#NetworkInterfaceNames
> This is a very important step, as it will introduce a whole new level of bricking that will most likely require installation of a JTAG connector and cable. You may be asking yourself, "Did this happen to the authors?" The answer is yes, it did. Refer to Chapter 8.

Figure 4.4 shows a graphical representation of how we are changing the default VLAN assignment on the WRT54G. The wireless interface *eth1* has been assigned to the VLAN associated to the WAN interface, requiring routing capabilities (instead of bridging) to send traffic from the Ethernet switch to the wireless network.

Figure 4.4 Routed Bridge Interface Configuration

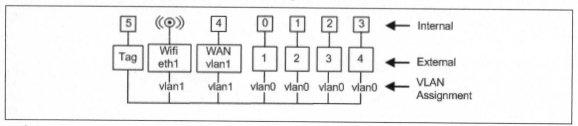

> ### NOTE
>
> Two documents in the OpenWrt Wiki do a fantastic job explaining the inner workings of the networking subsystem:
>
> **http://wiki.openwrt.org/OpenWrtDocs/NetworkInterfaces** In this document, the Asus WL-500G Premium device is used as an example to explain the inner workings of OpenWrt's networking subsystem.
>
> **http://wiki.openwrt.org/OpenWrtNVRAM** In the section titled "1. IP Interface Settings," this document goes on to explain the meaning behind all the interface names that precede all the interface settings (i.e., *lan* and *wan*).

Now you can configure your new WAN adapter (*eth1*) with a static IP address on the wireless network provided to you by wrt-livingrm. You could also configure this using DHCP; however, a static IP address lets you connect back to it easily for management.

```
# nvram set wan_proto="static"
# nvram set wan_ipaddr="192.168.1.56"
# nvram set wan_netmask="255.255.255.0"
# nvram set wan_gateway="192.168.1.1"
# nvram set wan_dns="192.168.1.10"
# nvram commit
```

Reload the wireless settings, which will now include reloading the WAN adapter:

```
# ifdown wan
# ifup wan
# /sbin/wifi
```

Configuring the Firewall

In order to manage the WRT54G that we are using as a routed bridge (Figure 4.3), we need to adjust the firewall rules that apply to the routing process inside the WRT54G. The default firewall rules do not accept connections on the WAN ports, and because we've put the wireless adapter in the WAN VLAN, we need to adjust the rules. You can easily adjust firewall rules on your WRT54G running OpenWrt by editing the /etc/firewall.user file. To allow management over port 22 Transmission Control Protocol (TCP) (SSH) and port 80 TCP (HTTP), add the following rules:

```
iptables -t nat -A prerouting_rule -i $WAN -p tcp --dport 22 -j ACCEPT
iptables         -A input_rule       -i $WAN -p tcp --dport 22 -j ACCEPT
iptables -t nat -A prerouting_rule -i $WAN -p tcp --dport 80 -j ACCEPT
iptables         -A input_rule       -i $WAN -p tcp --dport 80 -j ACCEPT
```

Then, execute /etc/firewall.user as follows:

```
# /etc/firewall.user
```

This script will clear all of the iptables firewall rules and reset them, including your new changes. If you have enabled HTTPS management on your WRT54G, be certain to allow port 443 instead of (or in addition to, depending on your level of paranoia) port 80, as follows:

```
iptables -t nat -A prerouting_rule -i $WAN -p tcp --dport 443 -j ACCEPT
iptables         -A input_rule       -i $WAN -p tcp --dport 443 -j ACCEPT
```

You may also need to open a port in the firewall that will map back to a host plugged into the LAN VLAN. For example, if you require FTP access to your game system, you should add the following rule:

```
iptables -t nat -A prerouting_rule -i $WAN -p tcp --dport 21 -j DNAT --to
10.10.10.10:21
```

```
iptables        -A forwarding_rule -i $WAN -p tcp --dport 21 -d 10.10.10.10 -j
ACCEPT
```

The preceding rules will take connections on the WAN adapter to port 21, and redirect them to the game system at the IP address of 10.10.10.10 on port 21.

Captive Portal-in-a-Box

A captive portal is a handy suite of technologies that allows you to redirect users on a wireless network to a page where you can ask them to register, authenticate, or simply accept an acceptable use policy. The various captive portals all do this using slightly different techniques. Numerous captive portal solutions are available to the WRT54G platform. Wifidog and Chillispot are two projects that have grown quite large and are well supported on both DD-WRT and OpenWrt. However, both require that you have an external authentication service, which can mean setting up a Remote Authentication Dial-in User Service (RADIUS) server and even Apache, along with MySQL or Postgres database applications. Other projects have taken it a bit further and integrated it into a hotspot community, and as a member you can join the hotspot network. Table 4.1 briefly describes many of the available hotspots.

Table 4.1 Available Hotspots

Hotspot	Web Site	Technology
Wifidog	http://dev.wifidog.org	An agent that runs on an access point to redirect users. Requires a PHP and Postgres backend for authentication and management.
Chillispot	www.chillispot.org	Uses a user space application to redirect users to an authentication Web server which can authenticate using RADIUS.
NoCat	http://nocat.net	The original NoCatAuth requires Perl and typically runs on a Linux server. NoCatSplash is a rewrite of this code in C, and it has been ported to many platforms, including OpenWrt. It is typically run without authentication.
Coova	www.coova.org	A custom firmware based on OpenWrt that uses Chillispot and/or Wifidog to provide a captive portal in various different configurations.
WorldSpot	http://worldspot.net/wk/	A social captive portal Web site that allows you to join the hotspot, or run your own for fun and profit. Based on DD-WRT and Chillispot.

Continued

Table 4.1 continued Available Hotspots

Hotspot	Web Site	Technology
Sputnik	www.sputnik.com/products/apf.html	A hotspot technology similar to WorldSpot; however, they sell pre-built routers with their own custom firmware.

NOTE

For a good overview of how the captive portal redirects traffic, refer to the Wikipedia article at http://en.wikipedia.org/wiki/Captive_portal, and specifically, the section titled "Implementation."

Although these solutions work well in many situations, they are a bit beyond the scope of this book and often require external servers and/or accounts with various hotspot providers, which would give all members access to your wireless network. Wouldn't it be nice if we had an all-in-one captive portal that ran on a WRT54G and didn't require any other servers or accounts? Using Ewrt with some customizations, we can achieve this rather easily.

In Figure 4.5, we see the hotspot network configuration, starting with the cable modem providing Internet access. The cable modem terminates to the WAN port of a WRT54G (wrt–inet), which provides network address translation (NAT) and DHCP services on the LAN side. This can be any router, running any kind of firmware that allows for this functionality. We then take another WRT54G, install Ewrt on it using the instructions in Chapter 2, and plug the network cable in between a LAN port on wrt–inet and the WAN port on the captive portal access point running Ewrt, wrt–cp.

Figure 4.5 Captive Portal Network Setup

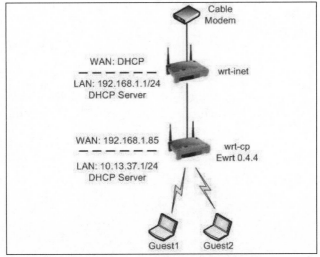

To configure the initial settings it is best to take a laptop or PC and plug it into the LAN side of wrt-cp. You will get a default, dynamically assigned IP address where you can then log into the Web interface using the default username of *admin* and a password of *admin*. Next, you need to use the Web GUI to change the IP address on the WAN interface, which can be either statically or dynamically assigned. You will also need to be certain that the default gateway and DNS servers are provided, or entered manually if you're using a static IP address. A static IP address can have an advantage, as you can restrict its access to the rest of the network as it will represent all wireless captive portal users. A static IP address also makes it easy to administer from the WAN side if you so choose. The LAN side of wrt-cp needs to be a different subnet from the WAN side; in this case, we are using 10.13.37.0/24 as the subnet. Once you change this setting, you will need to re-login to the Web GUI. You will need to be certain to configure a DHCP server on the LAN side as well so that clients can get an address, default gateway, and DNS server when associating to the wireless captive portal SSID, which can be called something like "MyHotSpot". By default, the SSID is ewrt, but you can change this by going into the wireless settings (**Wireless | Basic Settings**).

Now you can further configure your hotspot SSH to connect to the router's LAN IP address:

```
# ssh 10.13.37.1
```

NOTE

The SSH server takes a minute or more to produce a prompt as it generates the keys. Be patient.

Set the following NVRAM variables:

```
# nvram set lan_gateway_enable="0"
# nvram set lan_gateway=""
# nvram set lan_dns_enable="0"
# nvram set lan_dns=""
# nvram set lan_wan_proxy_arp="0"
# nvram set lan_wan_bridge="0"
# nvram commit
# reboot
```

These settings ensure that your default route or DNS on the WAN works properly and is not confused with a route or DNS server setting on the LAN port. Next, go to the GUI and enable NoCat, as shown in Figure 4.6.

Figure 4.6 NoCat Captive Portal Setup Page

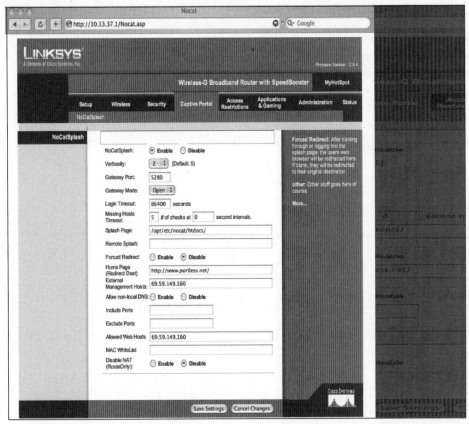

On the captive portal configuration page shown in Figure 4.6, you will need to click the **Enable** radio button next to the label **NoCatSplash**. You can leave the remaining options at their default values.

The next step is very important and you must do it before you make changes via the command line to enable local authentication, which will require that you again SSH to the router and enter the following commands:

```
# ipkg update
# ipkg install nocat-pwd libglib
# nvram set NC_DocumentRoot="/opt/etc/nocat/htdocs/"
# nvram set NC_binary_path="/opt/usr/sbin/"
# nvram set NC_binary_name="splashd-pw"
# nvram set NC_LeaseFile="/opt/etc/nocat/nocat.leases"
# nvram commit
# reboot
```

The first two commands will update your package tree (this version of Ewrt is based on OpenWrt). Then we install the nocat-pwd package along with the required libglib library (we got dependency errors due to a bug in the package, so installation of libglib is required). The NVRAM settings that begin with "NC" are read by Ewrt when starting the captive portal functionality. We tell the captive portal to use a specific Web directory and binary, splashd-pw, which provides not only the captive portal, but also the authentication. Now we can commit our changes and reboot.

Now we will need to edit the /opt/etc/nocat/nocat-pw.txt file to change the username and passwords. By default, Ewrt gives us the following usernames and passwords:

```
user1     user1     3600
user2     user2     3600
user3     user3     3600
user4     user4     3600
user10    user10    36000
user11    user11    36000
user12    user12    36000
user13    user13    36000
admin     nimda     0
```

Please do not leave the defaults, but create you own entries as follows:

```
# cd /opt/etc/nocat/
# cat > nocat-pw.txt
psw hacknaked 36000
<CTRL-D>
```

The first two columns represent the username and password. The third field represents the *Login Timeout* setting, which defines how long a client can stay authenticated (in seconds). A value of 0 will cause a user never to expire (until the NoCat server is restarted, including clearing the iptables firewall rules or rebooting the router). Optionally, you can edit /opt/etc/nocat/htdocs/splash.html to customize the login page to suit your needs. When you are done, associate to the SSID and browse to any Web page. You should be redirected to the captive portal login page, as shown in Figure 4.7.

Upon successful login, you will be redirected to the Web page you were trying to reach. You should see the following messages if the login was successful:

Figure 4.7 Ewrt Splash Screen with Login

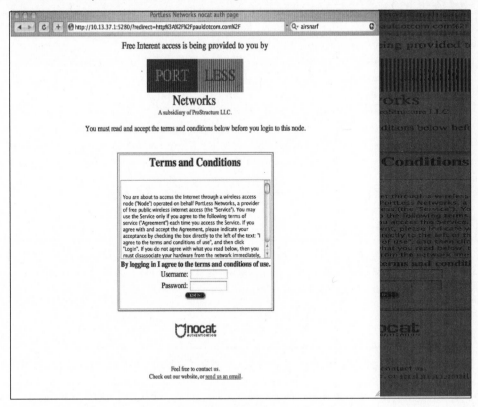

```
ewrt ~/var/log# grep NoCat /var/log/messages

Apr 29 12:41:59   daemon.notice NoCat[110]: splashd start

Apr 29 12:41:59   daemon.notice NoCat[110]: initialize_driver: No fetch required
(static splash page)

Apr 29 12:42:08   daemon.warn NoCat[110]: peer_file_reinit: Cannot open lease file
/opt/etc/nocat/nocat.leases for re-initialization!

Apr 29 12:42:42   daemon.warn NoCat[110]: File not found:
/opt/etc/nocat/htdocs//favicon.ico
```

**Apr 29 12:44:29   daemon.notice NoCat[110]: accept_peer: adding psw, on IP:
10.13.37.101**

The most important line is the last one, appearing in bold, that should say that the login was successful. Now you can impress all of your geek friends with your own personal hotspot. This is also a nice solution for small or even medium-size businesses looking to authenticate wireless users—for example, if you have vendors and contractors coming in on a temporary basis and you do not want to issue them credentials in your authentication system, but they need access to a wireless network. In this example, it would be best to terminate the hotspot (i.e., plug in the WAN port) to a DMZ network.

Asterisk for VoIP

Asterisk is a fully functional, free, open source Linux–based IP PBX phone system. It has every feature you can imagine from a commercial PBX solution (call hold, transfer, customized dial plans, etc.). Asterisk is infinitely configurable. As a matter of course for open source projects, the source code is available and portable to many different platforms; in our case, the WRT54G. Additionally, due to the highly configurable nature of Asterisk, it can be slimmed down to fit in a small space.

The initial install of Asterisk on a WRT54G must be very small, as after the installation of OpenWrt, there are only about 5.5MB of available space left. If desired, it is possible to eliminate some of the unused modules, and enable additional ones for more features, including voicemail, music on hold, and so on. You can apply the SD card mod to increase WRT54G storage capacity and take advantage of all of Asterisk's capabilities.

For more information about the Asterisk project, visit www.asterisk.com.

Installing Asterisk

Installing Asterisk under OpenWrt is a very trivial thing to accomplish! The OpenWrt package tree includes a version of Asterisk as an ipkg package. Although this version may not be the latest version of Asterisk, it is completely stable on the WRT54G platform.

> **NOTE**
>
> The current version of Asterisk in the OpenWrt package tree at the time of this writing is 1.0.10-1, whereas the current version released from the Asterisk project under a full Intel Linux installation is 1.4. You can obtain later versions of Asterisk for the WRT54G in the ipkg format from a number of places; however, you should treat them as Beta or unstable. We were able to use several of the unofficial OpenWrt packages to cause significant issues with the base OpenWrt install.
>
> If you want to use a later version, you can obtain one from various sources listed in the OpenWrt forums, by searching for "asterisk". You can find the OpenWrt forums at http://forum.openwrt.org.

You need to install the OpenWrt package of Asterisk with a connection on the WAN port to the Internet for package retrieval. First, you need to update your OpenWrt package list with the following command:

```
# ipkg update
```

To install Asterisk, issue the following command at the OpenWrt command line (via SSH):

```
# ipkg install asterisk
```

By performing this install, ipkg will also include any dependencies that have not been met previously. The dependencies for Asterisk include libncurses and libpthread.

Configuring Asterisk

Configuring Asterisk can be a monumental task, given its complexity and highly configurable nature. Although we won't be covering all of the options in this section, as it is beyond the scope of this book, we will lay the foundation for further customization. You can find more information on configuring all of the features of Asterisk at www.asterisk.org/support.

Configuring modules.conf

We need to begin by modifying a few of the configuration files located in /etc/asterisk. The first one we will need to modify is modules.conf, which instructs Asterisk which modules to load at startup. Obviously, the more modules you load at startup, the greater the impact on your memory usage. With limited RAM on the WRT54G device, you need to make some conscious decisions as to which modules you load.

The default modules.conf is an excellent start; you can, and should, remove a few other modules from the default startup. Asterisk has two methods for loading modules:

- Specify *autoload=yes* in the *[modules]* section of modules.conf, and Asterisk will load all modules in the Asterisk modules directory as specified in asterisk.conf (the *astmoddir* item which is set to /usr/lib/asterisk/modules by default), unless they are specified as a *noload* option, which will not load the specified module.

- Specify *autoload=no* in the *[modules]* section of modules.conf, and Asterisk will load only the modules specified with the *load* option.

By default, Asterisk uses the *autoload=yes* option, so that is the method we will describe here.

You should add the following line to modules.conf with *autoload=yes* set, in order to disable the module and save on system resources:

```
noload => res_musiconhold.so
```

At this time, you do not have any music copied to the WRT54G, and due to limited space, it is not recommended that you use the WRT54G as a music repository. You could provide appropriate music at an alternative location, such as a Server Message Block (SMB) share or SD memory card. Please see Chapters 3 and 7 for more information on configuring SMB shares and SD cards, respectively.

Additionally, in our example, we are using only a limited set of audio codecs and connection types, so we will leave only the ones we will need (in our case, Session Initiation Protocol [SIP] and ulaw). This will reduce our memory footprint, by removing these modules. However, your needs may vary depending on your VoIP provider, or on your client phone capabilities.

We should remove these modules, *chan_iax2.so*, *format_wav.so*, and *format_wav_gsm.so* (for iax2 and wav audio conversions), for our example, as we do not need them:

```
noload => chan_iax2.so
noload => format_wav.so
noload => format_wav_gsm.so
```

We also need to be very careful about the codecs that we use with our SIP (or other) clients, such as iLibC. These particular codecs can use a significant amount of processor horsepower, and can require a dedicated math processor. You may recall from Chapter 1 that none of the WRT54G models is terribly powerful, as none of the processors contains dedicated math processing. As a result, using these codecs will result in poor to no call quality.

Configuring VoIP Provider Connectivity

Next, we will configure our WRT54G to connect to a SIP provider on the Internet so that we can start to make calls with phones attached to our local Asterisk installation. Although there are several methods for connecting to various VoIP providers, the one we have elected to use in this example, BroadVoice (www.broadvoice.com), allows for only SIP connections.

Notes from the Underground…

Choosing a VoIP Provider

Due to the rise in popularity in Internet-based VoIP solutions, there has been a huge upswing in VoIP providers. As with many other industries, not all vendors are created equal. Take great care in selecting a VoIP provider!

With a local Asterisk installation it is very important to make sure that the VoIP provider you select allows for and supports Bring Your Own Equipment (BYOE). Certainly one could select a provider that does not support Asterisk, but the labor required to figure out how to make the installation work may be considerable. Why not just do the research upfront for a guaranteed solution! Additionally, some providers will not allow BYOE, and require that you purchase their equipment or purchase limited, compatible equipment. This would defeat our purposes of running our own PBX on our WRT54G.

As with any other technology purchase, it is good to read all of the reviews, and do your research upfront. A great resource for selecting a VoIP provider that will allow BYOE and is known to work with and/or support Asterisk is http://voip-info.org.

A great (and bad) thing about the market explosion of VoIP providers is consumer choice. Be sure to familiarize yourself with all of the plans and costs associated with each provider, and make sure they give you the correct plans for your needs. For example, many VoIP providers provide national service at decent rates, and international rates as well; just be sure that the countries you want to call are listed for your provider of choice. Picking the wrong provider for your needs could result in even higher costs than your current Plain Old Telephone Service (POTS).

BroadVoice has provided some great installation instructions for use with Asterisk. Be sure to check your selected provider's configuration instructions. With the instructions provided from BroadVoice, we will be utilizing SIP, but many other providers can utilize other connection types, such as Global System for Mobile Communications (GSM) or Inter-Asterisk Exchange (IAX).

NOTE

Although different providers may use different connection types, essentially the requirements for connections are the same: a connection point, a username, and a password. The different connection types do require different configuration files to be modified. These configuration files are also located under /etc/asterisk, and are named for the appropriate connection type, such as gsm.conf or iax.conf.

In our example for BroadVoice, we will be modifying the sip.conf file located in /etc/asterisk. This file can be easily modified with vi. The first thing you need to do with the sip.conf file is to register your device with BroadVoice so that you may begin using your WRT54G to route calls. The registration is configured with a *register* directive, which can be located anywhere in the configuration file. We have elected to include our particular *register* directive in the section pertaining to registration to make it easier for us to find later.

For BroadVoice, the *register* directive is as follows:

```
register => <VoIP Phone #>@sip.broadvoice.com:<password>:<VoIP Phone\
#>@sip.broadvoice.com/666
```

You do need to replace a few items in the configuration directive to items provided by your VoIP provider, such as your phone number and password. There are two other items to note that are important with your register configuration: sip.broadvoice.com and 666. sip.broadvoice.com does not refer to the actual DNS name, but to another section later in the SIP configuration file where you will define more information about the connection type to BroadVoice. The 666 refers to a local VoIP phone attached to our Asterisk installation. We used 666 as an extension, which will also match a section later on in our sip.conf file.

This *register* command is telling Asterisk that sip.broadvoice.com (as defined in the *[sip.broadvoice.com]* configuration section) should register its capabilities for extension 666. This will allow extension 666 to receive calls directly when a third party dials the VoIP phone number.

Now we need to define additional configuration sections for additional attributes for the two different connections: one for BroadVoice and one for our local extension 666.

BroadVoice has provided some excellent configuration instructions; however, we have made a few changes to our BroadVoice connection. Here is the configuration we used. Replace items as provided by your provider.

```
[sip.broadvoice.com]
type=peer
user=phone
host=sip.broadvoice.com
fromdomain=sip.broadvoice.com
fromuser=<VoIP Phone #>
secret=<password>
username=<VoIP Phone #>
insecure=very
```

```
context=from-broadvoice
authname=<VoIP Phone #>
dtmfmode=inband
dtmf=inband
disallow=all
;allow=gsm
allow=ulaw
;Disable canreinvite if you are behind a NAT
canreinvite=no
```

In our configuration, we added the option *disallow=all* and commented out *allow=gsm* by using a leading ;, which defines the line as a comment. We elected to do this because our VoIP phone supports ulaw as a codec, as does BroadVoice. When we perform conversion, it will require more processing power to convert from our local phone to BroadVoice, possibly reducing our call quality. Our local phone extension does support GSM as well, so we disabled it in order to make sure we are forcing ulaw.

TIP

GSM requires significantly less bandwidth than ulaw, but unfortunately, BroadVoice does not support GSM connections. If at all possible, use GSM when connecting to your VoIP provider, as the Internet connection that is used could have limited bandwidth. The reduced traffic footprint of GSM will perform much better over an Internet connection, resulting in better call quality.

The local connection to the VoIP phone, in many cases, will have a significantly faster connection to the Asterisk installation than our connection to the Internet. As a result, we can use the higher-bandwidth codec (in this case, ulaw) between the two. This will require additional processing power by the WRT54G to perform the codec conversion, which is why we elected to match the two connections with ulaw.

You should also note that the *[sip.broadvoice.com]* section declaration is a match to what was used in the *register* directive we defined earlier.

We also need to define the capabilities of our local phone extension 666 so that it can connect to our Asterisk installation. In order to accomplish that, we need to define an additional configuration section for our local VoIP phone:

```
[666]
; X-Lite - Mac SoftPhone
type=friend
context=default
host=dynamic
dtmfmode=rfc2833
```

```
disallow=all
allow=ulaw
callerid="Larry Pesce" <800-555-1212>
```

In a nutshell, we are defining our local phone extension so that it can connect to our Asterisk installation. Again, we are allowing only the ulaw codec to be used between Asterisk and the VoIP phone, and you will note that the configuration section header *[666]* matches the extension we defined as being allowed to directly receive calls with the *register* command. For more information on the other commands, refer to www.asterisk.org/support.

Are You 0wned?

VoIP Security

In our configuration examples for our Asterisk setup for our local VoIP phones, we assumed a trusted network. You may note that our local extension does not require authentication of either a username or a password. If a nefarious individual were able to gain access to our trusted network, he could effectively knock our local phone off the network with several different types of denial of service (DoS) attacks. If the phone were a soft phone (a VoIP phone based in software), it is even possible that the soft phone may not be running.

In these instances, an attacker could impersonate our phone and gain connectivity to our Asterisk installation with all of the same privileges that our regular VoIP phone would have, including the capability to answer and make calls! It can do this with very little captured network traffic. Keep in mind that if any phones are implemented over wireless, this traffic could be captured over the air.

In addition to our trusted network issues, VoIP traffic is notoriously difficult to secure. For example, SIP traffic over a network is essentially sent "in the clear," with no encryption. If this traffic were intercepted, it would be possible to impersonate the device establishing the call. Additionally, the Real-time Transport Protocol (RTP) traffic also travels "in the clear," which makes it possible to record the phone calls. One particularly easy tool to use under Windows is Cain and Abel, a multipurpose security auditing tool. Cain and Abel is able to sniff VoIP traffic off an appropriately configured network, and automatically convert and save the phone conversations into .wav files. Cain and Abel is available from www.oxid.it. You can perform the same type of VoIP traffic to phone conversation conversion through the standard Wireshark sniffer, available at www.wireshark.org.

Although the SIP standard, RFC 3261, defines secure extensions (called Secure SIP) based on Transport Layer Security (TLS), and there is another standard, called Secure Real-time Transport Protocol (SRTP), RFC 3711, focused on providing security to the RTP VoIP calls, their implementation is not widely adopted.

Continued

> For information on securing your Asterisk installation plenty of resources are available, including the various configuration files for Asterisk, guides at www.asterisk.org and www.voip-info.org, and *Practical VoIP Security*, from Syngress Publishing (ISBN # 1597490601).

We completed a significant amount of Asterisk configuration; however, we will still be unable to dial until we define our dial plan in the extensions.conf file.

Configuring extensions.conf

In order to be able to dial out from our local VoIP phone, we need to create a default dial plan. A dial plan on any PBX is just a mapping of what paths a phone call should take when specific numbers are dialed from one of the phones. In order to create some default dial mappings, we need to edit the extensions.conf file in /etc/asterisk.

The comments in extensions.conf are a valuable resource for understanding how to create customized dial plans that include voicemail, call transfers, and even multiple VoIP providers. This can come in handy for additional configurations, but those are beyond the scope of this book. We'll at least give you the basics to get outgoing calls working with our BroadVoice example.

In order for our local VoIP phone extension to make an outbound call, we need to tell Asterisk where to route the call. In the default setup, Asterisk does not have any general routing information. As a result, we need to add the following lines to our extensions.conf file:

```
exten => _1NXXNXXXXXX, 1, dial(SIP/${EXTEN}@sip.broadvoice.com,30)
exten => _1NXXNXXXXXX, 2, congestion()
exten => _1NXXNXXXXXX, 102, busy()
exten => 3,1,Dial(SIP/sip.broadvoice.com,20,tr)
```

The first three *exten* commands perform pattern matching for numbers dialed by local VoIP extensions. *exten* commands that begin with an underscore perform pattern matching. These particular examples are tailored to U.S. dialing examples; U.S. dialing starts with a *1*, a three-digit area code (*NXX*), and a seven-digit local number (*NXXXXXX*). So in the first command, when a U.S. number is dialed, Asterisk knows it must use SIP to place the call from the extension that started the connection (*${EXTEN}*, which in our configuration is 666), and that it needs to use the connection profile sip.broadvoice.com as defined in our sip.conf file. The second and third lines define how to deal with network overload and busy connections for U.S. dialing. The fourth line allows for any other connections that are not covered by the pattern matching to be routed via the sip.broadvoice.com connection profile.

It's easy to extend this dial plan to add functionality to utilize international dialing by adding additional pattern matching. For example, BroadVoice provides additional services for international calling to particular countries. Its recommended dial plan directly from BroadVoice for its international calling plan looks like this, and has been edited for space:

```
exten=_01130.,1,dial(SIP/${EXTEN}@sip.broadvoice.com,30)
exten=_01131.,1,dial(SIP/${EXTEN}@sip.broadvoice.com,30)
exten=_011.,2,congestion() ; No answer, nothing
exten=_011.,102,busy() ; Busy
```

You can find the full dial plan from BroadVoice at www.broadvoice.com/support_install_asterisk.html.

Configuring the X-Lite Soft Phone

Before investing a considerable amount of money in a physical IP phone, we suggest a software-based VoIP phone. There is no sense in spending your hard-earned money just to make sure Asterisk meets your needs. Although you have many options to choose from, the X–Lite soft phone from CounterPath (www.xten.com) is a great free alternative. The X–Lite Soft phone supports Windows, Linux, and OS X.

WARNING

As of this writing, the OS X X-Lite client (version 2.0 1105x, build stamp 21409) is very buggy. It will make and receive calls appropriately; however, it has a nasty habit of crashing when a call has ended. X-Lite is under constant development, so we expect many of these issues to be resolved in future releases.

For our example, we will be configuring the OS X client. Although the Linux and Windows clients have slightly different appearances, the menus and items needed for configuration are the same. With the OS X and Linux installations, when the X–Lite soft phone is first started it enters into a configuration wizard for determining appropriate sound configuration. We will skip the configuration wizard under OS X and Linux, as the reminder of the settings that do need to be configured are the same for all three clients.

Under OS X and Linux, you can find these settings under **Menu | System Settings | SIP Proxy**. We need to configure a few settings for our example in this menu, also reflected in Figure 4.8:

- **Display Name** Set this to whatever you want Caller ID to display.
- **Username** This is the extension as defined in sip.conf.
- **Password** In our example, this should be left blank.
- **Domain/Realm** This is the internal IP address of our Asterisk installation.
- **SIP Proxy** This is the internal IP address of our Asterisk installation.

Figure 4.8 OS X and Linux X-Lite Configuration

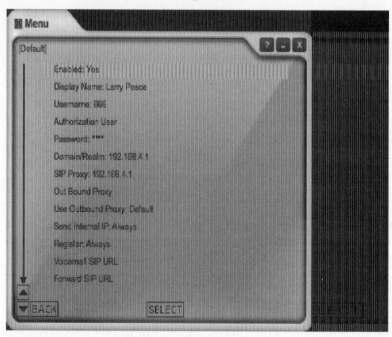

Under Windows, the configuration is a little bit different. You can find the settings under **Menu | SIP Account Settings**. To create a new connection click **Add**, and to modify an existing connection click **Properties**. The settings we need to define under the Account tab for our example, also reflected in Figure 4.9, are:

- **Display Name** Set this to whatever you want Caller ID to display.
- **User name** This is the extension as defined in sip.conf.
- **Domain** This is the internal IP address of our Asterisk installation.
- **Register with domain and receive incoming calls** This must be checked.
- **Proxy Address** This is the internal IP address of our Asterisk installation.

As you may note, Figure 4.9 references a different username (or extension) because we created this in our setup as a separate extension, allowing us to have multiple phones. You could easily change this setting to 666 to replace an OS X or Linux soft client.

Figure 4.9 Windows X-Lite configuration

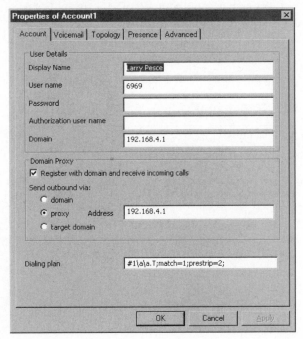

Once the client has been configured, it should automatically connect to the Asterisk server on your WRT54G, and you should be able to begin to make phone calls. If calls do not work, some troubleshooting is in order.

Troubleshooting Asterisk

As with every other option in Asterisk, troubleshooting options are numerous. There are troubleshooting options for every command and configuration option. Some of the best places to obtain information on how to troubleshoot various problems are the configuration files themselves. For example, if you suspect that you are having problems with SIP connections, check the sip.conf file comments! The configuration file for SIP has some common troubleshooting options for SIP. From the sip.conf file, you can see that you have some great options:

```
; Useful CLI commands to check peers/users:
;    sip show peers          Show all SIP peers (including friends)
;    sip show users          Show all SIP users (including friends)
;    sip show registry       Show status of hosts we register with
;
;    sip debug               Show all SIP messages
;
;    reload chan_sip.so      Reload configuration file
;                            Active SIP peers will not be reconfigured
```

In order to start troubleshooting Asterisk problems, you need to enter interactive mode with Asterisk. While connected to OpenWrt on your WRT54G through SSH, with Asterisk already running in the background, issue the following command:

```
# asterisk -r
```

You will then be given the interactive mode of Asterisk, as shown in Figure 4.10.

Figure 4.10 Asterisk Interactive Mode

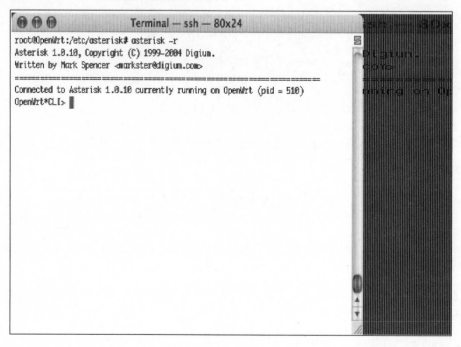

The first thing to do when troubleshooting any issue is to set very high levels for debug and info settings by using the following commands at the Asterisk prompt:

```
OpenWrt*CLI> set debug 100000
OpenWrt*CLI> set verbose 100000
```

These settings will output plenty of information about every connection that Asterisk makes in any direction. Errors in these outputs will be easy to discern.

NOTE

The debug and info settings will not be retained after you exit interactive mode, or if you restart Asterisk.

Auto-Starting Asterisk on Boot

By default, the packages used to install Asterisk do not set up Asterisk to survive a reboot. At this point, if our WRT54G were to reboot, Asterisk would not be running. This can be particularly frustrating, if you expect Asterisk to "just work" after you have configured it, or when the WRT54G is installed in an area where it is not readily accessible either physically or via the network. It is also not particularly helpful to have to log in and restart Asterisk when it is readily accessible and you are using it regularly!

In order to have Asterisk restart after a reboot, you need to add a script to the standard Linux startup framework under /etc/init.d. You also need to make sure the /etc/default/asterisk file contains *ENABLE_ASTERISK=yes*, which may already be set to *no*. It is possible that the file does not exist, and if it does not, you will need to create it.

You'll also create the following script with vi under /etc/init.d, and name it *S60Asterisk*:

```
#!/bin/sh

DEFAULT=/etc/default/asterisk
OPTIONS=""
[ -f $DEFAULT ] && . $DEFAULT
[ "$ENABLE_ASTERISK" = "yes" ] || exit 0

case $1 in
 start)
  [ -d /var/run ] || mkdir -p /var/run
  [ -d /var/log/asterisk ] || mkdir -p /var/log/asterisk
  [ -d /var/spool/asterisk ] || mkdir -p /var/spool/asterisk
  /usr/sbin/asterisk $OPTIONS
  ;;
 stop)
  [ -f /var/run/asterisk.pid ] && kill $(cat /var/run/asterisk.pid) >/dev/null 2>&1
  ;;
 *)
  echo "usage: $0 (start|stop)"
  exit 1
esac

exit $?
```

To make sure your startup script is executable, use:

```
chmod +x /etc/init.d/S60Asterisk
```

Summary

If you are interested in wardriving, the first sections of this chapter showed you how to build a self-contained wardriving-in-a-box kit. Combine this with some of the battery power projects found in Chapter 7, and you should be able to build a solution for wardriving on the go. Connect all of those new gaming systems and DVRs to a WRT54G for an extensible media adapter that supports either routed or bridge networking and WPA. Impress all of your friends with your very own captive portal or "hotspot" that is self-contained and does not require a subscription. Finally, make calls on the Internet by turning your WRT54G into a full-fledged phone system using Asterisk.

As you can see, the WRT54G platform is quite extensible, as shown in the projects in this chapter. Certainly, this is only the tip of the iceberg for projects! Through support from the OpenWrt developers and other package maintainers, you can extend the functionality of your WRT54G beyond the default configuration.

Solutions Fast Track

Wardriving-in-a-Box

☑ This mod requires a working serial port and a working SD card on your WRT54G. These two hardware hacks are described in Chapter 7.

☑ The Kismet server will capture all of your wardriving information, and save it to the SD card once it has been properly configured.

☑ The Kismet server will interact with GPSs to obtain latitude and longitude data from a serial GPS, and log this information when wireless networks are discovered.

☑ You can remove the SD card and analyze the captured information in a different system after your wardrive.

Setting Up a Wireless Media Adapter

☑ There are a few different ways to create a wireless bridge?namely, routed mode and bridge mode.

☑ Routed mode will support WPA2, whereas bridge mode supports only WPA.

☑ In routed bridge mode, you will need to edit /etc/firewall.user to allow management traffic and access to hosts behind the bridge.

Captive Portal-in-a-Box

☑ A wireless captive portal is a great way to provide guest access to your network. You can build a captive portal that runs entirely on a WRT54G.

☑ Ewrt is an OpenWrt-based firmware distribution that is focused on providing a captive portal. Although captive portals are convenient, they do not offer the protection of other security mechanisms, such as WPA.

☑ If you want to prompt the user for a username and password, you must make special modifications to the captive portal configuration. Be certain to change the default usernames and passwords.

Asterisk for VoIP

☑ Asterisk provides a fully featured VoIP PBX on your WRT54G with either software-based or hardware-based VoIP phones.

☑ A fully configured Asterisk server is a lot of work, but even a basic configuration will be useful for making inexpensive calls with the right VoIP provider.

☑ The X-Lite soft phone available for Linux, OS X, and Windows is a great, free way to get started with VoIP.

Frequently Asked Questions

The following Frequently Asked Questions, answered by the authors of this book, are designed to both measure your understanding of the concepts presented in this chapter and to assist you with real-life implementation of these concepts. To have your questions about this chapter answered by the author, browse to **www.syngress.com/solutions** and click on the **"Ask the Author"** form.

Q: What features does the WRT54G offer over the WGA54G Wireless Gaming Adapter, which was intended to be a gaming adapter?

A: The WGA54G does not support WPA, it contains only one wired Ethernet port, and it has no easy way to upgrade the antenna.

Q: WPA is not working on my WRT54G running OpenWrt. How come?

A: In order for WPA to work on your WRT54G running OpenWrt, you will need to install the wl package (*ipkg install wl*).

Q: How do I reload the wireless settings on my WRT54G running OpenWrt?

A: Simply execute the command *wifi* to reload the wireless adapter.

Q: I want to experiment with NoCatSplash on OpenWrt. Where should I look for information?

A: NoCatSplash is the program heavily modified by the Ewrt folks, and you can find more information at http://nocat.net/~sderle/README.OpenWRT.

Q: I really don't want my friends to authenticate. Instead, I want to just grab their passwords to laugh at them later. What should I use?

A: See Chapter 6, which covers Airsnarf–Rogue Squadron.

Q: Instead of the hardware mods to a WRT54G for a wardriving-in-a-box solution, couldn't I just use a WRTSL54GS with a USB drive and USB GPS?

A: Certainly! However, the major drawback to the WRTSL54GS for a wardriving-in-a-box solution is that it does not feature a removable antenna. The ability to swap antennas can mean the success or failure of any wardriving operation.

Q: A later version of GPSD is available. Can I use that version instead of the one used here?

A: The newer version had some code additions that have rendered it incredibly unstable for use with Kismet. It may work with your particular GPS unit, but it may not. You have been warned!

Q: Will Asterisk on the WRT54G support voicemail?

A: Yes, but due to space constraints of the onboard flash, you will want to set up an SD card or use an SMB share for voicemail storage.

Q: Which VoIP hardware and software clients will work with Asterisk?

A: Most will in one way or another, but they may require significant tinkering. For a list of compatible and community-tested devices, check www.asterisk.org.

## Chapter 5

Securing Wireless Using a WRT54G

Solutions in this chapter:

- **Basic Wireless Security**

- **Configuring WPA-Personal (PSK)**

- **Configuring WPA-Enterprise (and WPA2-Enterprise)**

☑ **Summary**

☑ **Solutions Fast Track**

☑ **Frequently Asked Questions**

Introduction

Wireless security has been a hot topic in the computer security community for years, for very good reasons. Unsecured wireless networks can be compromised quite easily, revealing your personal information and computer files and allowing your network to be used to attack others or to conduct various other inappropriate activities. By utilizing multiple layers of security, including (most importantly) Wi-Fi Protected Access (WPA) or WPA2, you can reduce those risks.

The examples in this chapter are based on the features of OpenWrt 0.9, the current release as of this writing.

Basic Wireless Security

In this section, we will discuss some very basic, fundamental security settings that you should use as part of an overall defense-in-depth security strategy. These security measures by themselves may not provide adequate security; however, when you combine them with each other, and with WPA/WPA2, you can offer improved security for your wireless networks. Of course, you must choose an encryption protocol (Wireless Encryption Protocol [WEP], WPA, or WPA2), with WPA2 being the best choice (the reasons for which should become clear by the end of this chapter).

Select a Secure Network Name (SSID)

Too many times we have seen organizations and individuals leak information about themselves in the form of the wireless network name, known as the SSID. To test this theory, all you need to do is enable your wireless adapter and review the list of available SSIDs. Inevitably, you will find some structured as *FirstName_LastName*, *CompanyName*, or *Name_Location*. This gives away that you are, in fact, Company X or Person Y, and that this is quite possibly your wireless network. Use an SSID name that does not give away information about you or your organization, if you can. For example, the following commands will set the SSID using OpenWrt:

```
# nvram set wl0_ssid="TheMatrix"
# nvram commit
```

Then restart the wireless subsystem to enable the settings with:

```
# /sbin/wifi
```

The most an attacker could glean from the preceding SSID is the name of your favorite movie. Additionally, if you want an extra level of security, you should change your SSID often to prevent dictionary attacks against WPA/WPA2, which we discuss later in this chapter.

Hiding Your SSID

Although this may not hide you from most attackers (and certainly not from anyone who is reading this book) it may prevent your neighbor from connecting to your network. Connections to wireless networks are managed by the operating system, and Windows XP especially is not selective about which networks it connects to. For example, if you have a wireless network with the SSID *linksys* and so does your neighbor you could be connecting to each other's networks without even knowing it!

In an effort to make it less convenient for unauthorized people to connect to your network, you can hide your SSID by doing the following, using OpenWrt as an example:

```
# nvram set wl0_closed="1"
# nvram commit
```

Then restart the wireless subsystem to enable the settings with:

```
# /sbin/wifi
```

Wireless networks that hide their SSIDs—that is, that do not include the SSID in the beacon frames broadcast by the access point—are known as **cloaked networks**.

> **NOTE**
>
> Microsoft Wireless Client Update, a patch for Windows XP with Service Pack 2, KB917021, available at http://support.microsoft.com/kb/917021, changed the default behavior in Windows XP. Among other things, it allows you to configure an SSID to "Connect even if the network is not broadcasting," which could reveal a hidden SSID wherever the client travels. Use this option with caution and be certain to review the aforementioned patch from Microsoft. This patch is not included in the default Microsoft updates at the time of this writing.

MAC Address Filtering

In conjunction with hiding your SSID, it might also be a good idea to build in another layer of access control in the form of Media Access Control (MAC) address filtering. This will configure your access point to allow only certain computers on your network based on their MAC addresses. MAC addresses can easily be spoofed, and a list can be obtained just from sniffing the wireless network, but why not make your attacker go through the trouble? To set a list of allowable MAC addresses, do the following:

```
# nvram set wl0_macmode="allow"
# nvram set wl0_maclist="01:02:03:04:05:06 0A:0B:0C:0D:0E:0F"
# nvram commit
```

Then restart the wireless subsystem to enable the settings with:

```
# /sbin/wifi
```

Note that multiple MAC addresses are separated with a space.

Configuring WEP

In the beginning of wireless network security, there was the Wireless Encryption Protocol (WEP). WEP was designed to provide an encryption layer on top of all data communications over wireless.

Unfortunately, the group that designed the encryption methods for WEP did so in a vacuum, and did not consult cryptographic experts. If they had, they would have been told that WEP would be quite trivial to compromise.

Although WEP is considered insecure, it is better than nothing. When utilizing older hardware that does not support WPA/WPA2, it is a good idea to use WEP. Although WEP won't keep out a determined attacker, it will keep out the casual "wireless thief"; neighbors, casual wardrivers, and others that may be looking for open access points. To configure WEP using OpenWrt, do the following:

```
# nvram set wl0_wep="enabled"
# nvram set wl0_key="1"
# nvram set wl0_key1="f3d6b754b345038414f2746531"
# nvram commit
```

Then restart the wireless subsystem to enable the settings with:

```
# /sbin/wifi
```

The preceding code shows a 104-bit (sometimes referred to as 128-bit) WEP key (26 hexadecimal characters). If you prefer to enter a string instead of hexadecimal characters, you can use the syntax *nvram set wl0_key1="s:mywepkeystring"*. Again, you should not use WEP if WPA is available; however, some specialized devices (such as Voice over IP [VoIP] phones) may support only WEP.

> **NOTE**
>
> A great site for generating WEP keys is www.andrewscompanies.com/tools/wep.asp. Many others are available on the Internet as well. If you prefer to generate your own keys, you could write a shell script; see this posting, www.securityfocus.com/archive/137/439531/30/300/threaded, for an example.

Configuring WPA-Personal (PSK)

Introduction to WPA/WPA2 (802.11i)

In response to the weaknesses inherent to WEP, the Wi-Fi Alliance created a new encryption scheme called Wi-Fi Protected Access (WPA). At the time, WPA was intended to closely follow the then-draft 802.11i specification that was in front of the IEEE. WPA was intended to be backward-compatible with existing hardware, access points, and wireless cards that had low processing requirements and capabilities. Although many wireless cards would benefit from WPA with a firmware upgrade, many access points would not support WPA.

WPA contained many significant upgrades in the encryption methods used, as well as some other protection methods that plagued WEP installations. In addition to the increased protections, WPA was designed to be implemented in two different modes: WPA-Personal, also known as WPA-PSK (Wi-Fi Protected Access Pre-Shared Key), and WPA-Enterprise. WPA-PSK was intended to be used by home and small-business consumers, by utilizing a single key implemented as a password for the wireless network on each access point and on each wireless client. WPA-Enterprise implements the key via an 802.1*x*/Extensible Authentication Protocol (EAP) backend authentication server (instead of the shared password), along with software on the wireless client (called the *supplicant*) to manage the WPA-Enterprise authentication and subsequent key exchanges.

WPA was only an interim measure until the full IEEE 802.11i specification was completed and ratified by the IEEE. When ratified, 802.11i became known as Wi-Fi Protected Access 2 (WPA2). WPA2 includes all of the same features as WPA, but provides stronger encryption for the underlying key exchanges. WPA2 also will function in PSK and Enterprise modes, just as WPA does. The only drawbacks with WPA2 are the new, more processor-intensive encryption techniques, which use the Advanced Encryption Standard (AES). The additional processor horsepower means that many older wireless networking cards and access points will not be supported, and must be swapped out for newer units in order to support WPA2.

It is theoretically possible to obtain the WPA-PSK or WPA2-PSK preshared key using brute force attacks; however, it is not terribly efficient. These attacks require incredible amounts of processing power, and years' worth of effort. It is possible because the preshared key is static, whereas the Enterprise implementation of either utilizes random and changing keys, making it virtually impossible to obtain the keys.

Are You 0wned?

Cracking WPA/WPA2 PSK

coWPAtty (www.churchofwifi.org/default.asp?PageLink=Project_Display.asp?PID=95) is a tool specifically designed to reveal WPA and WPA2 preshared keys. This tool works by comparing specific, precaptured wireless traffic, and cycling through comparisons utilizing a dictionary of possible keys. This operation can take several weeks (or longer) to complete, depending on the size of the dictionary.

In 2006, at DEFCON 14, the Church of WiFi (a wireless security research group) coordinated a release of a new version of coWPAtty that supports the cracking of WPA2-PSK, as well as the ability to precompute the comparisons against the specific wireless traffic needed to obtain the keys. In order to precompute the key comparisons, coWPAtty needs a dictionary and the SSID of the network in which you wish to crack WPA/WPA2-PSK. The SSID is utilized with PSK to calculate the final key that is transmitted over the network, so it is essential that it is included in the comparisons.

With this new release of coWPAtty, the Church of WiFi also released a set of precomputed comparison tables that was developed utilizing a 1-million-word dictionary in conjunction with the top 1,000 SSIDs discovered by wardrivers as reported to http://wigle.net. These precomputed tables, when utilized against a WPA/WPA2-PSK network with one of the 1,000 SSIDs, and utilizing relatively insecure preshared keys, can

Continued

be cracked in a few hours or less! The precalculated dictionaries and associated files have been made available as a torrent download. For more information, see the Church of WiFi's site regarding the release, at www.churchofwifi.org/Project_Display.asp?PID=90. Be warned that the entire tables download is just more than 8 GB!

This release clearly indicates how important it is, when using PSK, to pick a unique SSID and a very complex key. This will make attacks very time-consuming. It is also a good idea to change your SSID every so often, as this will help to thwart repeated attempts to compromise the preshared key.

Configuring WPA-PSK (and WPA2-PSK)

The easiest way to begin to provide a more secure wireless connection is to use WPA-PSK. To do so, we need to have clients that support WPA to connect to our WRT54G. In this section, we will configure WPA under OpenWrt, which will require command-line access to our WRT54G.

Before we can begin to set up WPA (including WPA-PSK or WPA-Enterprise) we must first install the nas package. The nas package contains the Broadcom proprietary nas utility that is used to set up the encryption required for the WPA and WPA2 connections. We'll also want to be sure that our package repository is up-to-date before we install the nas package, by issuing the following two commands:

```
# ipkg update
# ipkg install nas
```

As part of the installation, the nas install package will create a startup script, /etc/init.d/S41wpa, which passes the NVRAM variables that we will set to the nas utility. Although we should not need to modify this script under normal circumstances, when nas fails to start on boot, this script is a good place to investigate to determine the cause of the failure.

In order to define our WPA type, we need to set an NVRAM variable to a setting for our chosen WPA type. For WPA-PSK, we need to set *wl0_akm* to *psk*:

```
# nvram set wl0_akm="psk"
```

NOTE

To avoid conflicts and potential problems it is best to disable WEP before using WPA. You can do this easily by issuing the command *nvram set wl0_wep="disabled"* and then committing the NVRAM settings using the *nvram commit* command and reloading the wireless settings with the */sbin/wifi* command.

For WPA2-PSK, we need to set *wl0_akm* to *psk2*:

```
# nvram set wl0_akm="psk2"
```

NOTE

If you set *wl0_akm* to any value, it will override any WEP settings, regardless of what you set *wl0_wep* to. This will effectively override *wl0_wep*.

We also need to set an NVRAM variable with the encryption type for the WPA/WPA2 network. We have three choices: *tkip*, *aes*, and *tkip+aes*. You will want to choose the encryption type that is best for your environment, and is the minimum supported by all of your wireless clients. In this example, we'll use AES:

```
# nvram set wl0_crypto=aes
```

NOTE

Although the *aes* and *tkip+aes* settings may be slightly more secure, the cryptographic functions that utilize AES will put an increased load on the WRT54G processor. In environments with large numbers of wireless clients connected to the same WRT54G, using *aes* or *tkip+aes* may introduce significant wireless speed deficiencies. With AES and many connected clients, the processor will spend more time performing cryptography functions instead of processing network traffic.

The use of *tkip* will increase wireless speed with a large number of wireless clients, as the processing requirements for Temporary Key Integrity Protocol (TKIP) are reduced.

The second and final step to the PSK configuration is to set the preshared key on the router that we will utilize on all of the connected clients. The key we pick must be between eight and 63 characters long and can contain letters, numbers, and special characters. In order to counteract the dictionary attacks mentioned before using coWPAtty, it is recommended that we use a preshared key of more than 20 characters. Once we select it, we will set the key for either WPA or WPA2 on the router with the following commands:

```
# nvram set wl0_wpa_psk="haxorthematrix.com!"
```

TIP

You can find a great place to generate preshared keys with maximum entropy (randomness) on Steve Gibson's Web site, at www.grc.com/passwords.

In order to complete our WPA-PSK or WPA2-PSK setup, we need to save our NVRAM changes. If we do not, the changes will not survive a reboot. We can save the changes with the following command:

```
# nvram commit
```

If we want our settings to take effect immediately, we can execute the nas startup script manually with the following command:

```
# /etc/init.d/S41wpa
```

Alternatively, we can reboot our router. Upon restart, our selected WPA/WPA2 preshared key will be available for wireless clients.

Notes from the Underground...

Wi-Fi Settings at a Glance

As we have experienced already, there are many configuration options for wireless settings, and wireless security settings, on your WRT54G running OpenWrt. The *nvram* command line is very powerful, but it does not provide you with an easy way to take a snapshot of the current wireless settings on your router. Thanks to Raul Siles, and a handy little shell script, this task is now greatly simplified.

The script is currently hosted at www.wrt54ghacks.com. You can obtain it by issuing the following commands:

```
root@openvpn:~# wget http://www.wrt54ghacks.com/whiterussian/wifi_info.sh
Connecting to www.wrt54ghacks.com[213.194.149.156]:80
wifi_info.sh           100%
|*******************************************************| 3778        00:00
ETA
```

Once downloaded, we can then change the permissions and execute it:

```
root@openvpn:~# chmod +x wifi_info.sh
root@openvpn:~# ./wifi_info.sh


[ OpenWrt versions ]
- OpenWrt:  WHITE RUSSIAN (0.9)
- Busybox: BusyBox v1.00 (2007.01.30-11:42+0000) multi-call binary
- NAS:     nas - 3.90.37-17 - Proprietary Broadcom WPA
Authenticator/Supplicant
```

Continued

```
[ Basic OpenWrt Wireless settings ]


RADIO  TXPWR  MODE    CHANNEL SSID
------ -----  ----    ------- ----
    on    19  ap            6  HackNaked


[ Basic OpenWrt Wireless Security settings ]


CLOAKED  MAC Filter  MAC Addresses
-------  ----------  -------------
    no          off


[ Advanced OpenWrt Wireless Security settings ]


WPA TYPE  ENCRYPTION  WPA/WPA2 Key
--------  ----------  ------------
 wpa psk       tkip  hacknaked
```
You can obtain this script at www.wrt54ghacks.com/whiterussian/wifi_info.sh.

Configuring WPA-Enterprise (and WPA2-Enterprise)

WPA-Enterprise is intended for organizations that wish to use WPA and tie into a backend authentication mechanism such as Lightweight Directory Access Protocol (LDAP) or Microsoft's Active Directory. Instead of using a preshared key, WPA-Enterprise uses an EAP type to provide the authentication. We could go into many of the details of WPA-Enterprise; however, they are far beyond the scope of this book. We do believe it is the best option for wireless security for the following reasons:

- It is not vulnerable to dictionary attacks against the preshared key, because there is no static and user-selected preshared key.

- It is much easier to change the authentication credentials, as it is not done with a key that must exist on the client device, but rather via a central authentication point.

- A Remote Authentication Dial-in User Service (RADIUS) server is used for authentication, which can provide detailed accounting and logging, as well as advanced features that can be implemented for authorization.

With WPA-Enterprise come many different EAP types, each with their own characteristics. Table 5.1 displays some of the most popular EAP types from the long list of Internet Engineering Task Force (IETF) standards and vendor proposals.

Table 5.1 Available EAP Types

EAP Type	Authentication	Description
EAP-TLS (Transport Layer Security)	PKI; certificates on both, the client and server.	Requires that you generate a certificate for every client, which serves as the authentication mechanism.
TTLS (Tunneled Transport Layer Security)	PKI; only a server certificate is required. Clients are authenticated using a user password, and usernames are not disclosed in the network (as in PEAP).	Authenticates the server to the client. Requires a third-party supplicant to run in Windows.
EAP-GTC (Generic Token Card)	Smart card or other security token.	Developed by Cisco as an alternative to PEAP that did not require MSCHAPv2, but instead uses a smart card. Sometimes referred to as PEAPv1/EAP-GTC.
PEAP (Protected EAP)	PKI; only a server certificate is required. Clients are authenticated using MSCHAPv2, typically tied to Microsoft Active Directory.	Sometimes referred to as PEAPv0/EAP-MSCHAPv2, it uses the built-in supplicant on Windows hosts and is the most widely deployed EAP type.
EAP-MD5	MD5 hashing function.	Does not offer a high level of security; is vulnerable to dictionary attacks.

Much of the configuration surrounding WPA-Enterprise will be focused on the RADIUS server, which we will run on the router itself for a completely self-contained WPA-Enterprise solution for personal or small-business use. Larger organizations (10+ people) should utilize an existing authentication server, such as Microsoft's Internet Authentication Service (IAS) or FreeRadius, and the corresponding user repository infrastructure, such as Microsoft's Active Directory or other LDAP server.

NOTE

Although WPA-Enterprise offers better security than other options such as WEP and WPA-PSK, it does rely on user passwords for security. If you are using this option, be certain to enforce a good password policy. The SANS Institute has a good example of a password policy located at www.sans.org/resources/policies/Password_Policy.pdf.

Access Point Configuration

NOTE

This configuration can be a bit daunting to enter by hand. The authors have provided a tarball with all of the appropriate configuration files, which you can download from www.wrt54ghacks.com/whiterussian/wpa-ent.tar. Once you download it (/tmp is a good place to download it to), simply go to the root directory by typing **cd /** and execute the command *tar xvf /tmp/wpa-ent.tar*.

To configure WPA- Enterprise we first need to configure the wireless settings as follows:

```
# nvram set wl0_akm="wpa wpa2"
# nvram set wl0_ssid="shinobi"
# nvram set wl0_radius_port="1812"
# nvram set wl0_radius_ipaddr="127.0.0.1"
# nvram set wl0_radius_key="SecretKey"
# nvram set wl0_auth_mode="radius"
# nvram set wl0_crypto="aes+tkip"
```

NOTE

You can use the same utility mentioned earlier, located at www.grc.com/passwords, to generate the key for the RADIUS server and client (*wl0_radius_key*). However, the maximum length of a RADIUS shared key is 31 characters, so be certain not to use the entire 64- or 63-character string.

Another recommended Windows-based free tool for generating RADIUS shared keys is Password Amplifier, from Funk Software, which was acquired by Juniper Networks. You can download it from www.funk.com/Download/PassAmp.msi.

You must reboot after you make the preceding NVRAM changes. The first value should enable WPA and WPA2 (802.11i) in enterprise mode. Set the SSID to some value, just as you would when setting up any other wireless network.

Next, we will need to point to a RADIUS server. In this case, we are going to set up FreeRadius locally on the WRT54G to achieve a self-sustaining system. If you so choose, you could put the RADIUS server on any other machine and, if it's FreeRadius, reuse the configurations that follow. We will tell the access point to use the RADIUS server running on the local system—127.0.0.1 on port 1812 (UDP)—which is the standard RADIUS authentication port. RADIUS has what it calls *clients*, which are devices or systems that need to authenticate users (wireless access points), not the user's client systems. In our case, the RADIUS client and server are on the same machine, but we still need to share a secret key between them. Our configuration reflects that, by setting the key to *SecretKey*. We then set the *wl0_auth_mode* to *radius*, and use the combination of AES and TKIP for our keying protocol.

Now we can move on to the RADIUS server configuration. We start by installing the necessary packages:

```
# ipkg install freeradius freeradius-mod-eap freeradius-mod-eap-gtc freeradius-mod-
eap-md5 freeradius-mod-eap-mschapv2 freeradius-mod-eap-peap freeradius-mod-eap-tls
freeradius-mod-eap-ttls freeradius-mod-files freeradius-mod-mschap freeradius-mod-
chap
```

Once the packages have been installed successfully, we should have a new directory called /etc/freeradius, which contains all of our configurations. There are a few files which we need to replace to make WPA-Enterprise work on our WRT54G. First, we need to make a backup of the original files, as shown here:

```
# mkdir OLD

# mv radiusd.conf OLD/

# mv eap.conf OLD/

# mv clients.conf OLD/
```

The first file is the primary configuration file, radiusd.conf:

```
##
## radiusd.conf -- FreeRADIUS server configuration file.
##

prefix = /usr
exec_prefix = /usr
sysconfdir = /etc
localstatedir = /var
sbindir = /usr/sbin
logdir = ${localstatedir}/log/radius
raddbdir = /etc/freeradius
radacctdir = ${logdir}/radacct
confdir = ${raddbdir}
run_dir = ${localstatedir}/run
log_file = ${localstatedir}/log/radiusd.log
libdir = /usr/lib/freeradius
pidfile = ${run_dir}/radiusd.pid

max_request_time = 30
delete_blocked_requests = no
```

```
cleanup_delay = 5

max_requests = 1024

bind_address = *

port = 0

hostname_lookups = no

allow_core_dumps = no

log_stripped_names = no

log_auth_badpass = no

log_auth_goodpass = no

usercollide = no

lower_user = no

lower_pass = no

nospace_user = no

nospace_pass = no


security {

        max_attributes = 200

        reject_delay = 1

        status_server = no

}


proxy_requests  = no

snmp      = no


$INCLUDE   ${confdir}/clients.conf


thread pool {

        start_servers = 1

        max_servers = 4

        min_spare_servers = 1

        max_spare_servers = 3

        max_requests_per_server = 300

}


modules {

        pap {

                encryption_scheme = crypt

        }


        chap {
```

```
                        authtype = CHAP
        }

        $INCLUDE ${confdir}/eap.conf

        mschap {
                authtype = MS-CHAP
                with_ntdomain_hack = yes
        }
        files {
                usersfile = ${confdir}/users
                compat = no
        }

}

authorize {
        files
        mschap
        eap
}

authenticate {
        Auth-Type MS-CHAP {
                mschap
        }

        eap
}
```

NOTE

You can download this file from www.wrt54ghacks.com/whiterussian/radius.conf.

We've made several modifications to the standard configuration. The first modification includes some enhancements to make it run better on an embedded device with limited power capabilities:

```
thread pool {
        start_servers = 1
```

```
          max_servers = 4
          min_spare_servers = 1
          max_spare_servers = 3
          max_requests_per_server = 300
}
```

This tells FreeRadius to start only one *radiusd* daemon at boot time, and to never start more than four. The *min_spare_servers* and *max_spare_servers* define how many additional daemons FreeRadius will start. FreeRadius is very adaptive. It will dynamically adjust the number of servers running to handle the load, in addition to keeping a few "spares" around for other traffic and higher load conditions. The *max_request_per_server* is the maximum number of requests it will handle before cleaning up, freeing resources, and restarting. This helps ensure that a memory leak, which could be detrimental to an embedded device, does not get out of control and cause the system to crash.

We've included a file called clients.conf, which lists the clients that will use this RADIUS server for authentication (in our scenario, only the local system acting as a wireless access point):

```
client 127.0.0.1 {
          secret          = SecretKey
          shortname       = localhost
          nastype         = other          # localhost isn't usually a NAS...
}
```

Be certain that the value of the RADIUS parameter, *secret*, matches the value you selected in NVRAM for the access point. The remaining configuration is standard for a RADIUS server that will have to handle EAP types.

We've included a separate file, eap.conf, which contains the configuration for all the desired EAP types—in this case, PEAP and TTLS:

```
eap {
              default_eap_type = ttls
              timer_expire    = 60
              ignore_unknown_eap_types = no
              cisco_accounting_username_bug = no


              md5 {
              }


              mschapv2 {
              }



              tls {
                    #private_key_password = seekritpassword
                    private_key_file = ${raddbdir}/certs/client1.key
```

```
                          certificate_file = ${raddbdir}/certs/client1.crt

                          CA_file = ${raddbdir}/certs/cacert.pem

                          dh_file = ${raddbdir}/certs/dh

                          random_file = ${raddbdir}/certs/random

                          fragment_size = 1024

              }


              ttls {

                          default_eap_type = md5

                          copy_request_to_tunnel = no

                          use_tunneled_reply = no


              }


              peap {

                          default_eap_type = mschapv2

              }


      }
```

Again, most of the preceding configuration is standard. However, the section labeled *tls* requires some attention. You will have to generate certificates using a certificate authority (CA), and then move them, in addition to the CA certificate, to the WRT54G. In the preceding example, we keep all of the certificates in the ${raddbdir}/certs directory—that is, /etc/freeradius/certs. We are also required to have a Diffie-Hellman key, and a random file. We can generate these with the following *openssl* commands.

Diffie-Hellman key:

```
# openssl dhparam –check –text –5 512 -out dh
```

Random file:

```
# openssl rand -out random 1024
```

You can perform these commands on your CA and then copy the files to the /etc/freeradius/certs directory of the WRT54G. The same is true with the certificates and key files: Use your CA to generate them, and then copy the appropriate files to the router. We do not recommend that you use your router as a CA. Also, be certain to put a copy of the CA certificate on all of your clients.

NOTE

Creating your own CA may seem like a daunting task; however, numerous resources are available. Hack #69 in *Network Security Hacks, Second Edition,* by Andrew Lockhart, shows you how to create your own CA in just a few pages. We also found

a great tutorial at www.section6.net/wiki/index.php/Basics_of_using_
OpenSSL#Making_your_own_CA.

The next file we will need to populate is the users file, which contains the usernames and passwords for authentication when an external user repository, such as an LDAP server, is not used:

```
DEFAULT Group == "disabled", Auth-Type := Reject
        Reply-Message = "Your account has been disabled."
pdc     User-Password == "hacknaked"
larry   User-Password == "hax0r"
```

The preceding file creates two users, *pdc* and *larry*. You can enter more users by simply adding
lines as shown earlier, being certain that the password is enclosed in double quotes. When you add
new users, you will need to restart the RADIUS server before they will become activated.

The final configuration step is to create two necessary files that need to exist, but can be empty.
If these files do not already exist, create them using the following two commands while in the
/etc/freeradius directory:

```
# touch acct_user
# touch preproxy_user
```

To start the RADIUS server, we suggest that you run it in debug mode to be certain everything
is working:

```
# radiusd -X -A
```

The −X option will run with full debugging enabled, and the −A option will show the authentication requests. If you see the following messages, your RADIUS server is configured properly:

```
Module: Instantiated eap (eap)
Module: Loaded files
 files: usersfile = "/etc/freeradius/users"
 files: acctusersfile = "/etc/freeradius/acct_users"
 files: preproxy_usersfile = "/etc/freeradius/preproxy_users"
 files: compat = "no"
Module: Instantiated files (files)
Listening on authentication *:1812
Listening on accounting *:1813
Ready to process requests.
```

Client Configuration

The preceding configuration has been tested using a variety of clients, including OS X (which supports TTLS only), Windows XP, and even a Nokia N800 (using TTLS and PEAP with the built-in
supplicant). For Windows XP, you can use PEAP through the built-in Microsoft supplicant and TTLS

using the SecureW2 supplicant, freely available at www.securew2.org. You should be able to connect using any other client that supports TTLS or PEAP.

> **NOTE**
>
> Linux users can gain support for WPA using wpa_supplicant, which you can download from http://hostap.epitest.fi/wpa_supplicant/ and which is included in many Linux distributions.

OS X Configuration

One of the easiest configurations to implement uses TTLS on OS X. You simply need to associate to the SSID, choose **TTLS-PAP** from the menu, and enter your username and password, as shown in Figure 5.1.

Figure 5.1 OS X WPA Enterprise (TTLS) Configuration Screen

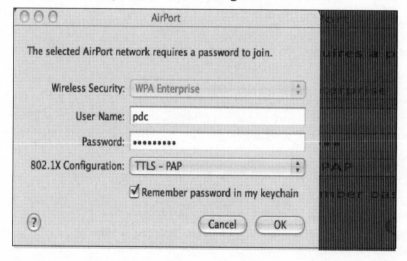

Figure 5.1 shows that OS X detects the network automatically as "WPA Enterprise". We've also checked the **Remember password in my keychain** box, which is completely optional; however, it makes it easier to connect to the network on a regular basis.

Windows Client Configuration

To configure a Windows client, follow the instructions for configuring an EAP-PEAP client. For example, you will add a new wireless network, and on the **Association** tab set the **Network Authentication** to WPA and **Data encryption** to TKIP. On the **Authentication** tab, set the **EAP type** to Protected EAP (PEAP). Click **Properties**, and then click **Configure**, and load your CA certificate or uncheck **Validate server certificate**. Under **Select Authentication Method**, choose **Secured password (EAP-MSCHAP v2)**, click **Configure**, and uncheck **Automatically use my Windows logon name and password (and domain if any)**, unless your Windows username and password are the same as the ones you entered in the users file on the RADIUS server. Click **OK** to all of the screens and connect to the wireless network. It should prompt you for a username, password, and domain. Enter the username and password in the dialog depicted in Figure 5.2 but leave the **Logon domain** field blank.

Figure 5.2 Windows XP PEAP Logon Screen

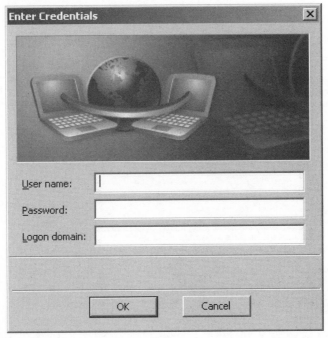

For more detailed instructions on configuring WPA clients, refer to the following resources:

■ **www.uwo.ca/its/doc/hdi/wireless/peap.html** Instructions, with full screenshots, on how to configure a PEAP client in Windows XP.

■ **www.uwo.ca/its/doc/hdi/wireless/mac-wireless/mac-wireless.html** Instructions on how to configure an OS X client for PEAP.

■ **www.oreillynet.com/etel/blog/2004/03/peap_support_on_linux_with_xsu.html** Configuring xsupplicant for Linux with PEAP.

■ **http://vuksan.com/linux/dot1x/wpa-client-config.html** Multiple guides on configuring TTLS for Linux, OS X, and Windows (SecureW2).

Finishing Up

Once you have a client successfully connected, you can configure FreeRadius to start automatically using the following commands:

```
# cd /etc/init.d/
# mv radiusd S76radiusd
```

You can also verify that clients are connecting by installing the wl package (*ipkg install wl*), and issuing the following command:

```
# wl assoclist
```

It will return the MAC addresses of successfully connected clients.

Summary

Wireless networks have become ubiquitous in our current environment, and security is becoming increasingly important as their usage grows. Unlike wired networks, wireless networks extend their range beyond the physical wire. As a result, we open ourselves to attack each time we set up a wireless network, whether at home, at work, or at the local coffee shop. By utilizing these security methods for our wireless networks, we can begin to protect our networks from unauthorized use. Although not all of the security methods are ideal, or terribly secure, they at least provide a deterrent.

Solutions Fast Track

Basic Wireless Security

☑ Choosing an appropriate SSID name is important, as you do not want to give out too much information about yourself within the namespace of your SSID.

☑ Hiding your SSID and configuring MAC address filtering, when used together and in conjunction with other wireless security mechanisms, can help to secure your wireless network.

☑ Some devices will support only WEP, and although WEP is not considered a secure protocol, it is still better than running an open wireless network.

Configuring WPA-Personal (PSK)

☑ WPA-PSK uses a shared secret to offer much better security than WEP and it is supported on most wireless hardware available today.

☑ WPA-PSK is vulnerable to dictionary attacks, so be certain to use a strong passphrase and change your SSID to something that is nonstandard.

☑ WPA2-PSK offers some enhanced security over WPA-PSK and should be used if the client hardware can support it. OpenWrt supports both WPA-PSK and WPA2-PSK.

Configuring WPA-Enterprise (and WPA2-Enterprise)

☑ WPA-Enterprise offers increased security over WPA-PSK because it does not use a static key, and it utilizes a central directory for authentication.

☑ There are many different EAP types. However, PEAP and TTLS are recommended for general use and offer a similar level of security and client support.

☑ Using TTLS in Windows requires that a third-party, open source supplicant, called SecureW2, be installed.

☑ Using OpenWrt, the standard wireless drivers, and FreeRadius, you can set up an access point as a self-contained WPA-Enterprise wireless network.

Frequently Asked Questions

The following Frequently Asked Questions, answered by the authors of this book, are designed to both measure your understanding of the concepts presented in this chapter and to assist you with real-life implementation of these concepts. To have your questions about this chapter answered by the author, browse to **www. syngress.com/solutions** and click on the **"Ask the Author"** form.

Q: I live really far away from other people. Do I still need to put security on my wireless network?

A: At the DEFCON 13 Wireless Shootout Contest, in 2005, the winning team was able to get a wireless signal to stretch 125 miles. We always recommend that people secure their wireless networks, regardless of their location (unless you have built a faraday cage around your house).

Q: In my environment, I am able to use only MAC address filtering and WEP as security mechanisms. What else can I do to help protect my wireless network?

A: You can do two things. You can implement Snort wireless (http://snort-wireless.org), and you can monitor the traffic coming from your wireless network carefully using the standard Snort, firewall logs, and traffic captures.

Q: I left my SSID at the default setting of *linksys* and enabled WPA with a password of *password*. Am I still safe?

A: If an attacker were to target your network, he would be able to crack the preceding SSID and password combination fairly quickly using the hacking tools mentioned in this chapter. It is best to set a unique SSID name and use a long random string of characters for the WPA/WPA2 pre-shared key.

Q: No matter what I do, WPA just will not work. What's wrong?

A: The most common problem is that people do not remember to install the nas package in OpenWrt. Do an *ipkg update* and then *ipkg install nas*.

Q: I upgraded to a more recent version of OpenWrt and now WPA is not working; how come?

A: When upgrading, sometimes the nas package needs to be reinstalled (enter *ipkg remove nas*, *ipkg update*, and then *ipk install nas*).

Q: I created my own certificates, but I am getting errors that state they are invalid. Why?

A: Be certain that you followed the instructions for setting the correct time on your routers, covered in Chapter 3. Certificates have an expiration date associated with them, so if the client and access point are not set to the correct time, you will get errors.

Q: I have more than 10 people connecting to a WRT54G running WPA-Enterprise using PEAP with AES encryption. What can I do to improve performance?

A: The first thing to do is to separate the RADIUS server out to a separate device. This could be another WRT54G box; however, it might be best to configure a Linux server. Also, you can experiment with WPA versus WPA2, and use TKIP instead of AES to save processing power.

Q: I have seen that both EAP types, PEAP and TTLS, require a digital certificate on the server and authenticate the user through the user's password. Apart from the built-in Windows support, what is the main difference between PEAP and TTLS?

A: PEAP discloses the usernames when establishing the secure TLS communication channel with the server. If you capture network traffic, you can see the usernames in the clear. TTLS uses a generic user instead, called *anonymous*, and then exchanges the real username inside the TLS tunnel. Therefore, TTLS is the preferred method from a security perspective.

## Chapter 6

WRT54G for Penetration Testers

Solutions in this chapter:

- Tunneling and VPN

- Wireless Security Tools Using OpenWrt

- WRTSL54GS CDMA Internet Connection

- WRT54G Wireless Captive Portal Password Sniffer

☑ Summary

☑ Solutions Fast Track

☑ Frequently Asked Questions

Introduction

In this chapter, we will explore how the WRT54G series hardware can help you perform penetration testing and vulnerability assessments. However, you do not have to use it for these purposes. We present the material in this fashion because this is how we are using it. Feel free to use the examples in this book for your own purposes; in fact, we encourage that you do so! Specifically, you can use the examples that follow to:

- Set up your own OpenVPN server for home or office use

- Set up your own WRT54G OpenVPN client to connect to other OpenVPN servers

- Deploy Kismet Drones and remote 2.4GHz spectrum analyzers for troubleshooting wireless connectivity problems

- Travel with your WRTSL54GS Code Division Multiple Access (CDMA) Internet connection and use it for general Internet access for you and your friends

The only project listed in this chapter that, other than having some fun with your friends, is solely geared toward penetration testing is the wireless captive portal that logs all usernames and passwords (Airsnarf–Rogue Squadron). However, you could also use this for demonstration purposes to show the risks of using open wireless hotspots, but remember, always use it with permission.

Tunneling and VPN

If you find that you need to transport data from one computer or network to another securely, you have probably looked into using some form of virtual private network (VPN) technology. VPNs make it easy to transport data securely, independent of higher-layer applications. For example, later in this chapter we will discuss Kismet Drone, which sends raw packets to a Kismet server across the network. The Kismet protocol does not implement encryption; however, if you send it across a VPN, the Kismet and wireless traffic will be secured by the VPN protocol and protected from prying eyes.

VPNs are also very useful for securely connecting remote clients to networks. For example, you may have a WRT54G at home that you would like to set up as an OpenVPN server. This will allow you to connect to your network at home from any point on the Internet over a secure tunnel, and access all of the computers and network resources available on your home network.

Notes from the Underground…

OpenVPN Bridge Mode versus Route Mode

OpenVPN offers two modes of operation: bridge and route. There are some significant differences in the way these two modes behave:

- Bridge mode provides a Layer 2 connection between clients and servers. This means that all broadcast traffic is shared between them, which could cause performance problems.

- Once a bridge is established, connectivity is pretty simple, as there are no routes to add because you are on the same Internet Protocol (IP) subnet.

- Route mode is a Layer 3 connection, and it requires that changes be made to your routing tables in order to provide connectivity to the remote end.

- Bridge mode is a bit more complicated to set up, as you need to be certain that the appropriate tunnel drivers are added to the kernel and that the correct interfaces are added to the bridge.

- Route mode performs better than bridge mode in most cases.

For the examples in this book, we are using bridge mode with a WRT54G set up as a client. You can apply this method of operation to many of the projects in this book, such as Kismet Drone and Wi-Spy, to tunnel data securely back to a central server.

Using the WRT54G As an OpenVPN Bridged Client

OpenVPN is a very popular open source software package that utilizes Secure Sockets Layer/Transport Layer Security (SSL/TLS) to create secure VPN tunnels. OpenVPN is very flexible, and it runs on a variety of different platforms, including Windows, OS X, Linux, and of course, various firmware on the WRT54G. In this example, we will use OpenWrt, as the OpenVPN packages are already compiled and available in the package repository.

As security professionals, we can use OpenVPN to our advantage in many ways. First, let's explore using the WRT54G as an OpenVPN client and the advantages this provides. Consider the diagram in Figure 6.1.

Figure 6.1 WRT54G As an OpenVPN Client

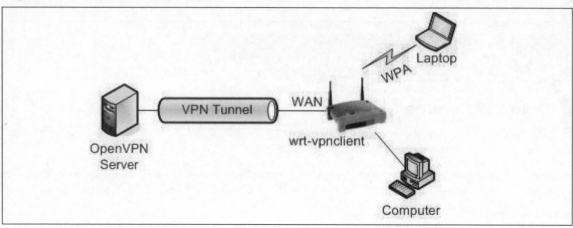

In the scenario described in the preceding section, you must first deploy an OpenVPN server. This server could be located anywhere on your network or on the Internet. There are a few differences between an OpenVPN server and an OpenVPN client with regard to configuration. The configuration steps are very similar when you set up OpenVPN on a regular Linux server, and instructions are readily available on the Internet from www.openvpn.org. Your network could be the network from which you perform penetration testing, or your company's corporate headquarters network. You can create the VPN tunnel across the Internet using any type of Internet connection (T1, xDSL, cable modem, etc.). The WRT54G in this case, wrt-vpnclient, would sit at the remote site location. The remote site could be the customer against whom we are performing the penetration test, or a remote site that needs a connection back to the corporate network (where the OpenVPN server is located).

> **NOTE**
>
> This setup, even though it uses the bridge mode, will still require that every device at the remote site have a route that tells them how to get back to the OpenVPN server network.

To configure a WRT54G as an OpenVPN client in bridge mode, do the following:

```
# ipkg install openvpn
```

Once the package has been installed, you will need to create the configuration:

```
# mkdir /etc/openvpn
# mkdir /etc/openvpn/keys
```

Next, you will create a client configuration file:

```
#Begin client.conf
client
dev tap
proto tcp
remote 192.168.1.250 443
nobind
user nobody
group root
persist-key
persist-tun
cd /etc/openvpn
ca keys/cacert.pem
cert keys/client1.crt
key keys/client1.key
cipher BF-CBC
comp-lzo
verb 3
mute 20
writepid /var/run/openvpn.pid
```

The preceding configuration will set the client to connect to 192.168.1.250 on port 443 to establish the VPN tunnel. Bridge mode is accomplished by the line *dev tap*. Next, you will need to create the keys and digital certificates and copy them to the /etc/openvpn/keys directory. You will need to do this on your certificate authority (CA) server, and then copy the key and certificate to the device. Next, you will create a startup file:

```
#!/bin/sh

case "$1" in
  stop)
    kill `cat /var/run/openvpn.pid`
    killall openvpn
    ;;
  *)
    if ! brctl show | grep -q tap0; then
      openvpn --mktun --dev tap0
      brctl addif br0 tap0
      ifconfig tap0 0.0.0.0 promisc up
    fi
    openvpn --config /etc/openvpn/client.conf
    ;;
esac
```

Once you run the preceding script, you should be connected to the OpenVPN server. For more help on troubleshooting connection issues at this stage, please visit http://openvpn.net.

NOTE

If you receive errors pertaining to certificates, you may want to check the date setting on the WRT54G and the OpenVPN server. If the date is too far off, the certificate will appear to be expired and the OpenVPN connection will fail. Refer to Chapter 3 for more information on setting the correct time on the WRT54G.

Notes from the Underground...

WRT54G As an OpenVPN Bridged Server

A fairly large cost is involved in sending penetration testers to remote sites, especially if it requires international travel and/or it is a large assessment requiring multiple days or weeks of stay. This could hold true not only for independent consultants or penetration testing companies, but also for large organizations with multiple remote sites wishing to do internal penetration testing or even simple vulnerability scanning. We talked about FairuzaWRT in Chapter 2, and we established that most security tools, and even more specifically, programs that use lots of memory, don't run well on the WRT54G platform. Using the WRT54G as a VPN gateway allows you to run your favorite security tools, and tunnel, or pivot, through a WRT54G to reach your targets. This eliminates the problem of trying to compile and run security tools on the WRT54G itself, and makes it much easier to reach the remote site (face it; no one likes to deal with the headaches of traveling, especially trying to get through TSA in the United States with two laptops, three wireless antennas, and an access point!). OpenVPN provides an easy way to do this, with a few different options with respect to security and routing. Once installed at the remote site with the VPN established, it will allow you to perform some of the major tasks in the penetration test, which include:

- Port scanning with Nmap
- Vulnerability scanning with Nessus
- Launching exploits with Metasploit
- Web application testing

The best way we have found to achieve this is by turning the WRT54G into an OpenVPN server (instead of being a OpenVPN client, as in the previous section) and, using bridge mode, creating a Layer 2 network connection between the client (the penetration tester) and server (the target network). This allows us to be on the same

Continued

Layer 2 network as the target, and run tools from our penetration testing systems, using the WRT54G as a remote gateway. We do not include example configurations here; however, switching between client mode and server mode is not that difficult. Check www.wrt54ghacks.com for updates and further information on using a WRT54G as a bridge mode server.

Remote Office Connectivity with vpnc

Connecting small, remote offices, especially ones that will be only temporary, can be challenging for many IT organizations. I have deployed small VPN devices to temporary remote locations, using firewall/VPN hardware devices that cost several hundred dollars, only to never recover the hardware. This is especially frustrating when the location may have only one or two employees. Using an inexpensive WRT54G, in the same configuration as Figure 6.1, you can accomplish the same goal. You also can extend this solution to include employees that are frequently traveling and require a VPN connection coupled with wireless connectivity for clients. For example, a trade show booth or hotel room is a likely scenario. Typically, hotels will offer either wireless or wired Internet access for a fee. These hotspot wireless networks are almost always open. The same goes for a trade show; you may have computers or other devices that are required to operate your booth at the trade show and need a secure wireless connection with access to your company's local network. Having your WRT54G provide you a secure VPN tunnel to the corporate network, and a secure wireless network for local clients, is a great way to solve this problem. You also will not break your budget when a marketing executive leaves the WRT54G behind (however, you will want to change your passwords and keys).

For this purpose, you could use either OpenVPN (SSL/TLS) or another IPSec-based VPN. A fantastic program called vpnc allows you to connect to Cisco VPN 3000 series concentrators, IOS routers, PIX/ASA appliances, and Juniper/Netscreen devices. This small program has been ported to many different UNIX/Linux operating systems, including OpenWrt! Consider the example network shown in Figure 6.2. This could be an individual or small, remote office location. The clients can be either wired or wireless in this case. The WRT54G itself provides the connection to the central office, terminating the VPN on any of the supported VPN server platforms mentioned previously.

Figure 6.2 Remote VPN Using a WRT54G and vpnc

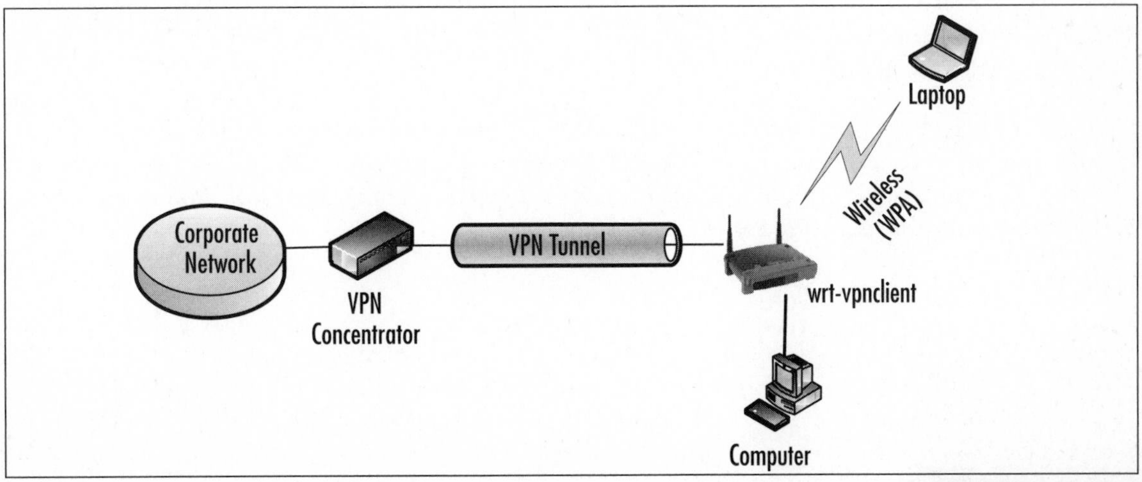

The configuration for the WRT54G is as follows. First you will need OpenWrt loaded with the Whiterussian 0.9 backports package repository. For more details on adding an additional package repository, see the section "Configuring the USB Bluetooth Adapter," later in this chapter.

Then you can begin to install the appropriate packages:

```
# ipkg install vpnc
Installing vpnc (0.3.3-1) to root...
Downloading http://downloads.openwrt.org/backports/0.9/vpnc_0.3.3-1_mipsel.ipk
Installing libgpg-error (1.0-1) to root...
Downloading http://downloads.openwrt.org/backports/0.9/libgpg-error_1.0-
1_mipsel.ipk
Installing libgcrypt (1.2.3-1) to root...
Downloading http://downloads.openwrt.org/backports/0.9/libgcrypt_1.2.3-1_mipsel.ipk
Installing kmod-tun (2.4.30-brcm-5) to root...
Downloading http://downloads.openwrt.org/whiterussian/packages/kmod-tun_2.4.30-
brcm-5_mipsel.ipk
Configuring kmod-tun
Configuring libgcrypt
Configuring libgpg-error
Configuring vpnc
Successfully terminated.
```

Once the packages have installed, you must reboot. This will properly load the kmod-tun package, which is a kernel module that provides the virtual tunnel interface needed to terminate the IPSec VPN connection. Once the router has rebooted, you should see a directory called /etc/vpnc. It contains two files: vpnc-script and vpnc.conf. In this example, you will be connecting to a Cisco VPN 3000 series concentrator. The vpnc.conf file should contain the following information in this case:

```
IPSec gateway 192.168.10.8
IPSec ID mygroupname
IPSec secret mygrouppassword
Xauth username myusername
Xauth password mypassword
```

The IPSec gateway should specify the IP address of your VPN concentrator or load-balanced IP address of multiple concentrators. The *IPSec ID* is your group name, specified in your existing VPN client configuration, along with the associated password specified as the *IPSec secret*. You should obtain this information from your VPN server administrator.

! **W**ARNING

Please do not go into your company's VPN configuration file (*.pcf) and take the encrypted password, then plug it into a Web page to decrypt. Many tutorials on the Internet will describe this as something you need to do in order to set up vpnc. This could very well violate your company security policies and get you in trouble, or even fired from your job.

The *Xauth username* is the username that you would use to authenticate to your VPN, and the same with the password. You can safely leave out the *Xauth password* parameter and vpnc will prompt you for your password each time it starts if you feel uncomfortable leaving your password on the router itself. The next file you will need to modify is vpnc-script. This script does not work with the shell on OpenWrt, Whiterussian RC6 or later, unless you install the patched version. To install the patched version, do the following:

```
# cd /etc/vpnc
# cp vpnc-script vpnc-script.bak
# wget http://wrt54ghacks.com/whiterussian/vpnc-script
```

This will install the latest version of the script that will set up the routing and connectivity for vpnc. It adds another feature as well and changes the SecureEasySetup (SES) button lights to indicate the VPN connection status. Table 6.1 lists the values and associated states.

Table 6.1 vpnc SES Button Color Status Codes

Status	SES Button Color
Not Connected	Off
Connecting	Orange
Connected	White

You will also need to create a file called /etc/init.d/S75vpnc, which should contain the following commands:

```
#!/bin/sh
mkdir -p -m777 /var/run/vpnc
vpnc --udp --disable-natt /etc/vpnc/vpnc.conf
```

The two parameters, —*udp* and —*disable-natt*, are totally optional and depend on your configuration. The —*udp* command will enable User Datagram Protocol (UDP) encapsulation, and —*disable-natt* will disable network address translation (NAT) traversal. Before we use the startup script, let's start vpnc in debug mode and be certain that it works. To start it in debug mode use the option —*debug 99* as follows:

```
# vpnc --udp --disable-natt --debug 99 /etc/vpnc/vpnc.conf
<snip>
DONE PARSING PAYLOAD type: 0c
PARSING PAYLOAD type: 00
PARSE_OK

S7.8
Connect Banner:
| You are now connected to the VPN.
|
| Use your tunnel wisely young grasshopper.
|
| PaulDotCom

<snip>

VPNC started in background (pid: 980)...
```

You will see a few pages full of output. The line that reads *PARSE_OK* is important; after this line is where you will see any error messages that were generated. If you see the *S7.8* and *Connect Banner:* lines that is a very good sign. The final line, *VPNC started in background (pid: nnn)…*, means you successfully established the tunnel and vpnc will run in the background and return you to the command prompt. From this point forward, if it works, you can use the provided startup script to start vpnc (/etc/init.d/S75vpnc). This script should also automatically start vpnc each time the router is rebooted. To disconnect vpnc, issue the following command:

```
# vpnc-disconnect
Terminating vpnc daemon (pid: 980)
```

Once you have the tunnel established, you have a few options for remote connectivity:

- Plug in and use the router's IP address as your default gateway.

- Associate wirelessly, using the router's IP address as the default gateway.

- Add routes to your local network that point specific traffic through the tunnel.

The option you choose will depend on your setup and intended use for the VPN. If you do choose the wireless option, and you intend to secure it using Wi-Fi Protected Access (WPA), you may run into performance problems.

> **NOTE**
>
> In our testing, we found the performance of vpnc to be pretty good. The majority of the time when the user is browsing to internal Web sites, using SSH to manage equipment and servers, and checking e-mail, the CPU on the WRT54G will not go

above 40 percent. However, when transferring large files, the CPU will spike to 100 percent, while still sustaining a 250KB/s transfer speed. This means it is best to dedicate a device for the VPN tunnel.

If you choose the routing option, you will need two routes. You will need to add one route for the IP address or subnet of your VPN concentrators. This route should point to your default gateway. You will need to add a second route for the subnet of your organization's internal network, which should point to the VPN gateway. For example, if your VPN gateway IP address is 192.168.8.10, and your WRT54G running vpnc is at 192.168.1.10, and your organization's internal address space is 192.168.0.0/16, the routes will be as shown in Table 6.2.

Table 6.2 vpnc Routes

Destination	Gateway
Default	192.168.1.1
192.168.8.10/32	192.168.1.1
192.168.0.0/16	192.168.1.10

This solution has many different options, so be certain to choose the one that is right for you. For example, if you want all users to route to the WRT54G VPN gateway running vpnc, this is what is called "split tunneling." Clients are able to connect to the Internet, then come across the VPN tunnel and potentially attack your network. You can solve this problem by forcing people to associate to the WRT54G or plug into it directly. On the server end, you may want to set up a separate group, with a separate group name and password just for remote connectivity devices, and restrict access into your network to only those resources needed by the users of the remote WRT54G clients. Perhaps one of the best applications is to give them to your already responsible network and security engineers so that they can more easily work remotely.

Wireless Security Tools Using OpenWrt

Not only are the WRT54G routers valuable to penetration testers for performing functions over their wired ports, but also the wireless capabilities provide additional valuable tools. You can utilize the wireless capabilities to perform wireless auditing and covert remote access, and to determine other appropriate wireless attacks. In this section, we'll illustrate a number of ways in which the wireless capabilities of the WRT54G can be an asset to a wireless penetration tester.

WRT54G Kismet Drone

A Kismet Drone is a little bit different from the install of Kismet that we performed for our "Wardriving-in-a-Box" setup in Chapter 4. A Kismet Drone performs same basic functions for wireless network discovery that a Kismet server installation does. However, a Kismet Drone does not log any data locally on the device on which it is installed, but rather serves up the data collected to a

Kismet server located elsewhere. This is helpful for placing Kismet Drones in a distributed fashion over a considerable area, and being able to centralize all of the information collected from multiple drones to a single, centralized Kismet server, through a wired network. Figure 6.3 shows an example of this type of installation.

Figure 6.3 Centralized Collection with Multiple WRT54G Kismet Drones

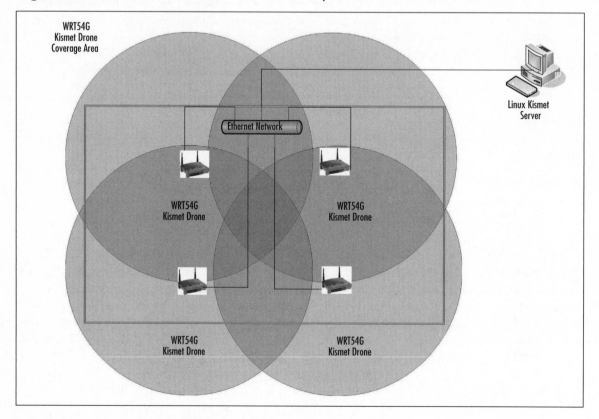

Installing and Configuring a Kismet Drone

With our earlier Kismet installation, premade packages are available for the Kismet Drone. The exception in this case is that the Kismet Drone package that resides in the default OpenWrt package repository works just fine. You don't have to jump through hoops to be able to get GPS support, as you will not be implementing it in this installation. You can install Kismet Drone with:

```
# ipkg install kismet-drone
```

This will install the Kismet Drone package and satisfy any missing dependencies such as *uclibc* and *libpcap*.

Once it is installed, you can configure your Kismet Drone installation by modifying /etc/kismet/kismet_drone.conf. Specifically, you need to pick the appropriate capture source for your WRT54G. By default, kismet_drone.conf has selected *eth1* as the capture source, as indicated with the *source* directive:

```
source=wrt54g,eth1,wrt54g
```

You should modify the *source* directive to be the appropriate capture source, as described in this chapter in the sidebar titled "My WRT54G Doesn't Work under Kismet." In most cases, the default value of *eth1* will be suitable.

You also need to allow the Kismet server permission to contact the Kismet Drone. By default, the Kismet Drone only allows connections from itself (localhost or 127.0.0.1). This default configuration will not be very helpful, as your Kismet server will likely be on a separate device such as a PC. In order to allow communication to a Kismet server over the network, you need to modify the *allowedhosts* configuration directive to allow connections from the Kismet server. In this example, we will allow a Kismet server with the IP address of 10.13.37.10 to access our Kismet Drones by modifying the *allowedhosts* directive in kismet_drone.conf, as shown here:

```
allowedhosts=10.13.37.10/32
```

Be aware that you will need to modify this setting to contain the IP address of your Kismet server.

Tools & Traps...

My WRT54G Doesn't Work under Kismet

Due to the significant wireless differences in the WRT54G versions, as discussed in Chapter 1, Kismet may not function as installed. The instruction in this chapter should support most versions of the WRT54G, WRT54GS, WRT54GL, and WRTSL54GS, but you can make the other versions work with a few minor changes.

You can make the other WRT54G versions work with Kismet quite easily. Kismet's configuration files instruct the software as to what capture source, or wireless card, to use while operating. As shown earlier, we defined a capture source for our WRT54GL in /etc/kismet/kismet_drone.conf as *source=wrt54g,eth1,wrt54g*. Here are the other combinations for some earlier WRT54G models:

WRT54G, versions 1.0 and 1.1:

```
source=wrt54g,eth2,wrt54g
```

WRT54G, version 2.0:

```
source=wrt54g,eth1,wrt54g
```

WRT54G, version 3.0:

```
source=wrt54g,eth1:prism0,wrt54g
```

Most versions will be able to use the default, as instructed earlier:

```
source=wrt54g,eth1,wrt54g
```

At this point in the installation process, your Kismet Drone should function as configured. As we indicated in Chapter 4, the WRT54G platforms do not support channel hopping, and we will likely miss important wireless traffic and information without channel hopping. The Kismet Drone will start and begin to listen on the last configured channel, likely the default channel 6. In order to provide channel hopping, you need to provide a manual method via a shell script. With this script you can also add the additional non-U.S. channels, as described in Chapter 4. In order for your script to function, you also need to install the wl package with:

```
# ipkg install wl
```

You now need to create your channel hopping script, identical to that in Chapter 4 in the "Wardriving-in-a-Box" section. If this will be a dedicated Kismet Drone device you will want the channel hopping to be performed at startup, again using the guide found in Chapter 4. To put the finishing touches on the automatic startup sequence, create a S93kismet_drone startup script in /etc/init.d with the following contents:

```
#! /bin/sh
/sbin/ifconfig eth1 up
/usr/sbin/wl ap 0
/usr/sbin/wl passive 1
/usr/sbin/wl promisc 1
/usr/sbin/wl monitor 1
/usr/bin/kismet_drone -f /etc/kismet/kismet_drone.conf > /dev/null 2>&1 &
```

Now, make it executable with the following command:

```
# chmod 755 /etc/init.d/S93kismet_drone
```

NOTE

Change *eth1* to the appropriate wireless interface for your device, which will differ depending on the model, type, and version. Refer to the sidebar in this chapter and http://wiki.openwrt.org for more information.

This script performs a number of steps to ensure that Kismet will start properly:

- It uses *ifconfig* to set the *eth1* interface up, or to an active state, in preparation for capture. This is just a precaution, as the interface should already be active.

- The *wl ap* command sets the AP mode to be that of a client, instead of acting as an access point.

- Passive mode is set with *wl passive* to prevent the transmission of any network or wireless packets during Kismet use and to prevent it from contacting unauthorized networks.

- *wl promisc* sets the wireless card in promiscuous mode, allowing all network traffic (at Layer 2) to be captured, regardless of source or destination Media Access Control (MAC) address.

- Monitor mode is enabled through the *wl monitor* command to capture all wireless traffic (at Layer 2), including management, control, and data 802.11 frames.

- Kismet is started utilizing the custom configuration in /etc/kismet.conf, and sends the unused console output to /dev/null (nowhere).

Now that you have the Kismet Drone and channel hopping starting at every bootup, you can configure a centralized server to connect to the Kismet Drone. Typically, you will want to connect the WRT54G with the Kismet Drone installed to your network using the wide area network (WAN) port, for ease of installation. The WAN port, in its default configuration, is already configured to obtain an IP address via the Dynamic Host Configuration Protocol (DHCP), and it provides some firewall capabilities. By using the WAN port, you will also possibly prevent a second DHCP server from becoming active on the attached subnet, which can cause network problems.

We do introduce a few problems when using the WAN port for connecting our Kismet Drone. First, we would not normally be able to connect to the Kismet Drone due to the IPTABLES firewall rules. We will change these settings shortly, so they will no longer be an issue. Second, we are electing to utilize DHCP on the WAN interface. This can cause issues should the WAN port receive a different IP address, as we would no longer be able to connect to our drone!

You can resolve the WAN port DHCP problems if you want, by assigning an appropriate static IP to the WAN interface. Do this by changing a few NVRAM values, as shown in the following code, that set the WAN port to be static (instead of DHCP), as well as set the WAN IP, netmask, gateway, and domain name system (DNS) server:

```
# nvram set wan_proto=static
# nvram set wan_ipaddr=<WAN IP Address>
# nvram set wan_netmask=<WAN Netmask>
# nvram set wan_gateway=<Gateway IP Address>
# nvram set wan_dns=<WAN DNS IP Address>
# nvram commit
# ifup wan
```

After you have changed these NVRAM settings, you will be able to use the statically assigned address as defined by *wan_ipaddr*. This has the potential to allow more controlled filtering for firewalls (on the WRT54G, or on a network inline), and better filtering on your server configuration.

You also need to change the default firewall configuration on your WRT54G to allow the Kismet server to connect to the Kismet Drone on the WAN-assigned IP address. You should also allow SSH connections on the WAN port as well, for remote management and configuration of the Kismet Drone. You can accomplish these firewall changes by editing /etc/firewall.user. In /etc/firewall.user, you need to locate the *Open Port to WAN* configuration section. In this section, note that two configuration lines exist for enabling SSH access via the WAN port, but they have been commented out.

You need to uncomment the two SSH configuration lines in the *Open Port to WAN* section, and create two additional, almost identical rules to allow traffic for the Kismet Drone port. The easiest way is to paste a copy of the two SSH rules, and modify them to reflect port 3501 (the default

Kismet Drone port) instead of port 22 for SSH. Your final *Open Port to WAN* section should look like this:

```
iptables -t nat -A prerouting_rule -i $WAN -p tcp --dport 22 -j ACCEPT
iptables        -A input_rule      -i $WAN -p tcp --dport 22 -j ACCEPT
iptables -t nat -A prerouting_rule -i $WAN -p tcp --dport 3501 -j ACCEPT
iptables        -A input_rule      -i $WAN -p tcp --dport 3501 -j ACCEPT
```

TIP

OpenWrt uses iptables for a firewall, and it is highly configurable. Instruction on iptables is beyond the scope of this book, but the Gentoo Linux wiki has a great resource on learning iptables at http://gentoo-wiki.com/HOWTO_Iptables_for_newbies. Additionally, you can find an online iptables rule generator at www.hideaway.net/iptables.

These firewall changes will be applied after a reboot, but you can make them active immediately by issuing the following command:

```
# /etc/init.d/S45firewall restart
```

You can now have your non-WRT54G-based Kismet server connect to your WRT54G Kismet Drone. Configuring the Kismet server under various operating systems is beyond the scope of this book; you can find installation guides at www.kismetwireless.net. In order to have a Kismet server connect to a drone, you need to modify the Kismet server's kismet.conf file to define a drone as a capture source. You can even define multiple drones, as shown in the following code. We'll assume in this example that we have two WRT54G Kismet Drones with IP addresses of 192.168.1.110 and 192.168.1.220:

```
source=kismet_drone,192.168.1.110:3501,drone1
source=kismet_drone,192.168.1.220:3501,drone2
```

Once you have made these configuration changes, you can start up a Kismet client, either on your Kismet server installation or on a separate PC, and connect to the drone over the network. Figure 6.4 shows an example.

Figure 6.4 Kismet Client Connected to a Kismet_Drone

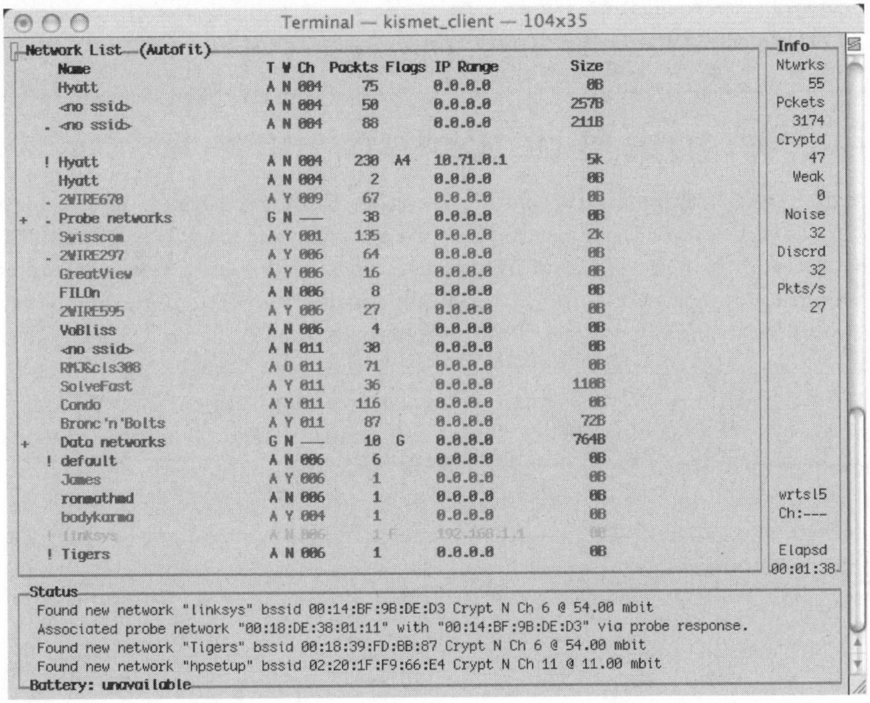

Notes from the Underground…

Signal Strength with Kismet on a WRT54G

One of the reasons you would deploy several Kismet Drones is to monitor for rogue access points. Rogue access points are wireless access points that may be installed in your environment, that are not permitted, and that may be providing unauthorized access to your network.

One of the best ways to determine the location of a rogue access point is to determine its signal strength as seen by the Kismet Drone. Unfortunately, the proprietary closed source wireless drivers provided by Broadcom for the WRT54G do not provide usable signal strength information! This puts a snag into rogue access point location using a Kismet Drone.

It is still possible to utilize Kismet Drones to locate access points, but it quickly becomes a complex process. At a minimum, Kismet Drones on WRT54G routers combined with a central Kismet server, and a laptop with a directional antenna, is still an effective method.

Continued

> You can find more information on locating rogue access points with Kismet, Kismet Drones, and WRT54G routers in a paper at the SANS Reading Room, at www.sans.org/reading_room/whitepapers/honors/1671.php.

WRT54G Remote Bluetooth Scanner

Bluetooth scanning is increasingly important for a wireless penetration tester, due to the proliferation of the technology and the devices, and the type of information that is used on a Bluetooth device. Devices with Bluetooth handle all sorts of information; phones have call records and address books, keyboards are used to type passwords and financial information, and Bluetooth telephone headsets carry audio communications. These types of information are valuable to an attacker, and Bluetooth devices are transmitting this information over the air.

Bluetooth is intended to be a short-range wireless technology, ranging from 1–100 meters, depending on the class of Bluetooth device. This would limit the range at which an attacker could intercept transmissions; however, an enterprising group of hackers have been able to create Bluetooth connections over distances greater than 1 mile, utilizing commodity hardware! Bluetooth utilizes the same 2.4GHz frequency range as Wi-Fi, so the antennas, and antenna design, are interchangeable between the two technologies.

NOTE

For more information on Bluetooth, including protocol information, frequencies, and distance information, check the Wikipedia entry at http://en.wikipedia.org/wiki/Bluetooth. You can find more information about long-range Bluetooth connections at http://trifinite.org/trifinite_stuff_lds.html and at www.smallnetbuilder.com/content/view/24256/98.

We will perform this hack on a WRTSL54GS due to the availability of a Universal Serial Bus (USB) port on this model. We will be utilizing a third-party USB Bluetooth adapter to perform our scans.

About the Bluetooth Adapter

The USB Bluetooth adapter that we have elected to use for this hack is a Linksys USBBT100, as shown in Figure 6.5, which is a Class 1 device capable of communicating up to 100 meters by default. This adapter features an external antenna; however, it has been replaced with a cable and an RP-SMA connector. We also mated the adapter with a 5dB omnidirectional antenna. Now, due to the modularity, we can select from different antennas as needed.

Figure 6.5 Modified Linksys USBBT100

TIP

You can purchase a premodified Linksys USBBT100 adapter and various antennas, either stand-alone or as a kit (which includes compatible antennas), from War Driving World at www.wardrivingworld.com.

This particular USB adapter is supported under OpenWrt; however, plenty of other adapters are supported by the Linux BlueZ drivers (www.bluez.org). We prefer this one due to the hackability of an external antenna, and the high power, as this is a Class 1 Bluetooth device capable of communicating up to 100 meters with the default antenna.

Preparing the WRTSL54GS USB Capabilities

In order to be able to use a USB device under OpenWrt, you need to install a few kernel modules to support the USB port. As the USB port is featured on only the WRTSL54GS model, the required kernel modules are not included by default in OpenWrt, in order to conserve space and memory. The USB modules have already been packaged for use with OpenWrt, and they are available through the default package repository.

In order to enable support under OpenWrt, you need to install the core USB kernel drivers as well as the specific Open Host Controller Interface (OHCI) kernel drivers. You can do this with the following command:

```
# ipkg install kmod-usb-core kmod-usb-ohci
```

NOTE

It is possible to use multiple USB devices on the single USB port on the WRTSL54GS, by using an inexpensive third-party USB hub. The authors have successfully used a USB Bluetooth adapter, USB spectrum analyzer, and two USB storage devices simultaneously! Depending on the hub's manufacturer, it may utilize the Universal Host

> Controller Interface (UHCI) USB standard controller instead of the OHCI controller in the WRTSL54GS. Kernel modules are available for UHCI devices by installing the kmod-usb-uhci package.

Once you have installed these kernel module packages, you will need to reboot the WRTSL54GS in order to have the kernel modules started. You can install these modules manually with the following two commands:

```
# insmod usbcore
# insmod usb-ohci
```

These modules allow OpenWrt to be able to communicate with the USB port and the host controller, in order to determine information about devices attached to the USB port so that the kernel can load the appropriate drivers.

Configuring the USB Bluetooth Adapter

Before you plug in and use the USB Bluetooth adapter, you need to make sure that you install the appropriate drivers for the Bluetooth adapter, and the Bluetooth utilities. First, you need to install the generic Bluetooth kernel modules and the kernel modules for the USB Bluetooth Host Controller Interface (HCI) from the default OpenWrt package tree:

```
# ipkg install kmod-bluetooth kmod-bluetooth-hciusb
```

You also need to install the Bluetooth utilities in the bluez utilities package. Unfortunately, the bluez packages are not in the default OpenWrt package tree, but they are available from the OpenWrt backports tree. In order to add these packages, you need to update /etc/ipkg.conf file with an additional repository. Add an additional *src* directive to /etc/ipkg.conf as follows:

```
src backports http://downloads.openwrt.org/backports/0.9/
```

This additional source directive provides a descriptive name (*backports*), and gives the location of the new repository that contains the BlueZ utilities. In order to install the BlueZ utilities, you need to make sure you update your package database to add the items from the new backports repository:

```
# ipkg update
# ipkg install bluez-utils
```

To begin using your USB Bluetooth adapter, you do need to modify some system configurations, as one of the modules does not automatically install after a restart, which is required for the Bluetooth adapter to function. You will need to add this additional module to the startup routines under /etc/modules.d. The files in this directory are processed in numerical order by the name of the file. You want this module to be added last, after the Bluetooth kernel modules, and after the USB port has been initialized. Create *70-hci* in the /etc/modules.d directory with the following contents:

```
hci_usb
```

The *hci_usb* module will initialize the Bluetooth HCI via the USB port so that you can interact with the Bluetooth adapter. This interaction will be extremely important in terms of Bluetooth device discovery. In order to complete the HCI installation, you need to ensure that the HCI daemon has been started, and is started during boot. Add this to the startup items under /etc/init.d, by creating *S70hcid* with the following contents:

```
#!/bin/sh
/usr/sbin/hcid &
```

You also need to make *S70hcid* executable with the following command:

```
# chmod 755 S70hcid
```

After all of these steps are complete, you should perform a full reboot of the WRTSL54GS in order to verify that all of your modules and your daemon start. Issue an *lsmod* command, and the output should reflect all of your new modules and their dependencies, as shown in the following code, including *bluez, hci_usb, l2cap, rfcomm, sco, usb-ohci* and *usbcore*:

```
Module              Size    Used by      Tainted: P
usbserial           24140   0
hci_usb             10520   1
usb-ohci            19236   0 (unused)
usbcore             74792   1 [usbserial hci_usb usb-ohci]
sco                 10196   0 (unused)
rfcomm              35128   0 (unused)
l2cap               18524   1 [rfcomm]
bluez               38936   3 [hci_usb sco rfcomm l2cap]
wlcompat            14896   0 (unused)
wl                  423640  0 (unused)
switch-robo         4444    0 (unused)
switch-core         4896    0 [switch-robo]
diag                3320    0 (unused)
```

Using the USB Bluetooth Adapter to Discover Devices

Earlier, you installed the bluez-utils package in order to make your Bluetooth device work with your WRTSL54GS. Included with the bluez-utils package are some utilities that are useful for finding and scanning Bluetooth devices. In addition to the scanning tools are some other tools that utilize some features of other Bluetooth devices, such as dial-up networking support, file transfers, and voice communications. In this case, we are primarily interested in using the scanning tools for penetration testing purposes.

The first step you need to perform is to locate some Bluetooth devices. You can do this using the *hcitool* included with the bluez-utils package. As shown here, you can initiate a scan for Bluetooth devices with the following command:

```
# hcitool scan
Scanning ...
        00:0F:86:34:8C:0A        BlackBerry 7520
        00:16:20:E8:A0:92        Z520a
        00:16:CB:8F:29:0C        NORAD
```

In the scanning output, we receive a list of three Bluetooth devices, along with their MAC addresses (or *baddr*) and the device name. Once you have been able to determine the *baddr*, you can use *hcitool info* to obtain more information about the device, as shown in the following abbreviated output against the NORAD device:

```
# hcitool info 00:16:CB:8F:29:0C
Requesting information ...
        BD Address: 00:16:CB:8F:29:0C
        Device Name: NORAD
        LMP Version: 2.0 (0x3) LMP Subversion: 0x7ad
        Manufacturer: Cambridge Silicon Radio (10)
        Features: 0xff 0xff 0x8f 0xfe 0x9b 0xf9 0x00 0x80
                <3-slot packets> <5-slot packets> <encryption> <slotoffset>
```

Now that you have the *baddr* of NORAD from your initial hcitool scan, you can utilize another tool to obtain some information about the Bluetooth services that are available on NORAD. The tool we will use to determines service information is *sdptool*. This tool will allow us to query the Bluetooth device and determine services that we could potentially utilize, including file transfers, dial-up networking, and potential interception of audio. Here is an abbreviated list of services available on NORAD:

```
# sdptool browse 00:16:CB:8F:29:0C
Browsing 00:16:CB:8F:29:0C ...
Service Name: OBEX Object Push
Service RecHandle: 0x10002
Service Class ID List:
  "OBEX Object Push" (0x1105)
Protocol Descriptor List:
  "L2CAP" (0x00000100)
  "RFCOMM" (0x0003)
    Channel: 10
  "OBEX" (0x0008)
Language Base Attr List:
  code_ISO639: 0x656e
  encoding:    0x6a
  base_offset: 0x100
Profile Descriptor List:
```

```
"OBEX Object Push" (0x1105)
    Version: 0x0100
```

> **NOTE**
>
> Palo Wireless has a detailed guide of Bluetooth services, available at www.palowire-less.com/infotooth/tutorial/k2_sdap.asp.

Now, you may have noticed that discovering Bluetooth devices is a manual process, and your information is not stored for further examination. Depending on your method for a penetration test, you may not have access to the device to repeatedly issue commands. Furthermore, you would need to constantly issue commands on your WRTSL54GS, which will be very time-consuming. The best way to obtain timely, relevant information about Bluetooth devices during the course of a penetration test is to implement a script to automatically scan for Bluetooth devices, and maintain the information for later review.

You can automate this process by creating a shell script, presented here as a basic proof of concept. We will create the following script as /usr/bin/btscan.sh:

```
#!/bin/ash
# Change these to reflect your environment
EMAIL="email@domain.com"
SMTP_RELAY=email-relay.domain.com
# These should be left alone
CR=$'\r'
VULN_MAC_FILE=/etc/btscan/VULN_MAC
TEMPFILE=/tmp/temp
#
# Make sure we have sendmail installed
#
if [ -z "$(ipkg list_installed | grep sendmail)" ]; then
        echo -e "ERROR: You must have the mini-sendmail package installed\ from
backports to use this script \n"
        echo -e "Add backports to /etc/ipkg.conf, then ipkg install \    mini-
sendmail \n"
        echo -e "Reference: http://wiki.openwrt.org/rsync-usb-sambaHowTo \n"
        exit 1
fi
echo "Searching For Bluetooth Devices..."
logger "BTSCAN: Searching For Bluetooth Devices..."
BTDEVICES=`hcitool scan | grep -v "Scanning" | awk '{FS = "\t" ; print $2\ "|" $NF
}' | tr -d ' '`
```

```
if [ ! -z "$BTDEVICES" ]; then
        echo "Subject:WRTSL54GS Bluetooth scan results" > $TEMPFILE
        echo "Device Adddress     Device Name     Vulnerable    Chipset" >> \
$TEMPFILE
        for i in $BTDEVICES; do
                MAC_PREFIX=`echo $i | cut -d":" -f1,2,3`
                if [ "$(grep $MAC_PREFIX $VULN_MAC_FILE)" ]; then
                        STR="$i|Yes"
                else
                        STR="$i|No"
                fi
                MAC=`echo $i | cut -d"|" -f1 `
                INFO=`hcitool info $MAC | grep Manufacturer | cut -d: -f2`
                STR="$STR|$INFO"
                echo $STR | awk -F"|" '{print $1 "     " $2 "       " $3 "     "\
                $4}' >> $TEMPFILE
        done
        cat $TEMPFILE | sendmail -f$EMAIL -s$SMTP_RELAY $EMAIL
else
        echo "No Bluetooth devices found"
        logger "BTSCAN: No Bluetooth devices found"
fi
```

Don't forget to make this script executable with:

```
# chmod 755 /usr/bin/btscan.sh
```

You also need to define a list of vulnerable Bluetooth devices, based upon the *baddr* prefix. You can populate the list of vulnerable devices with a list of Nokia phones determined to be vulnerable to attacks by the authors of the btscanner project (at www.pentest.co.uk). You can create the listing of vulnerable *baddr* prefixes in /etc/btscan/VULN_MAC:

```
00:60:57
00:0E:6D
00:02:EE
00:E0:03
00:0E:07
00:0A:D9
```

TIP

You can download both of the files described here with *wget http://www.wrt54ghacks.com/whiterussian/btscan.tar.gz* and extract them with *tar -zxvf btscan.tar.gz*. Once you've extracted the files, you can copy them to the appropriate locations.

NOTE

This list of vulnerable Bluetooth *baddr* (or MAC) prefixes is by no means comprehensive. You will need to add to this file any device prefixes in which you are interested.

For this script to function properly, you also need to install the mini-sendmail package. This will allow your script to send mail each time it is run, as defined by the *EMAIL* and *SMTP_RELAY* variables defined at the start of the script, after setting these variables to appropriate settings for your environment, or for the environment that will be audited for Bluetooth devices. Install the mini-sendmail package with the following command:

```
# ipkg install mini-sendmail
```

Now that you have all of the requirements for your automated script, you can test it by executing it with */usr/bin/btscan.sh*. Once a scan is complete, you should receive an e-mail with output similar to the following:

```
Received: (from larry@pauldotcom.com)
        by OpenWrt (mini_sendmail/1.3.5 16nov2003);
        Sat, 01 Jan 2000 01:00:31 UTC
        (sender root@OpenWrt)
Subject: WRTSL54GS Bluetooth scan results
To: undisclosed-recipients:;


Device Adddress    Device Name      Vulnerable  Chipset
00:0F:86:34:8C:0A  BlackBerry7520   Yes
00:16:CB:8F:29:0C  NORAD            No          Cambridge Silicon Radio (10)
```

Upon confirmation that your script is functioning, you'll probably want this script to execute with some frequency. We'll create a crontab entry so that cron can execute our script every 30 minutes. We will edit the crontab configuration file with the following command:

```
# crontab -e
```

This will bring up a vi session with a blank file to which we will add a single entry to have our Bluetooth scanning script running every 30 minutes, at zero minutes and 30 minutes past every hour. Here is our entry into crontab:

```
0,30  *  *  *  *  /usr/bin/btscan.sh
```

NOTE

For a concise description of the commands in the crontab file, the Admin's Choice Web site has a great guide at www.adminschoice.com/docs/crontab.htm.

Notes from the Underground…

Boardroom and Conference Room Bluetooth

One fantastic place to set up a WRTSL54GS for some effective Bluetooth scanning is in the boardroom, or in a popular conference room in the facility in which you are testing. This setup will have the "victims" bring their devices to you, in the boardroom. Clearly these types of rooms will frequently be occupied by company executives, or other individuals that may have access to privileged information.

We have intentionally set the scan interval to 30 minutes, as many meetings run about 30–60 minutes. During those times, we are likely to scan a room full of Bluetooth devices attached to important people! As an added benefit, any errors from Bluetooth scanning on the users' devices (such as asking for a pin) can easily be blamed on another device in the room, inadvertently trying to create a connection to a phone.

As an added benefit, many of the new conference room equipment is now being shipped with Bluetooth! It would be great to know that you could capture the latest confidential sales presentation transmitted with Bluetooth to the projector (such as Sanyo's PLC-EF10NZ or Toshiba's TLP-X20 or TLP-X21J), or via a Bluetooth microphone (such as the Sony ECMHW1).

In most cases, the modern boardroom or conference room will feature power and network connectivity built into the table! This makes for a convenient place to power and provide a WAN connection to a WRTSL54GS. A little duct tape to the underside of the table, and it is likely that no one will be the wiser.

WRT54G Remote 2.4GHz Spectrum Analyzer

The 2.4GHz spectrum is home to numerous networking and communications protocols, such as 802.11b/g, Bluetooth, and even cordless phones. Being able to analyze this spectrum in a cost-effective manner has many benefits:

- Troubleshooting wireless client connectivity problems

- Accurately choosing the least populated channel for your access points

- Detecting activity on all 14 802.11 channels (not limited by protocol)

- Detecting malicious or accidental flooding of the spectrum

- Analyzing and measuring anomalies that may cause interference (i.e., microwaves)

In order to accomplish these tasks, you will need the Wi-Spy USB dongle from MetaGeek (www.metageek.net), shown in Figure 6.6. It is a modified wireless USB keyboard dongle that has been given the capability to analyze spectrum information.

Figure 6.6 Wi-Spy Dongle

Currently, the Wi-Spy dongle works with Windows, Linux, and OS X, as both a client and a host for the USB dongle. For example, you could plug the dongle into your laptop and use the software to read the spectrum information, either locally or over the network.

The OS X version of the software is called EaKiu, and was authored by Dave, from Cookware, Inc. Cookware provides the OS X client for free, and includes a program called LINUXspy which allows you to plug the Wi-Spy dongle into any Linux host, and then connect to it remotely with the OS X client. This is a great concept; however, using the dongle on a laptop presents a couple of problems. First, you must dedicate a laptop running Linux for this purpose. Second, you have to get the laptop to the area where you want to analyze the 2.4GHz spectrum. This job is much better suited to the WRTSL54GS router. For this to work well for you, you will need the following:

- A WRTSL54GS router running OpenWrt Whiterussian 0.9
- A Wi-Spy USB dongle, version 1.2
- A USB extender cable
- A machine running OS X
- EaKiu Software, version 3.1

The first thing you need to do is to install OpenWrt Whiterussian 0.9 on the WRTSL54GS (hopefully you have gotten quite good at that by now). Next, install the appropriate USB packages:

```
kmod-usb-core - 2.4.30-brcm-5 - Kernel Support for USB
kmod-usb-ohci - 2.4.30-brcm-5 - Kernel driver for OHCI USB controllers
kmod-usb-uhci - 2.4.30-brcm-5 - Kernel driver for UHCI USB controllers
kmod-usb2 - 2.4.30-brcm-5 - Kernel driver for USB2 controllers
libusb - 0.1.12-1 - A library for accessing Linux USB devices
lsusb - 0.71-1 - A program to list USB devices
```

Once you have installed the packages, you will need to reboot. Once you're rebooted, plug the USB extender cable into the router, and then plug the Wi-Spy dongle into the other end of the cable. You should see a green light inside the Wi-Spy dongle once you're properly connected. To verify connectivity go to the command line and do the following:

```
# lsusb
Bus 004 Device 001: ID 0000:0000
Bus 003 Device 001: ID 0000:0000
Bus 002 Device 001: ID 0000:0000
Bus 002 Device 005: ID 1781:083e
Bus 001 Device 001: ID 0000:0000
```

In the output in the preceding example, you can see that Device 005 is on Bus 002 and has the USB ID 1781:083e. If you type the command *dmesg | grep 1781* you should see the following line in the output:

```
usb.c: USB device 4 (vend/prod 0x1781/0x83e) is not claimed by any active driver.
```

NOTE

With just about any other USB device, a report that the USB device is not claimed by any active driver often indicates a problem. In the case of Wi-Spy, the software will communicate directly with the device without the need for an additional driver.

Next, you will need to install LINUXspy, version 2.0.1, designed to work with Wi-Spy running on OpenWrt. To install this package run the following command:

```
# ipkg install http://wrt54ghacks.com/whiterussian/linuxspy_0.2-1_mipsel.ipk
```

This will install the LINUXspy binary, in addition to the dependencies (libusb and libpthread). Once you've installed the package, you can start the LINUXspy server by running the following command:

```
# LINUXspy

EaKiu LINUXspy Server - Version 2.0.1
-----------------------------------
LINUXspy: Wi-Spy USB device found!
LINUXspy: Starting threaded server on port 2400
```

When the server has started successfully, denoted by the line reading *LINUXspy: Starting threaded server on port 2400*, install the EaKiu OS X client according to the instructions. After it launches, click the button labeled **TCP** and enter the IP address of your WRTSL54GS, and then click **Connect**. If all goes well, you will see a screen similar to the one depicted in Figure 6.7.

Figure 6.7 EaKiu Client Connected to a Remote Wi-Spy Dongle

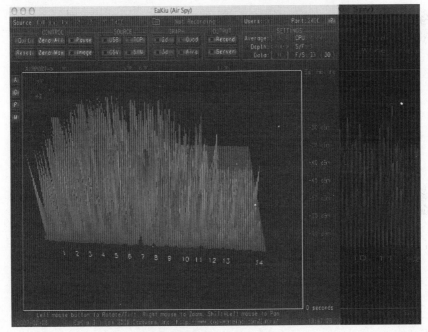

NOTE

We would like to thank Dave, from Cookware, Inc., for helping us port the LINUXspy program to OpenWrt and helping us test it. If you find this tool useful, be certain to visit www.metageek.net and www.cookwareinc.com for more information and updates. A new version of Wi-Spy hardware and software is being developed, but was not available in time for inclusion in this book.

WRTSL54GS CDMA Internet Connection

As penetration testers, occasionally we find ourselves in a situation where we are able to place a rogue device, such as a WRTSL54GS, at a client site in an inconspicuous location (i.e., tucked behind a printer or copier). This type of rogue device could give us backdoor access into a corporate network by making outbound connections, allowing us to bypass inbound firewall restrictions. Sometimes we may find ourselves in a position where a rogue device will not work for us, likely due to very restrictive outbound firewall rules. Finding that your client has good firewall rules is a good thing, but it is entirely possible that they have allowed anyone to attach a rogue device with an alternative routing path to their network, bypassing the firewall completely.

Enter cellular data networking! In the United States, Sprint maintains a CDMA cellular data network capable of reasonable broadband speeds. Early in 2007, Sprint released a new CDMA data modem, the Novatel Wireless Ovation U720, shown in Figure 6.8. The U720 becomes very useful to us, in that it features a USB connection. When we combine it with a WRTSL54GS, we can utilize it as a cellular router. Although Linksys has also released the WRT54G3G-ST, which is compatible with Sprint's EV-DO cellular data network, the cost of the WRT54G3G-ST is more than double the cost of the WRTSL54GS! Both solutions require the purchase of a cellular modem from Sprint (either USB or PCMCIA, at about the same cost). The PCMCIA version that is required for the WRT54G3G-ST is becoming increasingly incompatible with new mobile computing technologies, where USB and ExpressCard are the future standards.

Figure 6.8 The Novatel Wireless Ovation U720 CDMA Modem

In order to begin utilizing the U720 under OpenWrt, you need to install a few packages that enable the USB port, PPP communications, and serial modem drivers. In order to install these packages, perform the following commands:

```
# ipkg install kmod-usb-core kmosd-usb-ohci kmod-ppp chat kmosd-usb-serial
```

After the packages are installed, you need to make sure that a number of kernel modules are installed and loaded at startup. You need to customize the insertion of the *usbserial* kernel module, as the kernel module does not yet know about the U720. You need to specify the device vendor and product ID. To get your modules installed in the appropriate order, and to make your customized changes, you need to edit two files under /etc/modules.d. The first file to edit is 60-usb-serial, and you should modify it to look as follows in order to register the U720 with the *usbserial* module:

```
usbserial vendor=0x1410 product=0x2110
```

TIP

It is possible that these instructions will work with USB cellular devices other than the U720. In these other cases, you will need to change the vendor and product code passed to the USB serial kernel module. You can obtain the proper vendor and product ID for your device by issuing the *dmesg* command immediately after plugging in your USB device and examining the output.

In addition to the *usbserial* module, you need to create an additional set of modules to be loaded after *usbserial*. Under /etc/modules.d, create a new file named 80-ppp and populate it with the following lines to load these modules at startup.

```
slhc

ppp_generic

ppp_async
```

In order to create a working PPP connection, you need to provide a number of configuration options across several files. You need to define your connection port, the number to dial, routing information, and scripts for connection and disconnection. First you need to define your peer, or connection to dial, under /etc/ppp/peers. Create the settings indicated and described here as /etc/ppp/peers/sprint:

```
/dev/usb/tts/0   # Where our U72 Modem device is attached
921600           # Baud rate
defaultroute     # Utilize Sprint's default route
usepeerdns       # Utilize Sprint's DNS servers
crtscts          # Use hardware flow control
lock             # Lock the serial port so no other apps interfere
noauth           # No authentication to Sprint
local            # Don't use Carrier Detect or Data Terminal Ready
persist          # Redial if disconnected
user             # Sends no user name
ppp              # Use PPP protocol
holdoff 5        # Try a redial after disconnect after 5 seconds
```

```
lcp-echo-failure 4        # Prevents timeouts
lcp-echo-interval 65535 # Prevents timeouts
connect          "/usr/sbin/chat -v -f /etc/chatscripts/sprint-connect"
# Use this connect script when esablishing a PPP conenction
disconnect         "/usr/sbin/chat -v -f /etc/chatscripts/sprint-disconnect"
# Use this disconnect script when hanging up a PPP conenction
```

The Sprint peer script that we have just created references a connect and disconnect script at the very end, which also need to be created. These scripts provide commands to the modem portion of the U720 in order to dial and disconnect the PPP Internet connection. Here is the connect script, named sprint-connect, in /etc/chatscripts:

```
TIMEOUT 10
ABORT 'BUSY'
ABORT 'NO ANSWER'
ABORT 'ERROR'
SAY 'Starting Sprint...\n'
# Get the modem's attention and reset it.
""        'ATZ'
# E0=No echo, V1=English result codes
OK    'ATE0V1'
# List signal quality
'OK' 'AT+CSQ'
'OK' 'ATDT#777'
CONNECT
```

Here is the script named sprint-disconnect, in /etc/chatscripts, which will handle the disconnection:

```
"" "\K"
"" "+++ATH0"
SAY "Disconnected from Sprint."
```

TIP

You can download the peer file and both chatscripts with *wget http://www.wrt54ghacks.com/whiterussian/U720.tar.gz* and extract them with *tar -zxvf U720.tar.gz*. Once you've extracted the files, you can copy them to the appropriate locations.

Now that you have all of the configuration pieces in place, you need to make the final jump and set the U720 to connect at boot and become the default WAN interface, instead of the WAN port.

The first script that you'll want to add to the default startup scripts under /etc/init.d is called s80ppp. Create S80ppp as shown here to set up the serial port lock directory, and connect to Sprint with the pppd daemon:

```
#!/bin/sh
mkdir -p /var/lock
pppd call sprint
```

You also need to make S80ppp executable with the following command:

```
# chmod 755 /etc/init.d/S80ppp
```

As the last step in turning the WRTSL54GS into a CDMA router, you need to change the NVRAM variables to set a new network interface as the default WAN port. This will disable the current WAN port and set the new ppp0 interface, created by the connection to Sprint via the U720, as the new default WAN port. You can do this with two NVRAM commands, and a commit:

```
# nvram set wan_device=ppp0
# nvram set wan_ifname=ppp0
# nvram commit
```

> **NOTE**
>
> In order to restore to the default WAN port, if you no longer want to use the WRTSL54GS as a CDMA router, you need to revert the two NVRAM settings to the default values with:
> *nvram set wan_device=vlan1*
> *nvram set wan_ifname=eth1*
> *nvram commit*

A final reboot should result in a working CDMA router! If you were to unplug any cable from the WAN interface, you should still be able to connect to the Internet over the CDMA connection.

Now, you may have one slight problem with using your CDMA connection as part of a penetration test. Typically, you would be deploying this device in a covert manner, and you won't be able to log into the WRTSL54GS to determine the new WAN IP address assigned by the CDMA provider. You can create a script to query the interface and e-mail the new WAN IP every time a PPP connection is established to an e-mail address that you provide. In order for this script to work, you need to install mini-sendmail:

```
ipkg install mini-sendmail
```

Our script is fairly simple, as it sends the output of *ifconfig ppp0* in an e-mail via our defined mail relay to an e-mail address that we specify:

```
#!/bin/sh
# Change these to reflect your environment
```

```
EMAIL="emailaddress@domain.com"
SMTP_RELAY=smtp-mailhost.domain.com
# This should be left alone
TEMPFILE=/tmp/ppp-temp
#
# Make sure we have sendmail installed
#
if [ -z "$(ipkg list_installed | grep sendmail)" ]; then
    echo -e "ERROR: You must have the mini-sendmail package installed from
    echo -e "Add backports to /etc/ipkg.conf, then ipkg install mini-sendmail
    echo -e "Reference: http://wiki.openwrt.org/rsync-usb-sambaHowTo \n"
    exit 1
fi
sleep 10
echo "E-mailing CDMA IP information"
echo "Subject:CDMA IP Informations" > $TEMPFILE
ifconfig ppp0 >> $TEMPFILE
cat $TEMPFILE | sendmail -s$SMTP_RELAY -f$EMAIL $EMAIL
```

You can create this script as /usr/bin/ppp-ip.sh. You can make it executable with the following command:

```
chmod 755 /usr/bin/ppp-ip.sh
```

By running this script manually, you can verify that everything is working properly, and that you receive e-mail.

TIP

You can also download this script with *wget http://www.wrt54ghacks.com/whiterussian/ppp-ip.sh*, and copy it to the appropriate location, /usr/bin.

You will also want to set this script to be executed at startup, as this will be the first time that the interface will be activated. You can have your e-mail script run by creating S85ppp-ip under /etc/init.d, as shown here:

```
#!/bin/bash
/usr/bin/ppp-ip.sh &
```

Tip

> You may also want to add /usr/bin/ppp-ip.sh to your crontab, as shown earlier in this chapter. If your CDMA connection drops and reconnects, the ppp0 interface could obtain a different IP address from the provider. With a regular crontab entry, you will receive regular updates containing the IP address information. The startup script will run only at startup, and the CDMA disconnect could happen at any time. You should set the crontab entry to a time interval that is appropriate for your needs. For example, if you want the script to run every two hours, add **0 0-23/2 * * * /usr/bin/ppp-ip.sh > /dev/null 2>&1** to your crontab using the *crontab –e* command.

You would find at this point that if you attempted to connect to the WRTSL54GS via SSH on the CDMA WAN connection, you would fail. You need to enable SSH on the WAN port by modifying your firewall ruleset. You can accomplish these firewall changes by editing /etc/firewall.user. In /etc/firewall.user, you need to locate the *Open Port to WAN* configuration section. In this section, note that two configuration lines exist for enabling SSH access via the WAN port, but they have been commented out.

You need to uncomment the two SSH configuration lines in the *Open Port to WAN* section. Your final *Open Port to WAN* section should look like this:

```
iptables -t nat -A prerouting_rule -i $WAN -p tcp --dport 22 -j ACCEPT
iptables         -A input_rule      -i $WAN -p tcp --dport 22 -j ACCEPT
```

After either a reboot or a restart of the firewall with */etc/init.d/S45firewall restart*, you should be able to connect to your WRTSL54GS over the CDMA WAN connection. At this point, you can utilize the WRTSL54GS for whichever penetration tests you want to perform, and you will successfully bypass any potential external firewalls.

Note

> In order to make full use of the network connection, you will likely need to modify virtual LAN (VLAN) IP addresses, and get creative with routing entries. Each penetration testing environment will be different, so each modification will be unique.

WRT54G Wireless Captive Portal Password Sniffer

Captive portals are useful technology and are in widespread use throughout the world in various hotspots. Some charge for wireless Internet access, whereas others may just ask you to agree to an acceptable use policy (AUP). Most of these services do not provide for encryption on the wireless network, or any other such security mechanism, leaving them vulnerable to attack. One attack, dubbed the "evil twin" by popular media, works by creating an access point that broadcasts the same SSID as the hotspot and aims to steal people's credentials and sniff traffic. For example, a popular hotspot is provided by T-Mobile, whose SSID is typically "t-mobile". By creating a captive portal using the SSID "t-mobile" we can grab people's credentials as they will think they are logging into a real T-Mobile hotspot.

The Shmoo Group (www.shmoo.com) has documented this attack, dubbing it (more appropriately) airsnarf. In more recent versions, they have customized the Ewrt firmware such that it will grab users' passwords as they pass through the hotspot. They have released the firmware and call it Airsnarf–Rogue Squadron. You will need the following in order to set this up and use it (with permission, of course) in your penetration tests:

- A WRT54G, version 2.*x* or 3.*x*
- The Airsnarf/Rogue Squadron firmware
- A connection on the WAN port that provides Internet access
- The ability to customize Hypertext Markup Language (HTML) Web pages to impersonate a real captive portal

Airsnarf?Rogue Squadron installs like any other hotspot firmware. In fact, it is based on Ewrt firmware, 0.3 beta 1, by Portless Networks, which supports only the WRT54G, versions 2.*x* and 3.*x*. Once you have acquired the hardware, you can download the firmware from http://airsnarf.shmoo.com/rogue_squadron/index.html. Load the firmware, following the instructions provided in Chapter 2. Then go to http://192.168.1.1 and log in with the username *root* and the default password of *airsnarf*. If you're successful, the default administrative Web page should look like Figure 6.9. We used a screen shot from a real-world installation for this example, which references the IP address of 10.13.37.1. You will want to change from the 192.168.1.1 IP address, especially if the WAN IP address will be 192.168.1.0/24.

To change the LAN IP address go to the **Local IP Address field** and change it to a subnet that is different from the subnet on the WAN. For this example, we are using 10.13.37.1/24 as the LAN IP address and subnet. You will also need to enter an appropriate DNS server IP address in the **Static DNS 1: field** so that clients have the ability to resolve hostnames (in our example, we selected 192.168.1.10). Then click **Save Settings** and reconfigure your client computer to be on the 10.13.37.0/24 subnet. Once rebooted, go back into the Web interface and go to **Access Restrictions | Captive Portal (NoCat),** as shown in Figure 6.10, and customize the settings to your choosing by changing the **Gateway Name** to the name of your captive portal.

Figure 6.9 Airsnarf Configuration Page

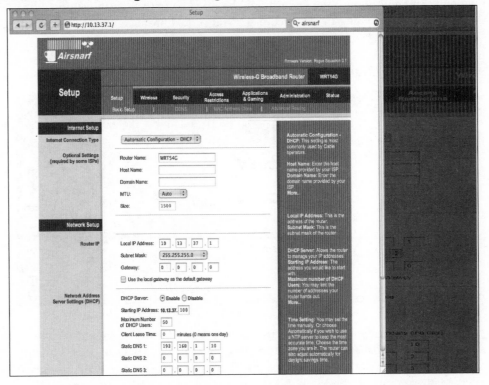

Figure 6.10 Airsnarf Captive Portal Setup Screen

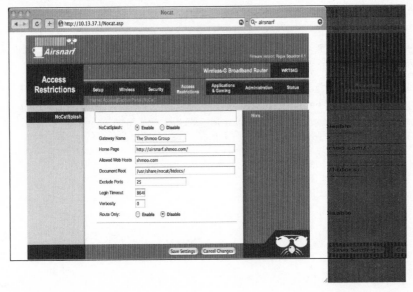

You may also want to change the **Allowed Web Hosts field,** which lists Web sites that are allowed without "authentication." Now you should be ready to test your captive portal by associating to the SSID "Airsnarf" and going to any Web page. This should produce a page as seen in Figure 6.11.

Figure 6.11 Airsnarf Login Screen

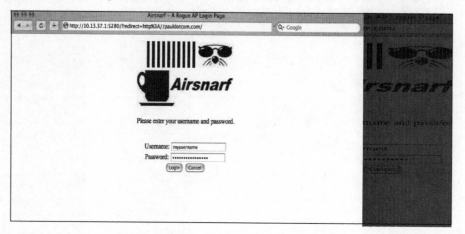

Log in with any username and password to test and click **Login.** You should then be redirected to the Web page you originally intended to visit. Next, SSH to the device and log in with the root username and password. The usernames and passwords are contained in the file /opt/airsnarfs.txt. You should see the username and password in this file, in addition to the Web site that was being redirected:

```
# cat /opt/airsnarfs.txt
redirect=http://pauldotcom.com/
username=myusername password=mystolenpassword accept_terms=yes
redirect=http://pauldotcom.com/ mode_login=Login
```

If you see the preceding data, you have successfully configured Airsnarf. The only thing left to do is get permission to run this in an organization that wants to have wireless security tested. You will want to customize the login page to look like a login page that users for that organization are familiar with. The Web pages are stored by default in /usr/local/share/nocat/htdocs.

Tools & Traps...

All Your Passwords Belong to dsniff

As far as password sniffing goes, few tools are as widely recognized as Dug Song's dsniff program, available at www.monkey.org/~dugsong/dsniff. dsniff allows you to capture traffic and pick out passwords from a long list of protocols, on the fly. dsniff supports many different protocols with respect to password sniffing, including FTP, Telnet, POP3, SMTP, IMAP, and HTTP. This is a perfect tool to install onto our fake captive portal device because not only could we obtain the passwords that the users enter on the splash Web page, but also we can potentially grab some of their other passwords when connecting to remote servers with dsniff. However, the preceding example uses an older version of Ewrt, and what follows is a tutorial that works with the latest stable version of OpenWrt (Whiterussian 0.9). To combine these two small projects would require some development effort, but would not be too difficult overall. To install dsniff, do the following:

```
# ipkg install dsniff

Installing dsniff (2.3-2) to root...

Downloading http://downloads.openwrt.org/whiterussian/packages/dsniff_2.3-
2_mipsel.ipk

Installing libnet (1.0.2a-7) to root...

Downloading
http://downloads.openwrt.org/whiterussian/packages/libnet_1.0.2a-
7_mipsel.ipk

Installing libpcap (0.9.4-1) to root...

Downloading
http://downloads.openwrt.org/whiterussian/packages/libpcap_0.9.4-
1_mipsel.ipk

Installing libnids (1.18-0) to root...

Downloading http://downloads.openwrt.org/whiterussian/packages/libnids_1.18-
0_mipsel.ipk

Installing libopenssl (0.9.8d-1) to root...

Downloading
http://downloads.openwrt.org/whiterussian/packages/libopenssl_0.9.8d-
1_mipsel.ipk

Installing libgdbm (1.8.3-0) to root...

Downloading http://downloads.openwrt.org/whiterussian/packages/libgdbm_
.8.3-0_mipsel.ipk

Configuring dsniff
```

Continued

```
Configuring libgdbm

Configuring libnet

Configuring libnids

Configuring libopenssl

Configuring libpcap

Successfully terminated.
```

Once you've installed dsniff, you should be aware of two files:

/usr/lib/dsniff.magic This file contains the regular expressions that correspond to the packets containing the passwords for a given protocol. For example, the line *0   string   AUTH\   pop* specifies that the offset into the packet is *0*, it is of type *string*, it searches for the string *AUTH*, and it displays a message of *pop*. This is a standard file format definition. For more information, you can type **man 5 magic** on any UNIX/Linux host.

/usr/lib/dsniff.services This file describes the services that dsniff uses, and it is structured the same as the /etc/services file on any UNIX/Linux host.

By modifying these two files, and using the *–m* parameter to dsniff, you can grab usernames and passwords from many different protocols. Let's look at how we would run dsniff to collect usernames and passwords going in clear text through our hotspot (or any other WRT54G):

```
# dsniff -dmn -s1500 -i eth1

<snip>

dsniff: trigger_set_tcp: port 8080 -> http

dsniff: trigger_set_tcp: port 8888 -> napster

dsniff: trigger_set_tcp: port 9898 -> aim

dsniff: trigger_set_tcp: port 65301 -> pcanywhere

dsniff: trigger_set_rpc: program 100005 -> mountd

dsniff: listening on eth1

[ 0 belong,=0,""]

dsniff: trigger_tcp: decoding port 23 as telnet

-----------------

01/13/00 23:16:35 tcp 192.168.1.249.39866 -> 192.168.1.1.23 (telnet)

root

admin


-----------------

01/13/00 23:18:26 tcp 192.168.1.249.58937 -> 192.168.1.42.80 (http)

GET /cgi-bin/webif/ HTTP/1.1
```

Continued

```
Host: wrt-office

Authorization: Basic cm9vdDphZG1pbg== [root:admin]


GET /cgi-bin/webif/ HTTP/1.1

Host: wrt-office

Authorization: Basic Og== [:]


dsniff: trigger_tcp: decoding port 80 as http

-----------------
```

In the preceding output, we ran dsniff in debug mode using the –*d* flag, and specified –*m* to tell dsniff to read from the dsniff.magic file, –*n* to disable name resolution, –*s1500* to specify the Maximum Transmission Unit (MTU) size to the maximum value for Ethernet networks, and the interface –*i eth1*, which is the WAN interface of our router. The interface will depend on how you have set up the router; in some cases, *br0* will work as well. In the output, you can see that someone (at 192.168.1.249) was using Telnet to get to a device at 192.168.1.1 with the username *root* and password *admin*. You can also see dsniff's capability to capture HTTP Basic authentication, as it catches the same user sending a username of *root* and a password of *admin* to what appears to be another router labeled wrt-office (at 192.168.1.42).

dsniff is a very powerful tool, and in fact it comes with a host of other tools for auditing your network, such as filesnarf, which captures files sent over the Network File System (NFS), and msgsnarf, which records messages from sniffed AOL Instant Messenger (AIM), ICQ 2000, IRC, and Yahoo! Messenger chat sessions. Please be certain you have the appropriate permissions before you run these tools on your network.

Summary

The WRT54G platform can be an invaluable tool for a penetration tester by providing alternative connection methods to a remote network to perform testing without having to travel. VPNs can be used to tunnel traffic for various purposes, such as remote network sniffing. For creating a backdoor into a network, a CDMA connection is most useful, allowing you to bypass the local network for remote connectivity.

You can use WRT54G routers to remotely monitor the wireless spectrum and Bluetooth traffic. These services will allow you to troubleshoot user problems, detect rogue devices, and monitor for vulnerable Bluetooth devices such as cell phones, which may contain sensitive information.

Finally, you can use Airsnarf Rogue Squadron to create fake hotspots for use in a penetration test, or just to have a little fun with your friends.

Solutions Fast Track

Tunneling and VPN

- ☑ OpenVPN is a great open source project that can provide a routed or bridge VPN connection using SSL/TLS tunnels.

- ☑ OpenVPN requires that you have a CA to generate certificates for clients and servers.

- ☑ There are limitations when using OpenVPN for remote penetration testing. Namely, in order to provide a true bridge between the client site and the penetration tester's site, you need to put the OpenVPN server at the client site in order to have full access to all systems available there.

Wireless Security Tools Using OpenWrt

- ☑ A Kismet Drone is useful for locating rogue access points and determining information about the wireless environment.

- ☑ Channel hopping is not supported in the wireless chipset, but a shell script can do the channel hopping instead.

- ☑ In order to connect to the Kismet Drone on the WAN port, you must modify the firewall ruleset.

- ☑ Modification of an inexpensive USB Bluetooth dongle can provide long-range Bluetooth scanning.

- ☑ The BlueZ utilities have been ported to OpenWrt, and they can provide basic Bluetooth discovery.

- ☑ With some scripting, you can perform continuous Bluetooth scans and e-mail them off-site for further analysis.

☑ You can perform Remote Spectrum 2.4GHz Spectrum analysis with a WRTSL54GS and a Wi-Spy dongle.

☑ EaKiu is the client tool to use with a remote Wi-Spy dongle attached to a WRTSL54GS.

WRTSL54GS and CDMA Internet Connection

v   You can use a CDMA rogue device, connected to the Internet, to bypass external firewalls.

☑ You can interface the CDMA modem with PPP.

☑ You use NVRAM variables to change the default WAN connection to the CDMA USB adapter.

WRT54G Wireless Captive Portal Password Sniffer

☑ Rogue Squadron from the Shmoo Group provides a customizable, fake portal for acquiring passwords.

☑ Passwords acquired with the Rogue Squadron portal are stored on the device, and must be periodically retrieved.

Frequently Asked Questions

The following Frequently Asked Questions, answered by the authors of this book, are designed to both measure your understanding of the concepts presented in this chapter and to assist you with real-life implementation of these concepts. To have your questions about this chapter answered by the author, browse to **www.syngress.com/solutions** and click on the **"Ask the Author"** form.

Q: Why isn't channel hopping supported natively with a Kismet Drone?

A: The proprietary nature of the drivers for the Broadcom wireless drivers have prevented native channel hopping. Due to the lack of documentation from the manufacturer, support for native channel hopping has not been able to be determined.

Q: Are other Bluetooth tools available under OpenWrt?

A: As of this writing, no other Bluetooth tools exist for OpenWrt. However, it may be possible to port some existing tools to this platform.

Q: Why should I pick a USB CDMA modem over a PCMCIA one?

A: Many new mobile technologies have dropped PCMCIA support for Express/34 slots, which are not compatible with each other. USB ports are featured on just about all modern (and not so modern) computing devices (including routers), and USB will maximize the potential alternative applications for the same CDMA modem.

Q: I am getting a lot of interference when I use the Wi-Spy dongle. What can I do?

A: Use a USB extension cable to put some distance between the WRTSL54GS and the Wi-Spy dongle.

Q: I am unable to see my USB Bluetooth dongle. What happened?

A: Be certain you have all the appropriate kernel modules installed, specifically *hci-usb*.

Q: Why does it take so long to connect via SSH to the Rogue Squadron WRT54G?

A: It appears that there are some issues with SSH under the Rogue Squadron setup. If you wait long enough, it will connect. This delay may be due to SSH needing to re-create session keys for each connection, which can take some time on a device with limited processing power.

## Chapter 7

WRT54G
Hardware Hacking

Solutions in this chapter:

- **Fun with Wireless Antennas**

- **Adding Ports: SD Card, Serial, and JTAG**

- **Powering Your WRT54G with Alternative Power Sources**

- **Attaching Your WRT54G to Your Laptop**

☑ **Summary**

☑ **Solutions Fast Track**

☑ **Frequently Asked Questions**

Introduction

In this chapter, we will cover the hacks that require hardware modification to the WRT54G routers. Although many people would consider some of these hardware hacks to be on the advanced side, we are here to show you that they can be easily accomplished by experts and amateurs alike. It will be helpful in the course of this chapter to have a little experience wielding a soldering iron and a power tool or two. Don't let that soldering iron scare you! With very little to no practice, you can master some basic soldering techniques.

TIP

> *MAKE* magazine released some fantastic tutorials on soldering as part of its "Learn to Solder Month." These tutorials will turn you into an expert in no time, and they are very easy to understand. You can find the tutorials, and other great soldering links, on the *MAKE* magazine blog at www.makezine.com/blog/archive/2007/01/its_learn_to_so.html.

Fun with Wireless Antennas

Antenna selection can be one of the make-or-break activities that will determine the success of your wireless network. For many, the default antennas that ship with the WRT54G are perfectly suitable. However, being the hackers that we are, we probably want something more from our wireless networks. By changing our antennas, we can achieve some very impressive results.

Components Needed for This Hack

This hack requires a few additional components that are provided standard with any WRT54G model. The additional components required are:

- An appropriate antenna
- A pigtail (optional)

Understanding RF

In order to understand how to pick an appropriate antenna, you need to understand a little about how the radio frequency (RF) signals can be affected by power settings and antennas. Because a comprehensive discussion of RF could fill more than half of this book, we'll be providing a very basic description.

Ultimately, the wireless signal that reaches your client will be affected by the amplitude, or power, of the signal that reaches it. Wireless signals work much like the ripples in a pond created by dropping a stone in the water. When the ripples extend farther out from the epicenter, they become softer and less powerful. We can make the ripples stronger farther from the epicenter by applying more initial force—in the case of wireless, with increasing transmission power, increasing antenna gain, or adding amplifiers. Effectively, all of these solutions will increase the range of a wireless network. When utilizing additional antennas for point-to-point links, it is important to note that antenna upgrades must be performed at both ends. Additionally, clients connected to a network where increased range is desired will also benefit from upgraded antennas.

The initial transmission power of the WRT54G radio card is 89mW (as determined by the wireless driver), and coupled with the default 2.2dB antenna will give us about 142mW of total transmit power at the antenna, using the RF math rules of the 3 s and the 10 s. This total output power of wireless card plus antenna is also known as EIRP (Equivalent Isotropically Radiated Power). The FCC determines the limits of WiFi radiation in the US based upon the EIRP, and they are rated at 1000mW (1 Watt) for indoor applications, or 4000mW (4 Watts) for outdoor applications.

TIP

Cisco has some great information on calculating EIRP using the RF math rules of the 3's and the 10's, at www.cisco.com/en/US/tech/tk722/tk809/technologies_ tech_note09186a00800e90fe.shtml. Additionally, RadioLabs offers a great online wireless calculator, useful for converting mW to dB, and so on. You can find the wireless calculator at http://radiolabs.com/stations/wifi_calc.html.

By simply upgrading our antennas on our WRT54G to some inexpensive 7dB replacements, we can increase the EIRP value to about 446mW! Aproximately, for every increase in our antenna gain by +9dB (or +6dB) outdoors, we effectively double our coverage area (or distance)

Antenna Types

Antennas come in many different shapes, sizes, and capabilities. However, you can break them down into two generic types based on their RF propagation methods. It is important to verify that the antenna that you select is suitable for the 2.4GHz (802.11b/g) and/or 5.8GHz (802.11a) bands, as antenna design depends on the intended frequency range.

Omnidirectional Antennas

Omnidirectional antennas, such as the default 2.2dB antennas, are the most common for indoor applications. As the name may imply, an omnidirectional antenna radiates RF signals in a circular, 360-degree pattern. This type of antenna, shown in Figure 7.1, makes perfect sense when trying to cover an area such as a home, apartment, or office with wireless signals.

Figure 7.1 Omnidirectional Antennas: 2.2dB, 7dB, and 9dB

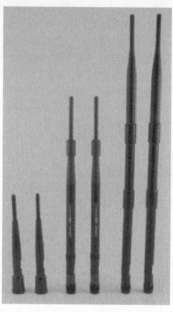

Directional Antennas

Directional antennas come in many different flavors, including Yagi, panel, sector, reflector, and parabolic. These different types all refer to the unique design in which they are constructed. These construction differences do have an impact on how the antenna functions or focuses wireless signals. In this chapter, we will be illustrating several types of directional antennas.

Directional antennas focus the wireless signal based upon their capabilities or design, and as a result, they increase the effective dB. By focusing the wireless signal, a directional antenna does not propagate signals in a 360-degree pattern (much like an omnidirectional antenna). Instead, it reduces the degree of propagation to typically less than 90 degrees. However, directional antennas can range from 5 to 180 degrees, depending on design. This reduction in propagation angle is referred to as *beam width*, and beam width varies for each antenna and design.

Directional antennas are perfect for implementing long-range wireless links between multiple WRT54G units in either a WDS or a WET configuration, as described in Chapter 4. The smaller directional antennas (shown with the larger antennas) in Figure 7.2 can also be extremely helpful as an aide in pinpointing other wireless networks, such as rogue devices, by utilizing the focused nature of the wireless signal. Some of these smaller antennas, such as the 9dB Yagi in Figure 7.2, are also capable of being installed on a compatible dish (as shown at www.netgate.com/product_info.php?cPath=23_36&products_id=382) to further increase their dB and narrow their beam width.

Figure 7.2 Directional Antennas: 9dB Yagi, 12dB Yagi, and 24dB Parabolic Dish (from Bottom to Top)

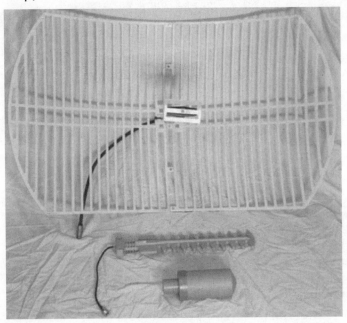

Attaching Antennas to the WRT54G

In Chapter 1, we indicated that both of the antenna connectors on the rear of the WRT54G are female RP-TNC connectors. By using an antenna with a male RP-TNC connector, you can attach it directly to the router. Of course, as you may imagine, there are many types of antenna connectors, and not all are compatible. In order to use antennas with a WRT54G, you need to utilize a pigtail. A pigtail is essentially an antenna connector converter.

For example, the WRT54G uses female RP-TNC connectors, but all of our directional antennas shown in Figure 7.3 utilize N female connectors (not to be confused with the U.S. N-type power connector). Therefore, we need to utilize a female RP-TNC to male N connector, as shown in our pigtail in Figure 7.3. Be sure to research and select your antennas carefully, and purchase the appropriate pigtail and connectors if needed.

Figure 7.3 RP-TNC to N Male Pigtail

Notes from the Underground...

When Diversity Is a Bad Thing...

In the default configuration of the WRT54G router, the included omnidirectional antennas are used in what is called *diversity mode*. In diversity mode, the router uses both antennas simultaneously to resolve any signal anomalies, called *multipath*. If you were to connect a directional antenna to only one antenna connector on the router, you might be able to send out plenty of data; however, you'd likely be unable to receive any data due to the lack of a long-range antenna on the other port, thus confusing the signal anomaly math to resolve multipath issues contained in the wireless radio chipset!

For a more detailed discussion of diversity and multipath, Cisco offers a detailed explanation at www.cisco.com/en/US/tech/tk722/tk809/technologies_tech_note09186a008019f646.shtml.

Although a hardware modification is available to resolve this issue, it is very difficult to reverse. You could remove the antenna diversity chip and replace it with a small piece of wire (check the forum thread at http://forum.bsr-clan.de/ftopic8743.html for more information), but there is a software modification that is much easier to implement, requiring that you issue only two NVRAM commands on the WRT54G:

```
# nvram set wl0_antdiv=x
# nvram commit
```

Replace *x* in the preceding command with the appropriate antenna designation that you want to use: *0* indicates the main antenna, and *1* is the auxiliary antenna. On the WRT54G, versions 1.0 and 1.1, and on the WRT54GS 1.0, the main antenna is

Continued

closest to the power jack. On the WRT54G, versions 2.0 and later, and on the WRT54GS, versions 1.1 and later, the main antenna is located closest to the reset button. Setting *x* to *3* resets to diversity mode, and setting it to *-1* sets it to auto-select. Once you have selected an individual antenna, both send and receive capabilities will be active on the selected antenna connector.

Adding Ports: SD Card, Serial, and JTAG

Of all of the hardware modifications in this chapter, some of the most useful concern the addition of other ports. These ports will allow you to add more storage to the device, add additional devices such as a GPS receiver, and add a JTAG connector in case you really screw up your firmware.

Opening the Router

In order to perform many of these hardware hacks, you first need to gain access to all of the juicy bits contained inside.

WRT54G and GL Series

WARNING

Opening your WRT54G will void your warranty! By opening the router, you will be passing beyond the point of no return.

First, you need to remove the two antennas from the rear of the router. You can do this by straightening the antennas, and sliding the plastic collar at the base of the antennas toward the tip. This will reveal the metal collar underneath, as shown in Figure 7.4, which you will use to manually unscrew the antennas.

Figure 7.4 Removing the WRT54G Antennas

Once you have removed the antennas, you can remove the light purple panel in the front from the rest of the casing. To remove the front panel, grip the side of the WRT54G on the gray portion, and pull on the front panel as demonstrated in Figure 7.5. Pull hard! Don't be afraid! It is not necessary to remove the foil warranty sticker, as it will be quickly rendered useless by a hard pull.

> ## WARNING
>
> Version 3 of the WRT54G does have a Phillips screw under each front leg that you need to remove before removing the front panel. They are located under the black rubber feet on the underside of the front panel.

Figure 7.5 Opening the WRT54G Front Panel

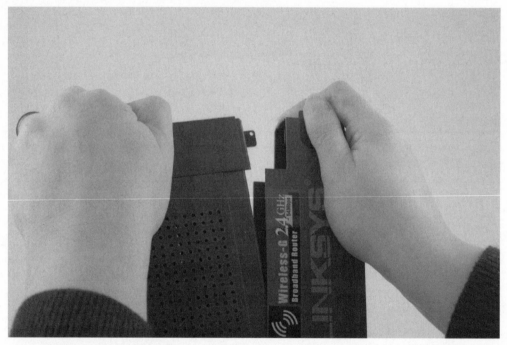

After you remove the front panel, separate the top of the remaining gray case from the bottom panel by sliding the top toward the rear of the router about one-quarter of an inch, and then lifting off the base. You will also need to remove the circuit board from the bottom of the case by removing the two Phillips screws located at the base of the Ethernet ports, as indicated in Figure 7.6.

Figure 7.6 WRT54G Circuit Board Screw Removal

> **NOTE**
>
> Depending on your WRT54G version, only one screw may be present instead of two. The examples here are based on the WRT54GL, version 1.1.

After you remove the screws, you should be able to separate the board from the base plate by sliding the circuit board to the front of the unit. You should now be left with just the circuit board of the router, as shown in Figure 7.7.

Figure 7.7 Circuit Board of the WRT54Gl, version 1.1

WRTSL54GS Series

Opening the WRTSL54GS is slightly different. First, you do not need to remove the antenna, as it is fixed to the unit. The WRTSL54GS is also screwed together with four Phillips screws located underneath the rubber feet, as shown in Figure 7.8.

Figure 7.8 WRTSL54GS Screw Removal

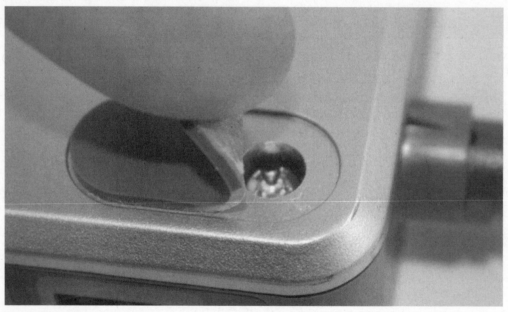

After you remove the four screws, the top and bottom halves of the case should separate, leaving the circuit board attached to the outer ring. The circuit board is held to the outer ring only by friction and by the label covering the Ethernet ports in the rear. It's easy to separate the circuit board from the ring, except for the attached, nonremovable antenna.

SD Card

Fortunately, the integrated processor offers a number of General Purpose Input/Output (GPIO) connectors that you can leverage to interface with a standard Secure Digital (SD) card. As a result, you can provide some additional storage to the WRT54G, in addition to the standard flash, usable as system disk.

Components Needed for This Hack

This hack requires a few additional components that are not provided standard with any WRT54G model. The additional components required are:

- Ribbon cable (or appropriate wire)
- An SD card
- An SD card connector (either a floppy drive edge connector, or a standard premade SD card connector)

You can order a premade SD card connector from an electronics supply house or, in the spirit of all good hardware hackers, remove one from an existing device. We opted to use one from an existing device that we were able to pick up at a local brick-and-mortar computer retailer in the discount bin for a few dollars. We will also show you how to use a floppy drive cable edge connector.

The standard tools that you will need for this project are the same for just about all hardware hacking projects: a soldering iron, rosin core solder, a #1 Phillips head screwdriver, a pair of wire cutters, a pair of wire strippers, and Dremel (or other rotary tool).

The Hack

For this hack, you need to connect the SD card reader to six points on the WRT54G board. In our example, we'll be performing this mod on a WRT54GL, version 1.1. This model is readily available as of this writing. These instructions will also work on the WRT54GL, version 1.0, and the WRT54G, version 4.0. Although many of the concepts are the same as with the other hardware versions not mentioned, there are some differences in GPIO locations on the other models.

NOTE

You can find the appropriate GPIO connections on the versions we do not mention in this chapter in the OpenWrt wiki, at http://wiki.openwrt.org/OpenWrtDocs/ Customizing/Hardware/MMC.

First, we need to note the pins on the SD card, as indicated in Figure 7.9.

Figure 7.9 SD Card Pin Out

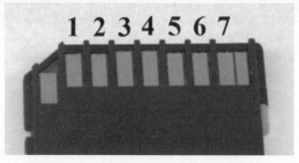

We need to attach some of these pins (via the SD card reader) to some specific points on the WRT54GL. Table 7.1 indicates which pins need to be connected to which points on the board, and Figure 7.10 displays this table in an approximate graphical representation.

Table 7.1 SD Card Pin to WRT54GL Board Assignments

SD Card Pin and Function	Connects to...
Pin 1, CS (Chip Select)	GPIO 7
Pin 2, DI (Data In)	GPIO 2 (With most other models, this will connect to GPIO 5.)
Pin 3, VSS (Negative Power)	Ground
Pin 4, VDD (Positive Power)	3.3V Power
Pin 5, CLK (Clock)	GPIO 3
Pin 6, VSS2 (Secondary Negative Power)	Ground
Pin 7, DO (Data Out)	GPIO 4

Figure 7.10 SD Card Pin to WRT54GL Board Approximations

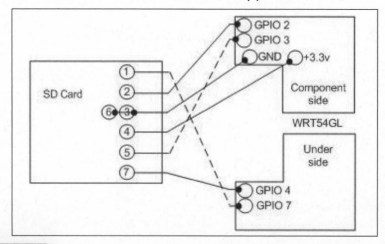

As you can see in Table 7.1, we will need a seven-stranded ribbon cable (an equal amount of 18ga to 28ga wire will work as well). We need to connect the appropriate pins on our SD card connector to each point on the board. First, we'll attach the ribbon cable to the SD card connector. Additionally, we've elected to keep our connector attached to the original board for some more stable mounting later on. It is possible that the rest of the components on the board will cause either the SD card or the WRT not to function. We were able to isolate the connector that we are attaching to by using a razor blade to cut all of the traces on the board around the connector.

We should note that we elected to identify pin 1 of the SD card connector with the red marked wire on the ribbon cable. It is important to make these distinctions to avoid mistakes when wiring your connections. When recycling a floppy drive cable for a ribbon cable, it is important to mark the cable for sanity's sake as well. A line drawn with permanent marker down the side of the ribbon cable works well.

With a floppy drive cable connector, the connection of the ribbon cable is a little bit simpler. Removing the back of the connector will reveal a series of metal teeth. The teeth are aligned in two rows, each corresponding to either side of the internal connector, as shown in Figure 7.11.

Figure 7.11 Teeth Corresponding to Floppy Connectors

We will need to pick a point on our floppy edge connector so that we can line up the pins on the card, and translate that to the teeth. We decided to use the key marker on the inside of the connector to line up with the unused pin 8 of the SD card, as shown in Figure 7.12.

Figure 7.12 Lining Up the SD Card to the Floppy Connector

connector key pin

Once we have the appropriate teeth on our floppy connector picked out on both planes, we can fan out the end of the ribbon cable just enough to line it up with the correct teeth. Be sure to put the marked wire in the ribbon where pin 1 should be. Insert the wire into the appropriate teeth, and place the back of the connector back over the teeth to hold the wire in place. When fully compressing the back of the connector, it is best to provide equal, even pressure over the length of the connector, especially where new wires are inserted in the teeth. A great way to accomplish this is to use a C-clamp between two pieces of wood, or a clamp with a large enough head to cover the length of the connector, as shown in Figure 7.13. Squeeze the back of the connector back on, using enough force to fully seat the cable into the teeth.

Figure 7.13 Using a Clamp to Squeeze the Floppy Connector

Now that we have our choice of SD card connector attached to our wire or ribbon cable, we need to attach the cable to the proper places on the board. As indicated earlier, we will be noting the proper locations for specific models.

We must attach pin 1 of the SD card via our ribbon cable to the WRT54GL board at the GPIO 7 location. We can find this location at the front of the board while looking at the LEDs. From the underside of the board, GPIO 7 is located on the left-hand pin of the DMZ LED. Solder pin 1 to the LED post, as shown on the right in Figure 7.14.

Figure 7.14 GPIO 7

We must connect pin 2 to GPIO 2, which we can find on the orange SecureEasySetup LED on the front edge of the board. When looking at the front of the board (at the LEDs), you can find GPIO 2 on the right-hand connection point of the white LED, as shown in Figure 7.15. Fortunately, Linksys has provided some test points on the board, and we can pass our wire through the top of the board and solder it on the underside.

Figure 7.15 GPIO 2

We should connect pins 3 and 6 to ground, and we'll complete both at the same time. It's easiest to locate ground on the serial port connection points, to the right of the front LEDs. Of the two sets of pads, the one we want is the one located to the rear of the board, and labeled JP2. You can find ground at locations 9 and 10 on JP2, as shown in Figure 7.16.

Figure 7.16 Ground Connections for Pins 3 and 6

Pin 4 of the SD card will require power to operate the card. We can find appropriate power of 3.3 volts on our serial pads as well. The 3.3 volt power can be found on pad 1, as shown in Figure 7.17.

Figure 7.17 3.3v Power Connector on Serial Pad

We should connect pin 5 of the SD card to GPIO 3 to provide an appropriate clock source. We can find GPIO 3 on the amber LED for SecureEasySetup on the front edge of the board. Again, Linksys has provided test points at the LED, and we can solder our GPIO 3 connection on the back side of the board to the right-hand side of the LED test point, as shown in Figure 7.18.

Figure 7.18 GPIO 3

The final connection that we need to make to finish the SD card mod is to attach pin 7 to GPIO 4. GPIO 4 is located on the SecureEasySetup switch itself, on the back of the board. While looking at the back of the board with the LEDs facing away from you, GPIO 4 is on the right-hand side of the switch connectors, toward the front edge of the board, as shown on the right in Figure 7.19. Solder directly to the pin that extends through the back of the board. Fortunately, there is a hole in the board to make passing the wire from the front side much easier.

Figure 7.19 GPIO 4

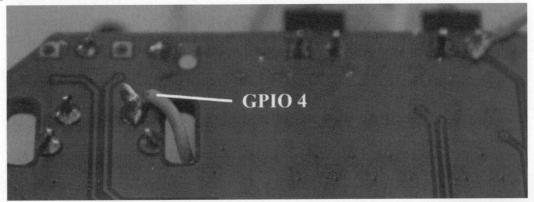

After completing our electrical connections, we need to securely mount our SD card reader to the case of the WRT54GL. First, we'll mount our real SD card connector to the top of the case. Find an appropriate point on the top of the case to lay the SD card reader flat, as shown in Figure 7.20, along the ridge molded into the top of the case.

Figure 7.20 SD Card Connector Mounting Placement

Mark the side edge of the case where the SD card will pass through to the outside so that you can swap SD cards without having to disassemble the WRT54G. We'll now utilize our Dremel (or other rotary tool) to make a hole in the side of the top portion of the case. A cutoff wheel is about the correct size for our SD card, and cleanup works well with a small, pointed sanding tip.

Perform a test fit of the SD card connector and verify that the SD card will clear the case and fit comfortably in the connector. Then apply a generous amount of hot glue to the top of the case in the mount location, and add additional hot glue around the edges for stability. This glue around the edges will provide some additional resistance for removing and inserting the SD card.

Once the glue has cooled and is providing a good bond, reassemble the case. Figure 7.21 displays the final result, which now provides ready access to the SD card.

If you used the floppy drive edge connector, you elected to externally mount the connecter so that each time you swap out the SD card, you can visually verify proper alignment. This is important, as the floppy drive edge connector does not have the appropriate keyed shape, and it is possible to insert the SD card upside down. In order to mount the floppy edge connector, you need to create a hole for the cable to pass through. Using your Dremel (or other rotary tool) with a small sanding bit, grind a shallow crescent, as shown in Figure 7.22, in the bottom plastic plate that the circuit board mounts to.

Figure 7.21 Final WRT54G SD Card External Connector

Test fit the size of the cable pass-through by placing the cable in the crescent that you just made, and reassemble the top to the base. You should have plenty of room, as shown in Figure 7.22.

Figure 7.22 Test Fit of Cable Pass-Through

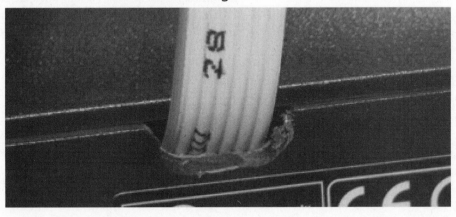

Once your test fit is successful, mount the floppy edge connector to the underside of the WRT54G with a generous amount of hot glue. The final result should look like Figure 7.23.

Figure 7.23 Final Mounting of Floppy Edge Connector

It is important to mount the floppy edge connector to the underside of the WRT54G in this case. If you were to mount it to the top of the unit, on the side near the cable pass-through, it would be very easy to damage the cable, or the crimp to the connector if you were to disassemble the unit again. By mounting the connector to the bottom plate, it remains in a fixed location when the top is removed. It is also important to note the proper alignment of the SD card when inserted. Although no damage will occur from a flip, a misalignment could cause damage to the SD card. It is wise to mount the floppy edge connector with the card inserted in order to note the proper insertion method for the SD card.

Using the SD Card under OpenWrt

Our new SD card reader won't be much use without some software to interface the hardware with the OpenWrt kernel. We need to provide a driver for the reader, and some support to read the contents.

First, you need to enable some file system support for the file allocation table (FAT). FAT file systems are typically associated with Windows systems, but we chose this file system format for inter-operability. A FAT file system can be read and/or written to under just about every modern operating system. In order to install FAT support under OpenWrt, you can use a package from the default OpenWrt package repository. In order to install the package, called kmod-vfat, to your OpenWrt installation, you need to make sure that you provide Internet connectivity to your WRT54G. Once connected, you need to update the ipkg repository, and then install the FAT kernel modules via an SSH connection. From the SSH command line, issue the following commands:

```
# ipkg update
# ipkg install kmod-vfat
```

After the installation of kmod-vfat is complete, you need to make sure that the modules are loaded, and that they reload after a reboot. As a benefit of installation through ipkg, the package installation will set the appropriate settings to make sure that FAT support is loaded at each boot. The best way to verify this is by performing a reboot, by issuing the *reboot* command.

After a reboot, you can verify that the *fat* and *vfat* modules have been loaded. You can check this by issuing the command *lsmod*. This command should give you output similar to the following (note that *fat* and *vfat* are listed under the Module column):

```
Module              Size   Used by    Tainted: P
vfat               11692   0 (unused)
fat                36840   0 [vfat]
wlcompat           14896   0 (unused)
wl                423640   0 (unused)
et                 32064   0 (unused)
diag                2560   0 (unused)
```

Now you can install the kernel module to interface with the SD card. Unfortunately, there is currently no ipkg for the driver, so you will need to install the MMC kernel module manually. First, download the kernel module to the appropriate place in the OpenWrt file system. Acquire the MMC module to your workstation, and unarchive the mmc.o file contained within using your favorite archive utility.

NOTE

In our example using the WRT54GL, we need to make sure that we download the appropriate MMC kernel module. On the WRT54GL, we utilize GPIO 2, whereas other models can utilize GPIO 5. GPIO 5 is subtly missing from the WRT54GL. You can download the GPIO 2 version of the MMC kernel module from www.frontiernet.net/~beakmyn/openwrt/mmc/mmc%20-%20gpio2.tar.

The different versions of the MMC kernel module are not interchangeable. The GPIO 5 version of the MMC kernel module is located at www.frontiernet.net/~beakmyn/openwrt/mmc%20-%20gpio5.tar.

Once the download and extraction are complete, we'll use SCP to copy the mmc.o kernel module to the appropriate location on the OpenWrt installation. The mmc.o file needs to end up in the /lib/modules/2.4.30 directory. You can do this with SCP using the following command:

```
# scp <full path to mmc.o>\mmc.o root@<WRT54GL_IP>\lib\modules\2.4.30\mmc.o
```

Now that you have the appropriate kernel module for your SD card copied in the device, you should load it and test that it works before you make it load after every reboot. You can accomplish this test by issuing *insmod mmc.o* from the /lib/modules/2.4.30 directory. This command should return:

```
using mmc.o
```

You can check the output of *dmesg* by issuing the *dmesg* command. The last few lines of output should look similar to the following:

```
mmc Hardware init
mmc Card init
mmc Card init *1*
mmc Card init *2*
Size = 1006080, hardsectsize = 512, sectors = 2012160
Partition check:
 mmca: p1
```

Notes from the Underground...

An All-in-One mmc.o Solution

Under OpenWrt Whiterussian, versions RC5 and later, the MMC driver is subtly broken because of the way that the newer versions of diag.o (the diagnostic driver) handle GPIO. Patches are available, as are precompiled MMC drivers that will work under RC5 and RC6.

These updated drivers still have the same issues concerning GPIO selection as GPIO 2 and 5. Nick DePetrillo has graciously provided us with an updated MMC driver that includes the patches for the diag.o issues, as well as the ability to select our GPIO settings on installation of the driver. So, instead of the commands listed earlier in this chapter, in our example we will perform an *insmod* of Nick's mmc.o for GPIO 2:

```
# insmod mmc.o gpio_sd_di_pin=2
```

We can also use the same driver for GPIO 5 as well with the appropriate module option:

```
insmod mmc.o gpio_sd_di_pin=5
```

If you intend to use Nick's updated MMC driver, you will also need to update /etc/modules.d/40-mmc to include the additions of the command-line options. In addition, Nick's updated MMC driver can reassign any one of the GPIO settings as long as your hardware supports it, and it reportedly supports SD cards greater than 2GB.

You can find the all-in-one MMC driver, with source code, at www.pauldotcom.com/wrt54g/all-in-one-mmc.tar.gz.

Upon installation of the MMC kernel module, the Cisco SecureEasySetup will be illuminated in amber. As noted earlier, you should have it auto-install after every reboot. You can accomplish this by creating a file named S20mmc under /etc/init.d. In the S20mmc file, you need to set up a GPIO mask, reference which driver to load, and mount the SD card. Edit the file using the vi editor so that S20mmc looks like this:

```
echo 9c > /proc/diag/gpiomask
insmod mmc
mkdir /mnt/mmc
mount /mnt/mmc
```

Save and close the file. The first line of the S20mmc file creates the /etc/diag/gpiomask file in order to alert the *diag* module not to monitor GPIO 1, 5, and 6. Because these GPIO lines are now used for the SD card, the *diag* module no longer needs to monitor them. Continuing to have the *diag* module monitor these GPIO lines will cause lockups and poor performance during access to the SD card. In cases where we utilize GPIO 2 instead of 5, we can replace the 9c with 7e to accurately reflect the appropriate values in hex.

Don't forget to make the script executable with:

```
# chmod 755 /etc/init.d/S20mmc
```

Now we can set the partition to automatically mount upon boot by creating a default mount point, and defining some default mount configuration. First, we need to use vi to edit /etc/fstab, and add the following line:

```
/dev/mmc/disc0/part1 /mnt/mmc vfat defaults 0 0
```

This will define a lookup table for OpenWrt so that the MMC file system can be mounted with considerable ease. Instead of typing the long, multipart command each time, /etc/fstab will allow us to shorten our command, by providing many of the configuration items beforehand.

A final reboot will verify that everything has worked properly. After the reboot, note that the SecureEasySetup amber LED does not stay lit, but does light momentarily during boot. It will become lit, and stay lit, upon the first read or write operation.

Now that the SD card is fully operational, you can use the extra storage just as you would for normal disk usage. You can also set up OpenWrt so that you can install packages to the SD card. In order to allow ipkg to use the SD card as a valid install location, you need to modify /etc/ipkg.conf to define a new destination. Using vi, add the following line to the end of ipkg.conf:

```
dest mmc /mnt/mmc
```

You also need to update some OpenWrt system variables so that any packages installed to the SD card will function properly, and the install locations will be added to the default path. You will need to modify /etc/profile to accomplish these two tasks.

First, you need to replace the existing *PATH* statement with the following, new *PATH* statement:

```
export PATH=$PATH:/mnt/mmc/bin:/mnt/mmc/sbin:/mnt/mmc/usr/bin:/mnt/mmc/usr/sbin
```

This will add the locations for binaries located on the SD card in typical binary locations to the default path.

Additionally, you need to make sure you update the *LD_LIBRARY* path to reflect the new possible locations for libraries installed by new packages on the SD card. Add the following line after the *PATH* declaration to /etc/profile:

```
export LD_LIBRARY_PATH=$LD_LIBRARY_PATH:/mnt/mmc/lib:/mnt/mmc/usr/lib
```

Because our profile is read only at login, the next time we log in to the WRT54GL via SSH it will reload our new profile. If we do not log in again, we will experience errors while installing packages, or running software from our SD card. We can also update the variables from our current session by reloading our profile with:

```
# ./etc/profile
```

In order to install or remove packages on the SD card, you need to specify a new switch to the ipkg command if you want the packages to end up there. For example, if we wanted to install tcpdump on our SD card, we would issue the following command:

```
# ipkg -d mmc install tcpdump
```

The *−d* switch is followed by our new shorthand location, as defined in /etc/ipkg.conf, to specify installation on our SD card.

Tools & Traps…

Why Doesn't My SD Card Package Work?

Many packages that you would want to install to the SD card come with their own, preconfigured configuration files that reference what would be a normal installation. Given that we've elected to install a package in a nondefault location, the software's own configuration files may need to be updated. For example, Asterisk contains its own configuration file that would reference specific locations for a default install, as shown here:

```
[directories]
astetcdir => /etc/asterisk
astmoddir => /usr/lib/asterisk/modules
```

Continued

```
astvarlibdir => /usr/lib/asterisk

astagidir => /usr/lib/asterisk/agi-bin

astspooldir => /var/spool/asterisk

astrundir => /var/run

astlogdir => /var/log/asterisk
```

If we have installed Asterisk to our SD card, clearly these files as referenced in asterisk.conf do not exist! We would have to update asterisk.conf to point to the file locations on our SD card instead:

```
[directories]

astetcdir => /mnt/mmc/etc/asterisk

astmoddir => /mnt/mmc/usr/lib/asterisk/modules

astvarlibdir => /mnt/mmc/usr/lib/asterisk

astagidir => /mnt/mmc/usr/lib/asterisk/agi-bin

astspooldir => /mnt/mmc/var/spool/asterisk

astrundir => /mnt/mmc/var/run

astlogdir => /mnt/mmc/var/log/asterisk
```

Some ipkg installations will also complete, but return errors, due to their inability to create symbolic links. You should be able to re-create these links, not with symbolic links but by copying the appropriate files (typically modules) from the MMC card to the main file system.

Additionally, the SD card is definitely intended to act as removable media. If you have configured specific software to start from, or write to, the SD card, operating or booting the WRT54GL without the card inserted can and will produce undesirable results.

Serial

Another very helpful modification to our WRT54G is the addition of one or more serial ports, which can be useful for attaching a GPS, as shown in Chapter 4. Most models do have the connectors for the serial ports contained on the circuit board. In our example, we will be demonstrating on a WRT54GL, version 1.1, as it is readily available and possesses the capability for serial ports

Components Needed for This Hack

This hack requires a few additional components that are not provided standard with any WRT54G model. The additional components required are:

- A 10-pin set of header pins in a 2-by-5 layout
- A 10-pin ribbon cable connector
- Ribbon cable or other appropriate wire

- The Compsys Workbench AD233BK serial kit, or other appropriate MAX232 implementation

- A 9-pin male serial connector

The Hack

NOTE

Very few WRT54G models do not have capabilities for adding a serial port to the circuit board. Particularly, the WRT54G, versions 1.0 and 1.1, do not contain the appropriate circuitry. You cannot add serial ports to these models.

The serial ports are populated in the form of a number of solder points on the board, aligned in two rows of five points. In most cases (as in our WRT54GL), the points are labeled JP2, as shown in Figure 7.24.

Figure 7.24 Unpopulated WRT54G Serial Ports at JP2

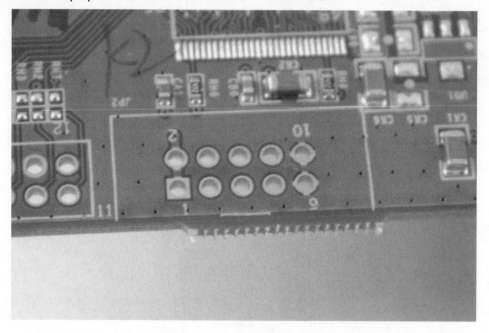

The easiest and best way for to begin to take advantage of our serial ports is to install a pin header in the appropriate location on the board, and use a connector attached to a ribbon cable to interface with it. Installing the pin header will enable us to detach our serial connector so that we can replace it if it breaks, or more easily disassemble the case at a later date.

NOTE

The pin header and pin connectors should be available from most well-stocked electronics supply houses. We obtained many of our parts from www.digi-key.com and from a local Radio Shack retail store. We'll provide a list of part numbers and suppliers where we obtained our parts in Appendix B.

After obtaining an appropriate pin header and connectors, you will need to place the pin header in the JP2 location and solder it to the board. If solder is already bonded to the connection locations, you will need to remove it with a solder sucker or soldering braid before inserting the pin header. Once you insert the pin header on the top side of the board, solder it from the underside of the board.

TIP

In many cases, once installed, the pin header will obscure the markings on the board that indicate the pin numbering at the JP2 location. As it will be important to us to be mindful of the pin numbering, it is helpful to make additional, visible markings designating one or more pins.

The JP2 header does contain the capability for two serial ports, each with different default capabilities under OpenWrt (or many other firmware distributions). The first serial port pin out, as shown in Table 7.2, is recognized as /dev/tts/0 under OpenWrt. This port is bound to a terminal session, and by connecting this to a serial terminal at 115200 baud N 8 1 (no parity, 8 data bits, 1 stop bit), we can gain command-line console access simply by pressing Enter. It should also be noted that neither serial port has hardware flow control enabled, and software flow control should be used.

The second serial port available on the JP2 header is available on the pin out, as indicated in Table 7.2. This serial port is usable at the same time as the first port; however, this port is not bound to a terminal session by default. This port is especially useful for connecting serial devices that do not require a terminal session, and will be the one we will utilize in this example in order to leave /dev/tts/0 available if we do require a serial terminal session.

Table 7.2 WRT54G JP2 Serial Port Pin Out

WRT54G JP2 Pin	Function
1	3.3 volts
2	3.3 volts
3	Tx (/dev/tts/1)
4	Tx (/dev/tts/0)

Continued

Table 7.2 continued WRT54G JP2 Serial Port Pin Out

WRT54G JP2 Pin	Function
5	Rx (/dev/tts/1)
6	Rx (/dev/tts/0)
7	Unused
8	Unused
9	Ground
10	Ground

Tools & Traps…

/dev/tts/0 Hangs My Serial Device!

Although it is possible to use /dev/tts/0 for any serial device, some devices may lock up due to unexpected data being sent to the device. Under OpenWrt, /dev/tts/0 is bound to a terminal session by default. As a result of the binding, all boot messages (such as those provided by any normal Linux system boot) are redirected to this serial port. Devices attached to this port at boot with the default binding enabled will receive the boot output, and some devices do not know how to interpret this data, causing them to lock up or become inoperable.

There are two options for dealing with these problems. First, you can attach the serial device after boot. However, although this is the simplest answer, it may not always be the most practical. Your WRT54G and serial device may be placed in an area that is not readily accessible. If power is lost to a WRT54G in this location, it may be difficult, or impractical, to detach the serial device, reboot the WRT54G, and reattach the serial device after the boot process has completed.

Alternatively, you can remove the default terminal binding from /dev/tts/0. This is a great solution, especially if you need to use both serial ports for devices, and both devices cannot appropriately handle the terminal output on boot. Although disabling the terminal session may solve your device problem, however, it is possible that it can cause an issue should you ever need a serial terminal session, as it will no longer be available. A serial terminal can be very useful in reviving a bricked router, so be aware of the benefits.

If you want to remove the terminal session binding, you can do so by editing /etc/inittab and commenting out the tts/0 line with a #, as shown here

```
#tts/0::askfirst:/bin/ash --login
```

In order to utilize the serial port on the WRT54G board, we need to provide some additional circuitry which will perform conversion from the default 3.3 volt (as delivered by the WRT54G) to a more standard 5 volt connection.

> ## ! WARNING
>
> Standard PC serial ports operate at 5 or 12 volts, whereas the serial ports on the WRT54G operate at 3.3 volts. Attaching a PC serial port directly to the WRT54G will seriously damage your router, possibly rendering it completely inoperable. As we have already passed beyond the point of any warranty service, you will just have created an expensive, yet geekily attractive, paperweight or doorstop.

One great way for to implement the appropriate hardware for our serial connection is to utilize the MAX232 chipset in a Transistor-Transistor Logic (TTL) to serial converter circuit. Compsys Workbench offers the MAX232 chipset in a TTL to serial kit with all the necessary components; perfect for our WRT54G. Compsys Workbench offers the AD233BK CTS/RTS kit as a do-it-yourself project. The fully assembled kit, as shown in Figure 7.25, is available for about $20, and is what we will be using in our example.

Figure 7.25 The Compsys Workbench AD233BK Serial Kit

Follow the instructions from Compsys Workbench for appropriate assembly of the AD233BK. We will need to make some slight modifications if we want to implement both serial ports with our single AD233BK. For instance, we need to cut two traces on the top side of the circuit board using a razorblade. The first is between the left-hand pin of J1 and pin 7 of the DB9 pads, and the second is between the right-hand pin of J2 and pin 8 of the DB9 pads. Do not install the four-pin header at J1 and J2, but reuse one of the attached jumpers and place it on J3.

> **NOTE**
>
> It is possible to build your own circuit from scratch, or by cannibalizing some common cell phone to serial port cables (often found in the discount bin at your local consumer electronics or office supply store for only a few dollars). You can find schematics for building your own TTL to serial converter at www.nslu2-linux.org/wiki/HowTo/AddASerialPort.

In order to connect our TTL to serial converter, we need to note the proper attachments from the pins on our converter to the pin header on the WRT54G board. Both serial ports will be attached to the AD233BK, and we can break each serial port out from the AD233BK as needed. Attach the AD233BK to the ribbon cable with the connector, as shown in Table 7.3 and depicted in a graphical representation in Figure 7.26.

Table 7.3 AD233BK to WRT54G Serial Port Pin Assignments

AD233BK Input Pins	WRT54G JP2 Pins
Rt	3
Tx	4
Ct	6
Rx	5
- (GND)	9 and 10
+5V	1 and 2
Unconnected	7 and 8

Figure 7.26 AD233BK to WRT54G Serial Port Connections

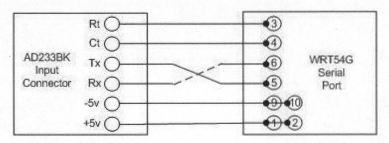

TIP

It is possible to utilize a single AD233BK kit for both serial ports at the same time, and we have modified the AD233BK appropriately. We will be completing the installation only for /dev/tts/1; however, we can complete /dev/tts/0 at any time. You can find the instructions for adding /dev/tts/0 at Rod Whitby's Web site, www.rwhitby.net/projects/wrt54gs. We elected to implement only the /dev/tts/1 option, as it is most easily used with a serial device, whereas the/dev/tts/0 device is typically reserved for a serial console connection.

When attaching the converter to the WRT54G board, you'll need to make sure that you pick an appropriate length of ribbon cable so that you can mount the serial connector on the outside of the case. You will need to pick an appropriate mounting location as well. Your mounting location should be such that the TTL to serial converter will not interfere with any of the other electronics, in order to prevent any shorts circuits.

One particularly good place to mount the serial port is in the front panel, on the right-hand side. Due to the L-shaped nature of the system board, this location will not interfere with any other electronics.

In other models, especially those that have full-size system boards, this front location may not be acceptable in the configuration that we have presented. With the WRT54GL model, we attached the serial pin header to the converter circuit board by utilizing some additional ribbon cable or some appropriately sized wire. When adding a second serial port, there may be enough room to mount them side by side, or you could use the center top of the casing.

Installation of the serial connector is the same for either mounting location; the steps are the same, just the location is different. For the first step, outline the outside connecting shield of the serial port connector on the outside of the casing. If your serial connector has screw terminal standoffs, mark the appropriate locations for the mounting holes as well. After marking your location, use your rotary tool with a small grinding bit cut out of the hole. You can clean it up with some medium-grade sandpaper and a small rounded file.

In order to create the optional holes for the screw standoffs, you can use an appropriately sized drill bit in your rotary tool. A small pointed grinding stone can also be used, but will deliver less-precise results. Figure 7.27 shows our final product.

Figure 7.27 Final WRT54G Serial Port Cutout with Optional Standoff Holes

Mounting the serial port connector will depend on your inclusion of the standoff screws. If you use the standoff screws, you will use them to mount the connector to the case. Insert the connector from the inside, and fasten it using the standoff screws and nuts. If you do not possess the standoff screws, you can glue the connector to the inside of the case. Using an epoxy will provide a much stronger bond for your connector, but using hot glue will allow you to remove the connector with an X-Acto knife should something go terribly wrong. Once you've mounted the serial port connector, you should have a result similar to that shown in Figure 7.28.

Figure 7.28 WRT54G Serial Port Installation Results

Using the Serial Port under OpenWrt

In order to utilize our serial ports for a device under OpenWrt, we need to make sure we have installed the serial package. Again, due to the fantastic package management under OpenWrt, we can issue the following commands in an SSH session on our Internet-connected device to install the serial package:

```
# ipkg update
# ipkg install setserial
```

By default, the serial ports are enabled at 115200 baud, N 8 1. Many serial devices that we want to install will not support this high speed. We can adjust this by installing the stty utility using the following commands, which will download the stty package, extract it, and place it in an appropriate location:

```
# cd /usr/sbin
# wget http://tobe.mine.nu/software/openwrt/stty.tgz
# tar -zxvf stty.tgz
# chmod 755 stty
```

In order to use a device on /dev/tts/1, we need to assign an interrupt request line (IRQ) to this serial port. We do not need to perform this on /dev/tts/0, as it has already been done in order to enable terminal output. We can accomplish this by executing:

```
# setserial /dev/tts/1 irq 3
```

Now we can successfully set the speed of /dev/tts/1 to 4,800 baud using the stty command *stty -F /dev/tts/1 raw speed 4800*, and we can perform the same task for /dev/tts/0 if we want with *stty -F /dev/tts/0 raw speed 4800*.

At this state, these setting are not permanent, as they will not survive a reboot. In order to have them take effect on every boot, we need to create the /etc/init.d/S91serial file using vi. The contents of S91serial should be as follows:

```
/usr/sbin/setserial /dev/tts/1 irq 3
/usr/sbin/stty -F /dev/tts/0 raw speed 4800
/usr/sbin/stty -F /dev/tts/1 raw speed 4800
```

After saving the file, we need to make sure it is executable at boot with

```
# chmod 755 /etc/init.d/S91serial
```

JTAG

Another useful port to install in a WRT54G is the JTAG port. The JTAG port will provide us direct access to the basic input/output system (BIOS) of the WRT54G. This connection will be extremely helpful in reviving a bricked WRT54G, a process that we will describe in Chapter 8. The JTAG port will typically be used only for troubleshooting and recovery purposes, so it may not be needed in every installation. The JTAG port is the safest method to recover from a bad flash, or to revive a bricked router, so in some cases, we may not have a choice.

Components Needed for This Hack

This hack requires a few additional components that are not provided standard with any WRT54G model. The additional components required are:

- A 10-pin set of header pins in a 2-by-5 layout
- A 10-pin ribbon cable connector
- Ribbon cable or other appropriate wire
- Four 100 Ohm resistors
- A 25-pin male parallel port connector, with hood

The Hack

You can find the JTAG connector in the form of a number of solder points on the board, aligned in two rows of six points. In our WRT54GL, version 1.1, the points are labeled JP1, as shown in Figure 7.29. With all WRT54G models, this will be the only 2-by-6 set of connection pads on the board.

Figure 7.29 Unpopulated WRT54G JTAG Port at JP1

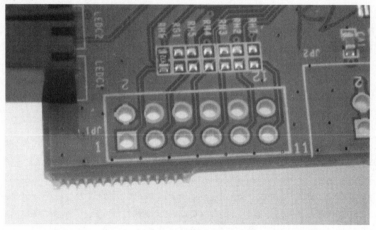

The easiest and best way to begin to take advantage of our JTAG interface is to install a pin header in the appropriate location on the board, and use a connector attached to a ribbon cable to interface with it. With the installation of the pin header, we will be able to attach our custom JTAG cable (shown later in this section) at will without a permanent and messy installation.

> **NOTE**
>
> The pin header and pin connectors should be available from most well-stocked electronics supply houses. We obtained many of our parts from www.digi-key.com and

from a local Radio Shack retail store. We'll provide a list of part numbers and suppliers where we obtained our parts in Appendix B.

After obtaining an appropriate pin header and connectors, place the pin header in the JP1 location and solder it to the board. If solder is already bonded to the connection locations, remove the solder with a solder sucker or soldering braid before inserting the pin header. Once you insert the pin header on the top side of the board, solder it from the underside of the board. Shown in Figure 7.30 is a completed set of pin headers for both JTAG and serial.

Figure 7.30 WRT54GL, version 1.1, JTAG and Serial Pin Headers

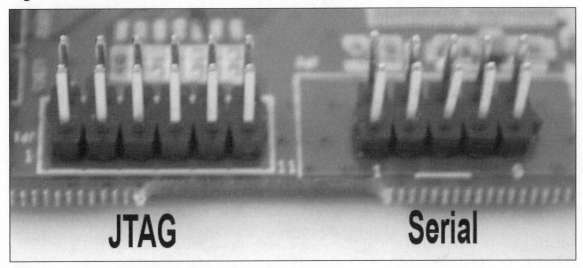

 Tip

In many cases, once installed, the pin header will obscure the markings on the board that indicate the pin numbering at the JP1 location. As it will be important to us to be mindful of the pin numbering, it is helpful to make additional, visible markings designating one or more pins.

Constructing a JTAG Cable

In order to interface with the JTAG port on the WRT54G, we need to construct a custom cable that will attach to a parallel port on a PC. There are two types of cables: buffered and unbuffered. Due to ease of construction and low cost, we'll be describing the unbuffered type of cable. This type of cable is based on the Xilinx DLC5 Cable III unbuffered JTAG cable, and costs about $5 in parts to construct.

NOTE

The buffered cable requires a few more parts and is a little more difficult to construct, but it is still within the abilities of an amateur. The parts for a buffered cable will cost around $25. For the schematics, see the OpenWrt wiki JTAG cable entry at http://wiki.openwrt.org/OpenWrtDocs/Customizing/Hardware/JTAG_Cable.

In order to construct our cable, we will need to obtain a 2-by-6 pin connector, a length of 12-element ribbon cable (or some recycled from a floppy or IDE cable), four 100 Ohm resistors, and a 25-pin male parallel port connector (see Figure 7.31).

Figure 7.31 JTAG Construction Parts

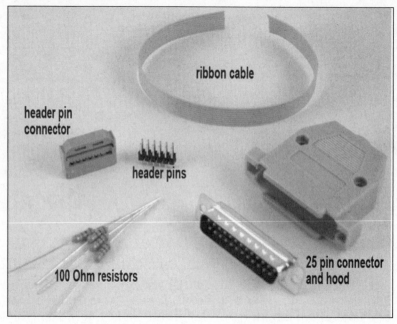

To begin construction, note the pin outs and required cross-connections for the parallel connector to the JTAG pin connector, as shown in Table 7.4.

Table 7.4 Parallel Port to JTAG Assignments

JTAG Pin	Parallel Port Pin(s)	100 Ohm Resistor Inline?
3	2	Yes
5	13	Yes
7	4	Yes
9	3	Yes
2, 4, 6, 8, 10, and 12	18, 19, 20, 21, 22, 23, 24, and 25	No

Begin by inserting the ribbon cable into the pin connector, noting the keyed cable marking (typically in red), as you can use it to keep track of pin 1. Next, trim the length of the resistors on one end so that they will fit snugly into the solder connection of the parallel port connector, and solder them to the appropriate pins. Also, create a bridge from parallel port pins 18 through 25 utilizing a trimmed off piece from the resistors. Lay the leftover resistor across the length of pins and solder the bridge to all of the pins. Figure 7.32 shows the results of our resistor and bridge installation.

Figure 7.32 Parallel Port Resistor and Jumper Installation

! **WARNING**

The Wiggler type of unbuffered cable is susceptible to electrical noise and interference. In order to reduce these problems, limit the length of the ribbon cable to the shortest practical length. A cable length of about 6 inches works well to connect to the WRT54G.

You can now solder the correct wires of the free end of the ribbon cable to the free end of the resistors and jumper, noting the pin outs in Table 7.4. You can then trim the extraneous wires on the ribbon cable and resistors, and install the connector into a housing. In Figure 7.33, you can see the result of our construction before the housing was closed.

Figure 7.33 The Final JTAG Cable

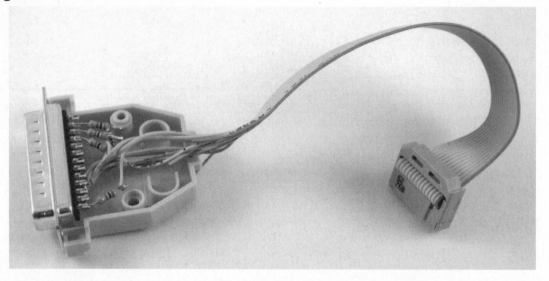

Tools & Traps

Testing Pin Connector Connections

It is extremely important to make sure that the pin connectors are wired properly in order to prevent damage to your router. One common way to so this is to verify electrical continuity from the end of the attached ribbon cable to the connector of the pin connector with a multimeter. Clearly, by examining the pin connector, you can see that most multimeter probes will not fit inside the connector.

In order to resolve this problem, you can utilize an additional, unused pin header inserted into the pin connector. This will extend the electrical connection outside of the connector where you can accurately test it with a probe. If a spare pin header is not available, you could utilize one already attached to the board by measuring the external point on the reverse of the circuit board. In a pinch, a paper clip or the left-over wire from a trimmed resistor can be inserted into the pin connector and used for measurement.

Continued

It may also be helpful during the test process to mark the underside of the pin connector where the pins are inserted to indicate pin 1. This will make measuring the remaining connectors much less error-prone.

We will cover testing and use of the JTAG cable for system backup and recovery in depth in Chapter 8.

Powering Your WRT54G with Alternative Sources

Powering a WRT54G with an alternative power source can have several advantages. You can carry your device in a backpack for covert testing, perform untethered wireless distance testing, or even use the device where wall power is not readily available. The possibilities are endless!

In terms of consumer use, the WRT54G is intended to be installed with a hardwired power connection delivered through the included "wall wart" power adapter. The included power adapter operates at 12 volts DC at 1 amp. Because these are relatively modest power requirements, you can power the WRT54G with a battery, which also produces DC power.

Components Needed for This Hack

This hack requires a few additional components that are provided standard with any WRT54G model. Not all of the parts listed are required for each hack, but rather are specific to the method selected. The additional components required are:

- Appropriately sized wire
- N–type power connector
- Batteries (dependent upon method)
- Battery holder that holds eight AA batteries
- 9 volt battery connector
- USB connector or USB cable
- FireWire connector or FireWire cable
- Solar panel (optional)
- Automotive 12 volt to USB power converter
- CAT 5 solid core network cable
- CAT 5 jacks
- CAT 5 jack housings
- N–type power receptacle

The Hack

The power connector provided with the power adapter is a standard N-type power connector which is readily obtained from most electronics supply houses. You can also source a connector from a broken or other unused power adapter, possibly from a completely different application. In the case of a cannibalized power connector to be reused, the power output of the sacrificial power adapter will not be important; we are only after the connector. The power connector is wired for a specific polarity for application with a WRT54G. As shown in Figure 7.34, the positive power lead is attached to the tip, or center connector, whereas the negative lead is connected to the ring, or outside connector. For testing all of the methods described in this book, we built a single N-type connector with a short length of cable and some quick disconnect connectors so that we can swap power methods at will without the need for individual cables.

Figure 7.34 N-type Connector Polarity for the WRT54G

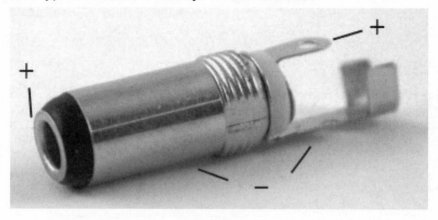

Upon entering the WRT54G, the incoming power source is immediately split into two different power regulation chips, as shown in Figure 7.35. These power regulation chips deliver reduced voltage requirements to all of the components to the board. The Anachip 1509-33 chip delivers 3.3 volts DC at 2 amps as an output, and the Anachip 1509-50 chip delivers 5 volts DC at 2 amps. The power regulation chips are being driven by 12 volts at 1 amp from the default power adapter and are delivering the appropriate output voltage. According to the chip manufacturer, the chips will deliver the required voltage and amperage when driven with up to 22 volts DC and up to 2 amps, with a minimum requirement of the lowest output voltage. This means that at the absolute minimum, we need to power the WRT54G before conversion with 5 volts. During testing in preparation for this book, we determined that a WRT54G under moderate load and with wireless set to the default power draws only about 30 milliamps!

Figure 7.35 WRT54G Power Regulation Chips

Now that we know what our minimum power requirements are, we can begin to determine what other power sources we can use. We'll want to use power sources that can deliver 5 volts DC with appropriate amperage.

Alkaline Batteries

The first obvious choice for power is some readily available alkaline batteries. Most alkaline batteries output 1.5 volts, so whether we pick AAA, AA, C, or D cells, we will need to use a minimum of four batteries (for a total of 6 volts). In our alkaline battery example, we have elected to utilize eight AA batteries, as this will effectively double the length of operation time over the four-battery solution. In the eight AA battery configuration, we can expect to power a WRT54G with wireless enabled at the default power level for about four hours. The battery holder shown in Figure 7.36 was readily available from our local Radio Shack, which also featured a 9 volt battery style of connector.

Figure 7.36 AA Battery Pack and 9 Volt Adapter

The 9 volt style connector is very convenient for our battery pack construction. Also at our local Radio Shack, we were able to obtain 9 volt battery connectors and some N-type jacks. By soldering an N-type jack directly to the leads from the 9 volt battery connector, we created an adapter from our battery pack to the WRT54G, as shown in Figure 7.36. Not only can we use this with our eight AA battery pack, but also we now have a quick swap-out method for another battery pack, or even a 9 volt battery. Our adapter can now utilize any battery or battery pack with the 9 volt style of connector.

Rechargeable Lithium-ion Battery Pack

Lithium-ion battery technology offers a significant upgrade over traditional alkaline batteries. First, the power output from a lithium-ion cell is rated higher per size as compared to traditional alkaline technology and can provide longer output. Second, lithium-ion batteries are rechargeable!

The rechargeable nature of lithium-ion batteries makes them a bit more practical from a cost perspective. When alkaline batteries are discharged, they must be disposed of and replaced with a new set. Rechargeable batteries, however, can be refreshed. Granted, lithium-ion batteries have a higher cost of entry (our example battery and charger, shown in Figure 7.37, cost about $40 combined), but they will easily outlive several hundred (if not a thousand) dollars' worth of alkaline batteries.

Figure 7.37 Lithium-ion Battery and Charger

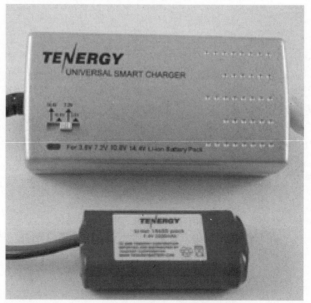

Our example, as shown in Figure 7.37, will output 7.4 volts at the desired amperage for our WRT54G. Obviously, 7.4 volts is greater than the 5 volts required to power the router, but it should power the WRT54G under moderate use for about 72 hours! It may not be obvious, but our example lithium-ion battery is just about one-quarter the size of the eight AA alkaline pack. With that performance improvement, we could implement four identical lithium-ion batteries in a series, and deliver about 288 hours in a form factor that is about the same. That is a huge improvement over alkaline batteries.

Lithium-ion technology is not without its dangers. It is important to note that when purchasing lithium-ion batteries, you should ensure that they contain a built-in protection circuit. If this circuit is not included, it is a very real possibility that while the battery is recharging, it will explode in a dramatic fashion, quite possibly causing a fire.

12 Volt Lead Acid Battery

A lead acid battery will function quite well in terms of powering our WRT54G. Delivering 12 volts at the appropriate amperage, lead acid batteries will provide more than adequate power. Appropriate recharging is also available for lead acid batteries.

Quite clearly, these batteries will not fit comfortably into our pants pockets, however! Most of these batteries can be sourced from motorcycles and riding lawn mowers. Even for those of us who are more technically inclined, a great source of 12 volt lead acid batteries is UPS units. The battery shown in Figure 7.38 was salvaged from a broken UPS unit.

Figure 7.38 Small Lead Acid Battery and Solar Panel

This repurposed UPS battery can power a WRT54G using the default wireless power setting for about 24 days (roughly 573 hours). Combined with an appropriate charger, possibly recycled from a UPS unit, an emergency lighting unit, or via solar power, a WRT54G could be powered almost indefinitely. Couple that with a waterproof enclosure and an appropriate antenna, and it would be a perfect setup for a remote wireless bridge.

Battery Comparison

Clearly from the preceding examples, we should expect to see some different usage times from different types of batteries. Our testing in preparation for this book revealed the capacities shown in Table 7.5.

Table 7.5 Battery Usage Times

Battery Operation	Approximate Rating	Approximate Length of
AA alkaline (quantity 8)	2.2mAh (each)	4 hours
9v alkaline	5mAh	2 hours
Li-ion	2,200mAh	72 hours
Lead acid	17.2Ah	573 hours

USB

The Universal Serial Bus (USB) found in most modern PCs and laptops provides the capability to deliver 5 volts of power per powered hub, at a maximum of 500 milliamps. This is an appropriate amount for powering a WRT54G, as the power regulation chips will upscale the power to the appropriate levels to operate the router.

> **NOTE**
>
> Not all USBs are created equal. Although there are some specific standards, many implementations do not follow them to the letter. There are also some different interpretations on the implementation specifications, depending on manufacturer. For more information on the caveats on USB power, read the USB power section of Wikipedia: http://en.wikipedia.org/wiki/Usb#Power_supply.

We can derive power from the USB by using an appropriate USB connector and matching the appropriate polarity to the N-type connector. Figure 7.39 shows the USB standard A type pin out. We built our cable from an unused USB cable we had on hand, and we removed one end with a pair of wire cutters and stripped the outer shielding back to reveal the internal cabling. As an alternative, unassembled USB connectors are readily available from most electronics suppliers, such as Digi-key.

Figure 7.39 USB Pin Out

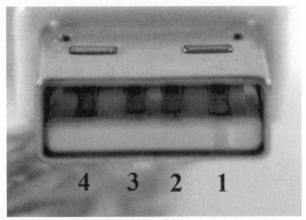

From our pin out, we can see that power is delivered via pins 1 and 4. Pin 1 delivers +5v and pin 4 delivers ground in order to complete the circuit.

It should be noted that when a WRT54G is powered with mobile technology such as a laptop, if the portable device is not actively attached to a charger, the powering of a WRT54G via USB will drastically affect the battery life of the portable device. Additionally, the USB has a maximum delivery of 500 milliamps to the entire bus, which can adversely affect any other devices that require power and may prevent either the WRT54G or the other device from operating properly. Despite these challenges, a USB-powered WRT54G can be very useful when attaching to a laptop from a mobility perspective.

FireWire 400

The FireWire 400 port found in many modern PCs and laptops provides the capability to deliver up to 30 volts at more than appropriate amperage to power a WRT54G.

NOTE

Although FireWire 800 can deliver the same power requirements, we will cover only the more common FireWire 400 type connections.

You can derive power from a FireWire port by using an appropriate FireWire connector and matching the appropriate polarity to the N-type connector. Figure 7.40 shows the standard 6-pin FireWire type pin out. We built our cable from a broken cable we had on hand, by completely disassembling the 6-pin connector. It should be noted that 6-pin to 4-pin cables do not utilize power at the 4-pin end (as determined by the specifications), and many cable manufacturers do not provide the appropriate cabling at the 6-pin end. As an alternative, unassembled FireWire connectors are readily available from most electronics suppliers, such as Digi-key.

Figure 7.40 FireWire 400 Pin Out

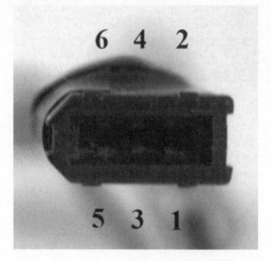

> **WARNING**
>
> It is strongly advised that any FireWire cables utilized for power be thoroughly tested for short circuits before use. It is possible to seriously damage any PC or laptop if a short exists. This could seriously damage the system beyond repair.

From our pin out, we can see that power is delivered via pins 1 and 2. Pin 1 delivers up to +30v and pin 2 delivers ground in order to complete the circuit.

It should be noted that when a WRT54G is powered with mobile technology such as a laptop, if the portable device is not actively attached to a charger, the powering of a WRT54G via FireWire will drastically affect the battery life of the portable device. Many portable devices also do not feature 6-pin FireWire connectors, with the exception of the new Intel-based Mac laptops. In these cases, where these ports are not available, USB may be a reasonable alternative.

Automotive Power

Automotive power is typically derived from technology identical to that of lead acid battery power, usually delivering 12 volts DC at more than adequate amperage. There are, however, some additional challenges with utilizing power from an automobile electrical system.

The first challenge is ground interference caused by engine operation. This symptom often is indicated by a quiet whine while operating a radio. This whine will rise in pitch as the engine revs. Ground interference can be eliminated with some additional, often expensive, electronics. The second challenge is some significant voltage fluctuation during operation. While starting the vehicle, the voltage can drop as low as 8 volts, and while the vehicle is running the output typically is around 13.5 volts.

> ! **WARNING**
>
> Attaching a WRT54G directly to your automotive electrical system without voltage regulation or isolation can render your router inoperable, and potentially damage it beyond repair.

In order to overcome these challenges, we could build our own circuit to perform voltage stabilization and regulation. In true hacker fashion, we could also use technology in a manner for which it was not intended! In our example, we will utilize the knowledge learned from our USB power section to power our WRT54G connection.

Many devices are powered via USB, and now there are plenty of cigarette lighter adapters that provide a USB power port. These USB power adapters, for whichever device they were intended, must also overcome the same power issues that we must. In our example, we were able to obtain a cigarette lighter to USB power converter from an automotive kit to provide simultaneous power and sync capability to an older Palm organizer, shown in Figure 7.41, for just less than $10. We could not assemble the circuitry and adapters at the same cost.

Figure 7.41 Automotive USB Power Converter

Contained within our automotive power converter is the appropriate circuitry to maintain a constant 5 volts DC at USB amperages (100 to 500 milliamps). By using the adapter and our USB cable modification, we can safely provide appropriate voltage to the WRT54G as well as isolate the router from the automotive electrical system.

Homebrew Power over Ethernet (PoE)

Power over Ethernet (PoE) is a technology that can deliver power over standard Ethernet cables by utilizing the unused pairs in the Ethernet cable. We refer to this as a homebrew PoE configuration, as it will not conform to the IEEE 802.3af standard. The 802.3af standard requires some significant power output, complex signaling, and some serious software implementation. In our nonstandard implementation, we will be injecting power directly into the unused Ethernet pairs.

In most standard 10-baseT and 100-baseT Ethernet networks, the white-blue/blue pairs (pins 4 and 5) and white-brown/brown pairs (pins 7 and 8) are unused. With this knowledge, we can use these pairs to transmit power utilizing these unused pairs. We'll be constructing a pair of adapters using readily available components, including consumer category 5 (CAT 5) jacks and mounting supplies, CAT 5 cable, and N-type power connectors.

At the power injection end (where we plug in our standard Linksys power adapter), we will need three ports, as shown in Figure 7.42. One port will be a male, N-type connector to receive power. The remaining two will be for network connections; incoming from our switch, and the output to our WRT54G over a length of CAT 5 cable. In Table 7.6, we indicate the three ports for the power injection adapter, and the connection matrix.

Table 7.6 Power over Ethernet Injector Wiring Table

Output to WRT54G (Ethernet)	Input from Network (Ethernet)	Power Input (N-Type Male)
1	1	
2	2	
3	3	
4	Unused	+12
5	Unused	+12
6	6	
7	Unused	- Ground
8	Unused	- Ground

It is important to note that pins 4, 5, 7, and 8 are not connected on our network end. We do not want to inject power back to our switch by accident, so the best way to ensure that is to not connect them. Also, we will utilize both wires in the pair to connect to our power source. If we need to provide larger voltages, we will have effectively provided a larger diameter of wire.

Figure 7.42 Internals of a Power Injection Adapter

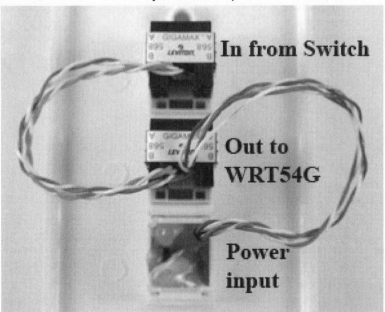

> **NOTE**
>
> The length of the CAT 5 cable between the power injector and power retrieval adapter can affect the voltage delivered to the WRT54G on the far end. We may need to provide increased power by utilizing a third-party power adapter. You can find a great calculator for determining the voltage required at www.gweep.net/~sfoskett/tech/poecalc.html. When performing your calculations, every 100 feet of CAT 5 cable between the injector and retrieval adapters will introduce about 3 ohms of resistance.

At the power retrieval end, we need to provide three ports as well. We will provide a power connection by attaching a female N-type connector to a length of extra CAT 5 cable. Two Ethernet ports will provide an incoming network connection containing power, and a network connection without power to our WRT54G. Figure 7.43 shows the connection for our power retrieval unit; Table 7.7 provides the details.

Table 7.7 Power Retrieval Wiring Table

Input from Power Injector (Ethernet)	Output to WRT54G (Ethernet)	Power Output (N-Type Female)
1	1	
2	2	
3	3	
4	Unused	+12
5	Unused	+12
6	6	
7	Unused	- Ground
8	Unused	- Ground

Figure 7.43 Internals of a Power Retrieval Adapter

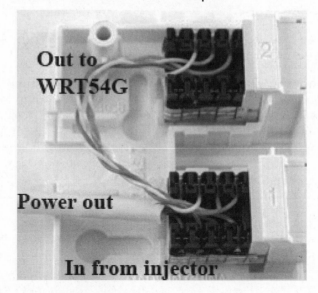

Alternative Power Summary

We described a number of options for alternative power sources for out WRT54G series routers, and they all have different price points, length of use, and applications. In Table 7.8, we compare all of the options described in this section.

Table 7.8 Alternative Power Comparisons

Battery	Approximate Cost	Approximate Length of Operation	Possible Applications	Pros/Cons
AA alkaline (quantity 8)	$6	4 hours	Penetration testing, temporary remote installation, distance testing, wardriving	Pros: inexpensive, small, mobile, readily available parts Cons: short lifespan
9v alkaline	$4	2 hours	Penetration testing, temporary remote installation, distance testing, wardriving	Pros: inexpensive, small, mobile, readily available parts Cons: short lifespan
Li-ion (with charger)	$40	72 hours	Penetration testing, temporary remote installation, distance testing, wardriving	Pros: small, mobile, decent lifespan Cons: higher cost, parts not readily available
Lead acid (with solar panel)	$100	573 hours (indefinite with solar panel)	Penetration testing, temporary remote installation, distance testing, wardriving, remote point-to-point network, remote hotspot	Pros: mobile, great lifespan Cons: higher cost, parts not readily available, mobile but heavy
USB	$40 to $4,200, depending on USB power source (USB charger versus laptop)	Varies, depending on source	Normal usage, wardriving, distance testing, temporary remote installation	Pros: mobile, great lifespan Cons: higher cost, parts not readily available
FireWire	$40 to $4,200, depending on USB power source (USB charger versus laptop)	Varies, depending on source	Normal usage, wardriving, distance testing, temporary remote installation	Pros: mobile, great lifespan Cons: higher cost, parts not readily available

Continued

Table 7.8 continued Alternative Power Comparisons

Battery	Approximate Cost	Approximate Length of Operation	Possible Applications	Pros/Cons
Automotive	$10 to $150, depending on power source	Varies, but likely indefinite	Wardriving, distance testing, temporary remote installation	Pros: mobile, great lifespan Cons: only as mobile as vehicle it is attached to
Power over Ethernet	$30 to $1,000, depending on PoE device (homebrew versus commercial device)	Indefinite	Remote installation, remote hotspot, remote point-to-point link	Pros: great lifespan, home brew cheaper than wiring AC power Cons: not mobile

Attaching Your WRT54G to Your Laptop

By far, attaching your WRT54G to your laptop is the easiest hardware hack in this book, and can certainly be helpful. In many of the applications used in this book, it can certainly be very helpful to either go mobile with your router, take up less room during use, or give us another free hand while on the move. Clearly, from our power hacks, we should even be able to power our WRT54G from the laptop itself.

Component Needed for This Hack

This hack requires an additional component that is not provided standard with any WRT54G model. The additional component required is:

- Industrial-strength Velcro, or other hook and loop fastener

The Hack

This book is about hacking the WRT54G series of routers, and successfully voiding those warranties, so that is where we will focus our direction. Given the vast differences in laptops, we won't actually be hacking the laptop, not to mention keeping the laptop warranty intact!

The easiest way we have discovered to attach a WRT54G to a laptop is with good old, industrial-strength, self-adhesive Velcro (or other hook and loop fasteners), obtained from a local home improvement store. This solution is completely reversible, and "temporarily permanent": It will perform the task at hand, and keep you from disassembling your laptop!

The best place to attach the Velcro on the WRT54G is the underside of the feet, which will likely provide the largest surface area. The black rubber inserts on the bottom of the feet are removable with a little bit of prying, and you can use them to trace a pattern on the Velcro for both the hook and the loop halves. Fortunately, you also can cut Velcro with a pair of sharp scissors to the appropriate size. Figure 7.44 shows the rubber foot pattern we made out of Velcro.

Figure 7.44 Rubber Foot and Velcro Cutout

Next, separate the protective paper from the hook (rough) portions of the Velcro, and apply them to the underside of the feet of the WRT54G. In order to eliminate any problems with lining up the hook (soft) part of the Velcro on the laptop, affix the loop portion to the hook portion already attached to the feet. Peel off the protective paper from all four loop portions, line them up to the backside of the laptop screen, and affix away! Apply gentle pressure to ensure proper contact to the laptop. Figure 7.45 shows the results.

WARNING

Applying too much pressure to the back of your laptop screen can crack the LCD panel inside, rendering the screen useless. Be careful!

Also, note the appropriate placement of the WRT54G so that it does not interfere with the operation of the display hinge. Mounting the router too low can interfere with obtaining an appropriate view of the laptop screen.

Once you have mounted the WRT54G to your laptop, you can power it via alternative sources, go mobile, and still have two hands to type with, or wield various antennas.

Figure 7.45 Velcro Mounting Success!

Summary

Many of our hardware hacks are much easier to perform than people make them out to be. In addition, the little bit of work that we can put in will offer huge returns in combination with some other hardware and software hacks. The antenna hacks can increase our wireless network range, and alternative power can extend our range away from a power outlet. We can use serial ports to connect all sorts of devices, and JTAG will help us out in a pinch!

Solutions Fast Track

Fun with Wireless Antennas

☑ An appropriate antenna can be used to increase the distance of your wireless signal, in either a 360-degree pattern or a very focused manner.

☑ The narrower the beam width of a high-directional antenna, the more focused the wireless energy will be concentrated, resulting in communication over longer distances.

☑ Antennas use a multitude of different, standardized connectors, but you can use an appropriate pigtail to convert between different connector types.

Adding Ports: SD Card, Serial, and JTAG

☑ Adding an MMC/SD card reader is an excellent way to expand the local storage on a WRT54G that normally wouldn't be expandable.

☑ Serial ports can be useful for adding a terminal to your WRT54G for troubleshooting purposes, or as a method of acquiring data from a device such as a GPS.

☑ A JTAG port won't help you expand the capabilities of your router, but it will be indispensable should something go wrong with your router.

Powering Your WRT54G with Alternative Sources

☑ Using alternative power sources will allow you to take the WRT54G mobile for even more possibilities: wardriving, remote connectivity, and penetration testing applications, to mention a few.

☑ Due to low power requirements during use, it is possible to derive power from alternative sources for significant periods of time; up to more than 20 days in some instances.

☑ Be sure to test all of your electrical connections before connecting alternative power to your router, as incorrect wiring can fry your WRT54G, rendering it inoperable.

Attaching Your WRT54G to Your Laptop

☑ Velcro is a great temporary fastener for attaching your WRT54G to your laptop.

☑ Be careful of your mounting location for your WRT54G, as it can interfere with the lid hinge or other peripherals and power connected to your laptop.

☑ Attach the Velcro to the WRT54G first, and then attach the other half of the Velcro to the WRT54G. This will eliminate possible alignment issues during the mounting process.

Frequently Asked Questions

The following Frequently Asked Questions, answered by the authors of this book, are designed to both measure your understanding of the concepts presented in this chapter and to assist you with real-life implementation of these concepts. To have your questions about this chapter answered by the author, browse to **www. syngress.com/solutions** and click on the **"Ask the Author"** form.

Q: Will opening my WRT54G void my warranty?

A: Definitely! Opening your WRT54G is going beyond the point of no return.

Q: Which antenna should I use?

A: You should use an omnidirectional antenna to increase your wireless footprint over a 360-degree area, such as an apartment, residence, or business. A directional antenna is better suited to long-range outdoor network-to-network connections, or for penetration testing applications.

Q: Should I turn up my wireless power by increasing the milliwatt output of the WRT54G, or by adding different antennas with increased dB?

A: Ideally, you should do a little bit of both by increasing power output (mW) and antenna gain (dB) a little at a time. Too much power or gain (or both) can actually degrade your wireless signal instead of making it better.

Q: Why is there a difference in GPIO port selection for MMC/SD card installation?

A: Most models of the WRT54G and WRT54GS have GPIO 5 available on the board, but it seems to be missing on the version 4.0 WRT54G and WRT54GL models, where GPIO 2 is available instead.

Q: How many serial ports can I add to a WRT54G?

A: The WRT54G models have the capability for two serial ports, and with some slight modification you can tweak the AD233BK single-port serial board to support two ports.

Q: What else can I use the JTAG port for besides fixing my broken router?

A: In most cases, it will not be useful for any other purposes; however, you could use it to do in-depth hardware debugging.

Q: What is the minimum power requirement for powering a WRT54G?

A: A WRT54G can be safely powered with a steady 5 volts DC at about 100mA. It may be possible to power one with less than 100mA, as a WRT54G typically draws only about 30- to 40mA under standard load.

Q: Is the WRT54G compatible with 802.3af Power over Ethernet (PoE) standards?

A: No, the WRT54G does not directly support any PoE specification, but you can use it with third-party PoE solutions that are either proprietary, homebrew, or 802.3af standard devices.

## Chapter 8

Troubleshooting WRT54G

Solutions in this chapter:

- **Using OpenWrt Failsafe Mode to Unbrick Your Router**

- **Using JTAG to Unbrick Your Router**

- **Getting Further Help**

☑ **Summary**

☑ **Solutions Fast Track**

☑ **Frequently Asked Questions**

Introduction

Occasionally, you'll be in a position where you've done something bad to your router and you can no longer interact with it. This can happen by flashing your router and then losing power on the router or on the PC in the middle of an upload, or if you have set some NVRAM settings that are not valid or are incorrect. A router that is not fully booting or is in an unknown operational state is "bricked"; the router is as useful to you as a brick in this state (that is to say, it is useless). Fortunately, you can usually recover from these problems using one or more of the methods discussed in this chapter.

WARNING

There is significant discussion online about the ability to recover by shorting some pins on the flash chip, known as the voidmain's method. This method invalidates the flash checksum and sends the router into failsafe mode. Although this method may work, it has the potential to destroy the router's circuit board. In the initial stages of researching this book, the authors rendered two routers inoperable and beyond repair using the pin-shorting method. There are better and safer ways to accomplish recovery, which we outline in this chapter. For a complete discussion, refer to the OpenWrt forum posting at http://forum.openwrt.org/viewtopic.php?pid=78.

Using OpenWrt Failsafe Mode to Unbrick Your Router

In the course of your WRT54G hacking adventures, you may become brave enough to start to make some serious changes to NVRAM (VLANs, etc.), customize your firewall rules, and back up or restore firmware images, JFFS partitions, and NVRAM partitions. All of the aforementioned activities could potentially "brick" your router. It is convenient to be able to get into the router to fix your problems without having to start over or make a JTAG cable.

Enter failsafe mode, a handy feature built into the OpenWrt distribution. During the boot process, OpenWrt will give you a short window of opportunity to use the Reset button and enter failsafe mode. The Reset button does not have any preprogrammed function by default in OpenWrt, once the OS is running. However, during the kernel boot process (i.e., when the DMZ light is solid when the router is booting up), OpenWrt will respond to the Reset button being pushed. Be careful; if you push the button too soon (i.e., before the DMZ light is lit and when the Power light is flashing), it could send the "Reset button pushed" command to the bootloader. The bootloader may cause your router to restore to factory defaults!

WARNING

Failsafe mode works only with OpenWrt Whiterussian RC5 and later. This means you must already have this firmware installed in order to use this feature. If you have some other firmware installed, the Reset button may do something different, such as restore to factory defaults!

To enter failsafe mode, do the following:

1. Unplug the power from the WRT54G router. Using the same precautions as listed in the Trivial File Transfer Protocol (TFTP) installation instructions in Chapter 2, plug a laptop or PC into any of the local area network (LAN) assigned ports. Even if you have switched the wide area network (WAN) port to be a LAN port, you must be certain to plug into the predefined LAN ports.

2. Install the recvudp program onto your computer. This is a small program that will listen for the special User Datagram Protocol (UDP) packets as they are sent by the router during the boot process. You can find the source code at http://downloads.openwrt.org/people/nbd/recvudp.c. In addition, precompiled binaries for UNIX and Windows are located at http://downloads.openwrt.org/people/florian/recvudp. An alternative to this program is to use tcpdump (or windump on Windows) and capture packets on UDP port 4919. You may wonder why they chose 4919 as the port. If you convert decimal 4919 to hexadecimal, you get 0x1337.

3. Once you've installed the program, you can run it by typing **./recvudp** (or **recvudp.exe** in Windows) from the command line, or start your packet capture with tcpdump, with the command *tcpdump –i <interface> –X –nn –s100 'udp port 4919'*. This command will grab the first 100 bytes (*–s100*) of each UDP packet on port 4919. The *–X* parameter tells tcpdump to output the hex and ASCII equivalents of the packet payload, and *–nn* says to not resolve hostnames or services.

4. Now power on your router, and as it boots, you will see a message that reads *Msg from 192.168.1.1: Press reset now, to enter Failsafe!*. Immediately press and hold the Reset button for two seconds.

5. If successful, you should see the message *Msg from 192.168.1.1: Entering Failsafe!* and booting should continue.

6. Once the router has finished booting, you can Telnet to 192.168.1.1 without a password and have access to the command line. During failsafe mode, the Power and DMZ LEDs will keep blinking.

> **NOTE**
>
> There are no precompiled recvudp binaries for Linux, so you will need to compile one yourself. Assuming that you have the gcc C compiler on your Linux system of choice, you can compile it with the command *gcc –o recvudp recvudp.c*. This command calls the gcc C compiler, and will create the output file (with –o) of recvudp, from the source file of recvudp.c.

> **NOTE**
>
> Pressing the Reset button at the right time might be tricky, so don't become frustrated if it doesn't work the first time. Try it again, being certain to press and release the Reset button according to the instructions.

Your router will contain only the settings from the SquashFS (read-only) file system, and not any changes written to the JFFS (writable) partition. From here, you can reset your NVRAM variables (*mtd –r erase nvram*), or revert back to the original JFFS partition using the *firstboot* command. Additionally, you can mount your JFFS partition with the */sbin/mount_root* command.

Failsafe mode also allows you to restore from a previous backup, as outlined in Chapter 3.

Notes from the Underground...

The "Other" Hardware

Although this book is focused on the WRT54G series hardware, you can successfully recover other hardware platforms using OpenWrt's failsafe mode.

First, let's start with the WRT54G family. You can recover the WRTSL54GS using OpenWrt's failsafe mode. However, the timing might be slightly different on this model. Timing in general will depend on the router's bootloader version, so don't be afraid to experiment with different timings.

Other hardware, such as the Asus WL-500G Premium, is fully supported by OpenWrt, and uses very similar hardware. Recovery on this device requires some experimentation with timing:

- When you initially press the Reset button
- How long you wait before pressing it again

Continued

- How long you hold it for the second time

In each case, you should see the same messages as described earlier. We used the failsafe method very effectively throughout the course of this book for different types of hardware, both Linksys and non-Linksys.

Using JTAG to Unbrick Your Router

In more severe cases where failsafe mode won't allow you to correct your bricked router, you will need to utilize a JTAG cable, which we constructed and to which we enabled the connection on our router in Chapter 7. In order to fully utilize the JTAG cable and port, you need to provide some additional software on a PC.

The required software, called HairyDairyMaid's Debrick Utility, is available for both Linux and Windows. The source code for Linux and binaries for Windows are contained in the same package, which you can find at a mirror at http://downloads.openwrt.org/utils. You can download the HairyDairyMaid's Debrick Utility, from now on referred to in this text as the *debrick utility*, with a Web browser under your OS of choice. The PC on which you use the debrick utility must have a parallel port in order to connect the JTAG cable.

The Windows installation is quite trivial. After downloading the tool, unzip the executable to a directory of your choice and execute it from the command line. To obtain a command line under Windows XP, select **Start | Run** and in the **Run** dialog box type **cmd.exe** and then click **OK**. In the new command prompt window, be sure to navigate to the correct directory to which the debrick utility was extracted.

Before you use the Windows version of the debrick utility, you need to load an input/output Windows driver. In the debrick utility directory, you can start the driver load utility with the following command:

```
loaddrv
```

This will create a new window. In the **Full pathname of driver** field, you need to enter the full path to giveio.sys, also located in the debrick utility directory. In our example, giveio.sys is located in c:\hdm\, as shown in Figure 8.1. Once you've entered the full path, click **Start**.

TIP

The LoadDrv utility appears to be subtly broken. It would be intuitive for the Install button to allow you to permanently install the driver, but it does not. You need to restart the driver using the aforementioned process after a reboot if you want to use the JTAG cable again.

Figure 8.1 The LoadDrv Utility

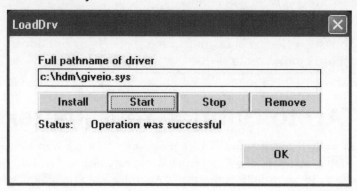

Under your Linux installation of choice, you need to extract the debrick utility after navigating to the directory where you downloaded it to. You can extract it using *unzip*:

```
# unzip HairyDairyMaid_WRT54G_Debrick_Utility_v48.zip
```

Once you've extracted the utility, you need to change to the newly created directory containing your extracted files, and then compile the utility with the following command:

```
# make
```

> **NOTE**
>
> Under Linux, you need to change kernel parallel port drivers before the debrick utility will work. You need to unload the *lp* kernel module and load the *ppdev* kernel module. You can do this with these two commands:
> # *rmmod lp*
> # *insmod ppdev*

Once the utility is extracted and built, you can attach it to your router. With the power off on the WRT54G, attach the pin connector end of the JTAG cable to the router, making sure to note the location of pin 1. With the power still off to the WRT54G, attach the 25-pin connector to the PC parallel port.

> **WARNING**
>
> Be sure to properly line up pin 1 on the circuit board with pin 1 on the JTAG cable.

After you've successfully connected the cable, as shown in Figure 8.2, you need to start the debrick utility. Navigate to the correct directory where the debrick utility is located under the command line. Under Windows, you can execute it and test the functionality of your cable with this command:

```
C:\>wrt54g.exe -probeonly
```

Under Linux, use this command:

```
#./wrt54g -probeonly
```

Figure 8.2 Installed JTAG Cable

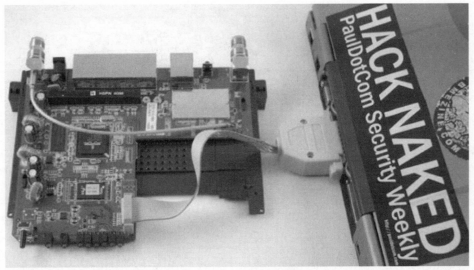

Apply power to the WRT54G and start the debrick utility with the appropriate command listed earlier. Once executed, the debrick utility will automatically connect and detect the WRT54G chipset, as shown in Figure 8.3.

Figure 8.3 Debrick Utility Auto-Detection

```
C:\WINDOWS\system32\cmd.exe - wrt54g.exe -probeonly                     _ □ X

C:\hdm>wrt54g.exe -probeonly

=========================================
WRT54G/GS EJTAG Debrick Utility v4.8
=========================================

Probing bus ... Done

Instruction Length set to 5

CPU Chip ID: 00000100011100010000000101111111 (0471017F)
*** Found a Broadcom BCM4702 Rev 1 CPU chip ***

   - EJTAG IMPCODE ....... : 00000000100000000000100100001000 (00800908)
   - EJTAG Version ....... : 1 or 2.0
   - EJTAG DMA Support ... : Yes

Issuing Processor / Peripheral Reset ... Done
Enabling Memory Writes ... Done
Halting Processor ... <Processor Entered Debug Mode!> ... Done
Clearing Watchdog ... _
```

TIP

If the debrick utility does not auto-detect your hardware, you can force it to use a specified chipset by specifying the */fc:<value>* switch on the command line when executing the utility. To determine the correct value for your chipset, execute the debrick utility without any command-line options to display the built-in help. The built-in help contains all of the appropriate values for the chipsets that are supported.

Tools & Traps...

Watchdog Guard Dog

During all of your JTAG operations with the debrick utility, you will see some output about Clearing Watchdog. This watchdog is a protection mechanism built into the CFE (discussed in Chapter 2) to determine whether any undesired access to the CFE is being performed (your activity may be considered undesired according to the manufacturer). This watchdog is set to a predefined internal timer, and when the timer is triggered, the watchdog terminates all JTAG operations.

This termination will be quite detrimental to flash-writing operations! Without the watchdog disabled, a write of CFE to flash will halt, and will fail at about 3 percent. This partially written state will be nonfunctional!

In order to perform a successful write, and for you to gain "undesired" access, you will need to disable the watchdog. The debrick utility will try to disable the watchdog by default. Occasionally, it will fail, and some success can be had by adding the */noemw* option. The *noemw* switch is intended to disable memory writes, but it still allows memory writes and apparently provides some additional interaction with the watchdog shutdown.

If your JTAG cable does not detect that a router is installed, or is unable to communicate with the flash chip, refer back to Chapter 7 and verify the construction of the JTAG cable. This is the cause for most communication problems between the PC and the router when using a JTAG cable.

In order to begin reviving your bricked router via JTAG, you will want to back up your current flash memory contents. As you may remember from Chapter 2, the flash chip is divided into three major sections: CFE (or basic input/output system [BIOS]/bootloader), kernel (or firmware or operating system, possibly OpenWrt), and NVRAM (where configuration variables are stored). Typically, you will want to back up your CFE and NVRAM, while ignoring the kernel. You typically ignore the kernel backup, as the kernel is quite large, and due to the speed of the JTAG interface, it can take up to six hours to perform a backup (or install) of the kernel. Later in this chapter, we will show you a more effective method for writing the kernel and foregoing a backup.

In order to begin your backups, you need to add some command-line switches to the execution of the debrick utility. First, back up the CFE with the following command:

```
# wrt54g -backup:cfe
```

The debrick utility will connect to the router and begin copying the contents of the CFE to a file on the PC, named CFE.BIN.SAVED_<datestamp>_<timestamp>, in the same directory as the debrick utility. Once complete, it will notify you of the completion status and return you to the command line. Now, back up your NVRAM with the following command:

```
# wrt54g -backup:nvram
```

Again, the debrick utility will connect to the router and begin copying the contents of NVRAM to a file on the PC, named NVRAM.BIN.SAVED_<datestamp>_<timestamp>, in the same directory as the debrick utility. Once complete, it will notify you of the completion status and return you to the command line.

! WARNING

Before executing multiple debrick utility commands that read or write to the flash chip, it is always a good idea to reboot the router in between commands. This will ensure that the router and the CFE are in an appropriate state for each command.

Notes from the Underground...

Backing Up the Entire Flash Chip

Although we suggest that you skip backing up either the kernel or the whole flash chip, it is certainly possible to do so. Even though the usefulness of backing up the entire flash on a bricked unit is dubious, it may be useful for other situations.

In order to back up the entire flash chip, you can still utilize the debrick utility. To perform the backup, issue the following command.

```
# wrt54g -backup:wholeflash
```

Depending on the size of the flash chip of the WRT54G model you are attempting to back up, this process can take from six to 24 hours to complete! This is because of the limited amount of bandwidth over the JTAG connection, and the large size of the whole flash.

Another reason, besides time constraints, you should avoid backing up the whole flash on a bricked router is that the three major flash sections are combined into one file instead of being split into individual, easily restorable files. Although it is possible

Continued

> to split all of the flash backup images into the individual files using some other utilities, it quickly becomes an exercise in inefficiency.

Once you have completed all of your backups, you can begin to restore your router configuration back to a working state. You will start with the simple problems, and work up to the more difficult ones.

The easiest problem that you can fix with the JTAG cable concerns NVRAM. It is very easy to turn a working WRT54G into a brick by setting NVRAM variables to incorrect settings and making the router inaccessible! During the course of writing this book, the authors successfully locked themselves out of a WRT54G by incorrectly defining virtual LAN (VLAN) assignments, and no Internet Protocol (IP) communication to the router was possible. To clear NVRAM settings issue the following command:

```
# wrt54g -erase:nvram
```

After a very short period of time, the debrick utility should report a success. If this is all you need to fix your router, a reboot should restore the WRT54G to the default configuration.

! WARNING

It is not safe to perform an NVRAM erase on all models, as the CFE on some models does not re-create the minimal NVRAM settings. Please refer to Chapter 3, which discusses on which models it is unsafe to erase NVRAM. If you have erased NVRAM on a model that is unsupported, you can use the debrick utility to restore your previously backed-up NVRAM settings (you did make a backup, right?) with the following command, which you should issue after renaming your backup NVRAM file to NVRAM.BIN:

```
# nvram -flash:nvram
```

The debrick utility will upload only specific files (there is no option to change the filename). The files to upload via JTAG must be named CFE.BIN, KERNEL.BIN, NVRAM.BIN, or WHOLEFLASH.BIN, depending on the type of write to be performed.

On models where erasing NVRAM is not a good idea, access via a serial console to change NVRAM settings may be possible after performing the serial port mod covered in Chapter 6.

If you have corrupted your operating system through one or more means (deleting needed files, creating a startup loop, or any other method), you can resolve this situation with a little more work. Start by utilizing the debrick utility to erase the kernel (or operating system) partition:

```
# wrt54g -erase:kernel
```

This command will complete the kernel erase. Once the utility reports a success, you will need to reboot the WRT54G. During the reboot, the CFE will notice that there is no operating system, and will revert to failsafe mode. In failsafe mode, you can once again upload new firmware to the router. For a full tutorial on how to flash your router with TFTP, please see Chapter 1. Unfortunately, if you have made customized changes to your previous firmware installation, they will be lost during the reflash operation, but what good was a bricked router to you anyway! After performing a TFTP upload, the router should be fully functional.

The last problem that you would need to rectify is a corrupted CFE. Although this does not happen often, it is certainly possible to corrupt the bootloader. You can restore the bootloader with the same debrick utility using the following command:

```
wrt54g -flash:cfe
```

You may notice that you did not need to erase the CFE before writing. The debrick utility automatically erases the CFE before writing the working one from CFE.BIN.

You may be asking yourself at this point why you would want to reflash your backed-up, corrupt CFE. Certainly, you wouldn't! The next question you may ask is where you can obtain a new CFE, as they are not part of most firmware distributions. That question is a little trickier to answer.

Every version of the WRT54G series routers contains a different version of the CFE to account for differences in hardware. Most CFE repositories are incomplete and may not have the CFE that you need. There is one repository that is as complete as possible, and it comes with a few extra utilities as well. This repository, part of the Skynet Repair Kit, is a full-featured set of Windows utilities from the wlan-skynet folks. You can download the most up-to-date version of the utility at http://wlan-skynet.de/download/index.shtml.

NOTE

At the time of this writing, there did not appear to be a version of the Skynet Repair Kit utility for any platform other than Windows.

The Skynet Repair Kit is easy to install: Simply download and run the setup executable. Once you've installed it, you can access the CFE creation utility from the Start menu by selecting **Start | All Programs | Skynet Repair Kit | Bootloader Creator 2.0**, which will display a new window, as shown in Figure 8.4.

Figure 8.4 Skynet Bootloader Creator

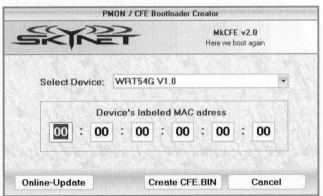

Before you can select a device for which to create a CFE, you need to update the CFE images by selecting the **Online-Update** button, and then clicking **Start** in the **Online updating** window. Once the update is complete, you can utilize the drop-down menu, **Select Device**, to pick your device. Next, you will need to provide a Media Access Control (MAC) address in the **Device's labeled MAC address** field. You can find this MAC address on the label on the bottom of the WRT54G. After you've filled in all of the fields, click the **Create CFE.BIN** button, which will display a standard Windows file save dialog box. Save the CFE.BIN file in your desired location, and proceed with the JTAG CFE flash.

Getting Further Help

Throughout this book, we used many different online resources to get help with various projects and technical difficulties. In this section, we provide a guide to getting help with WRT54G hacking.

Resources for This Book

First, we created a Web site, www.wrt54ghacks.com, dedicated to this book, which provides further insight, projects, and information related to WRT54G and other embedded device hacking. You can find additional information at the sources listed in the following sections.

OpenWrt

- **Wiki (http://wiki.Openwrt.org)** The OpenWrt wiki contains most of the project's documentation, How-Tos, and other related information.

- **Forum (http://forum.openwrt.org)** If you need to ask a question, the forum is the place. Also, you can find answers to many questions, and solutions to many problems, by searching the forum.

- **IRC (#OpenWrt on irc.freenode.net)** The IRC channel is a great place to talk with other OpenWrt users and developers. This is not a support channel, but if you have done the proper research and you want to ask questions about choosing the right solution, make suggestions, or take part in other intelligent discussions, this is the place for you. Be certain to read the "Getting help on IRC" page, located at http://wiki.openwrt.org/irc, before posting questions to the channel. You can sometimes find the authors in this channel as well (Paul Asadoorian uses the name *pauldotcom*, and Larry Pesce uses the name *haxorthematrix*, also in the #pauldotcom channel on the same server).

DD-WRT

- **Wiki (http://dd-wrt.com/wiki)** The DD-WRT wiki is a great resource to answer your questions, and is even available in multiple languages.

- **Forum (http://dd-wrt.com/phpBB2)** The DD-WRT forum covers a wide range of topics, with specific sections for different types of hardware.

Ewrt

- **FAQ (www.portless.net/ewrt/source/FAQ)** At the time of this writing, this was the best documentation available on Ewrt, and it answered most common questions.

- **www.wrt54ghacks.com** While we were writing this book, the Ewrt authors at Portless Networks closed the project. The binaries, source code, patches, and packages are still available from www.portless.net/ewrt. Paul and Larry will continue to work with Ewrt, and will document their successes at www.wrt54ghacks.com.

WRT54G Hacking Help

- **Linksysinfo.org (www.linksysinfo.org)** This is a great site for general information about the Linksys WRT54G platform and many of the different firmware options.

- **WRTrouters (www.wrtrouters.com)** This site is dedicated to hacking the WRT54G series routers.

- **Learning to solder resources from *MAKE* magazine (www.makezine.com/blog/archive/2006/04/how_to_solder_resources.html)** This site provides all you could ever need to learn how to solder.

- **Using a multimeter (www.doctronics.co.uk/meter.htm)** This is a short, simple guide to the basics of using a multimeter to make measurements from circuits when testing electronics.

Summary

There are many ways to break your WRT54G, and a few ways to fix them. Utilizing the methods in this chapter, you should be able to revive most dead WRT54G routers that have had software errors. If nothing else, there is always more help available online.

Solutions Fast Track

Using OpenWrt Failsafe Mode to Unbrick Your Router

- ☑ You must have OpenWrt Whiterussian RC5 or later in order to use failsafe mode.

- ☑ Failsafe mode works great if you are trying to recover from a corrupt JFFS partition or NVRAM setting gone wrong.

- ☑ When in failsafe mode, be certain to set your local IP address to something in the 192.168.1.0/24 subnet (other than 192.168.1.1, which will be the IP address of your router).

Using JTAG to Unbrick Your Router

- ☑ The HairyDairyMaid's Debrick Utility is the tool of choice for both Windows and Linux users who want to perform JTAG read and write operations for the CFE, kernel, or NVRAM.

- ☑ Always make a backup of your CFE and NVRAM. It is impractical to back up your kernel or the whole flash chip.

- ☑ You can obtain new copies of the CFE from the Skynet Repair Kit Bootloader Creator.

Getting Further Help

- ☑ The OpenWrt project has many excellent online resources, such as a wiki, forum, and IRC channel.

- ☑ The DD-WRT project has online resources as well, covering a wide range of topics.

- ☑ The Web offers other resources that will help you if you get stuck. For example, the Linksysinfo.org Web site has information about hacking the WRT54G platform, including support for many different firmware distributions.

Frequently Asked Questions

The following Frequently Asked Questions, answered by the authors of this book, are designed to both measure your understanding of the concepts presented in this chapter and to assist you with real-life implementation of these concepts. To have your questions about this chapter answered by the author, browse to **www. syngress.com/solutions** and click on the **"Ask the Author"** form.

Q: I pushed the Reset button before the DMZ light came on. How come my router has been reset to factory defaults?

A: When the router is booting, the bootloader may respond to the Reset button being pushed, forcing the firmware to return to factory defaults (using the NVRAM values stored in the CFE) or even brick your router (depending on the model and version). Always be certain that the Power light has stopped flashing and that the DMZ light is solid before pushing the Reset button.

Q: When my router powers on, the Power light flashes and nothing else happens. What is wrong?

A: You may have bricked your router, in which case you need to use a JTAG cable to diagnose the problem.

Q: I used voidmain's method to debrick my router. However, now it won't power on. How come?

A: We hate to say we told you so, but we told you so. You should short out the pins on the board itself only when all else (failsafe, JTAG, etc.) fails.

Q: Can I upload a new kernel via JTAG?

A: Yes, it is possible to upload a new kernel via JTAG from a TRX file (http://downloads.openwrt.org/whiterussian/0.9/default/OpenWrt-brcm-2.4-squashfs.trx), but it can take up to 24 hours. It is more practical to upload it via TFTP.

Q: How do I specify a different file to upload via JTAG with the HairyDairyMaid's Debrick Utility?

A: In the current releases, it is not possible to specify an alternative filename to upload. It will upload only the specifically named files (CFE.BIN, NVRAM.BIN, KERNEL.BIN, WHOLEFLASH.BIN) located in the same directory as the utility. Therefore, you need to rename the file you want to upload.

Q: Is there another way to obtain CFE images?

A: Yes, there are a few online repositories, but most are incomplete. You can find the one that was most complete as of this writing at http://lonewolf.hacker-nin.com/wrt/cfe.

Q: I asked a question on the OpenWrt IRC channel, but no one responded. How come?

A: Be certain to read the guidelines, "Getting help on IRC" (http://wiki.openwrt.org/irc), before posting to the channel. One of the most common problems is asking a question that has already been answered in the wiki or forums, so be certain to look there first before posting a question in IRC.

Q: Someone answered my question in IRC, but I forget what the answer was. Is there a log?

A: Yes, it is located at http://openwrt.org/logs.

Q: Do the OpenWrt developers and the Sveasoft developers hate each other?

A: *Hate* is a strong word, but you can read more about the situation here: http://openwrt.org/logs/openwrt-meets-sveasoft.

NVRAM Command Reference

Solutions in this chapter:

- **nvram Command Usage**
- **IP and Networking**
- **VLANs**
- **Wireless**
- **File System**
- **Miscellaneous Hardware and Custom Software Options**

Introduction

In this appendix, we'll list the NVRAM variables used throughout this book, broken down by category. This appendix is not intended to be an all-encompassing listing, but includes just the variables that were important enough to be included elsewhere in the book. For a full list of all OpenWrt NVRAM commands, visit http://wiki.openwrt.org/OpenWrtNVRAM. Additionally, http://downloads.openwrt.org/docs/hardware contains a listing of manufacturers with default NVRAM settings for some devices listed in the nvram.txt file for each hardware version (Table A.1).

nvram Command Usage

Table A.1

Command	Description
nvram show	Lists all NVRAM variables and values. The list is typically quite long, so *nvram show	sort	more* is a good way to make the output more readable. Also, these values are stored in /dev/nvram and you can access them with the command *strings /dev/nvram	sort	more*. If you need to send your NVRAM variables to someone (e-mail, forum, etc.) you can run either of the two preceding commands and pipe them to a file (e.g., *strings /dev/nvram | sort > /tmp/nvram.out*).
nvram get <variable>	Gets the value of a specific variable and displays it on the screen. If you do not know the entire variable name, you can use the command *nvram show	grep <string>*. For example, to see all of the wireless settings, use the command *nvram show	grep wl0_***.
nvram set <variable>= <value>	Sets a variable to a specified value. NVRAM set commands apply only to the running memory on the router. They do not take effect until they are committed to flash through the *nvram commit* command. You can clear the value of any variable using an empty string, as in *nvram set wl0_ssid=""*.
nvram unset <variable>	Deletes a variable from NVRAM. It is very useful to undo the creation of new variables with invalid names, such as *wl0_sid* instead of *wl0_ssid*.
nvram commit	Saves NVRAM settings from memory to flash.

NOTE

You must include multiple values in double quotes—for example, *nvram set lan_ifnames="vlan0 eth1 eth2 eth3"*.

IP and Networking

NVRAM variables relating to the Internet Protocol (IP) and networking appear in Table A.2. In this table, the "*" can refer to the interface name, which is, by default, *lan*, *wan*, or *wifi*.

Table A.2 IP and Networking NVRAM Variables

NVRAM Variable	Expected Value	Description
*_ifname	<port>	Assigns the network interface name for this category/group. Valid values for <port> include (but are not limited to) *eth1*, *eth2*, *eth3*, *eth4*, *eth5*, and *ppp0*.
*_ipaddr	<ip address>	Sets the IP address of the network interface, where <ip address> = valid IP address in x.x.x.x format.
*_netmask	<mask>	Sets the subnet mask of the network interface, where <mask> = valid subnet mask in x.x.x.x format.
*_gateway	<ip address>	Sets the IP address of the network interface default gateway, where <ip address> = valid IP address in x.x.x.x format.
*_dns	<ip address>	Sets the IP address of the domain name system (DNS) server for the network interface, where <ip address> = IP address of a valid DNS server in x.x.x.x format.
*_proto	<text>	Defines the protocol for obtaining IP information for the interface. Valid values for <text> include *none*, *static*, *dhcp*, *pppoe*, and *pptp*.

Continued

www.syngress.com

Table A.2 continued IP and Networking NVRAM Variables

NVRAM Variable	Expected Value	Description
wan_hostname	*<text>*	Hostname for the wide area network (WAN) interface, where *<text>* = up to 64 alphanumeric characters and some special characters, including underscores and the minus sign. This also changes the name on the command prompt. The default value in OpenWrt is *OpenWrt*.
lan_dhcp_enabled	*<number>*	Enables or disables the Dynamic Host Configuration Protocol (DHCP) server on the local area network (LAN), where *<number>* = 0 for disabled or 1 for enabled.
lan_gateway_enable	*<number>*	Enables or disables the LAN interface as the default gateway for LAN clients, where *<number>* = 0 for disabled or 1 for enabled.
lan_dns_enable	*<number>*	Enables or disables the LAN interface as the DNS server for LAN clients, where *<number>* = 0 for disabled or 1 for enabled.
lan_wan_proxy_arp	*<number>*	Enables or disables routed mode for a proxy ARP bridge, where *<number>* = 0 for disabled or 1 for enabled.
lan_wan_bridge	*<number>*	Defines whether the LAN and WAN ports should be bridged, where *<number>* = 0 for disabled or 1 for enabled.
wan_device	*<name>*	Sets the default virtual LAN (VLAN) for the WAN interface. Valid values are any valid VLAN in the *vlan<x>* format, where *<x>* = the VLAN number.

VLANs

NVRAM variables relating to Layer 2 networking (VLANs) appear in Table A.3.

Table A.3 VLAN NVRAM Variables

NVRAM Variable	Expected Value	Description
wan_iface	<port>	Assigns the network interface for use as the WAN interface. Valid values for <port> include (but are not limited to) eth1, eth2, eth3, eth4, eth5, ppp0, and any valid VLAN in the vlan<x> format, where <x> = the VLAN number.
*_ifnames	<interface(s)>	A space-separated list of interfaces to be added to the bridge identified by the "*". For example, by default the wireless interfaces are in the same bridge as the LAN interfaces, so the parameter reads lan_ifnames=vlan0 eth1 eth2 eth3. This applies only to interfaces that are bridges.
vlan0ports	<ports>	A list of interfaces assigned to VLAN 0. Valid values for <ports> include (but are not limited to) eth1, eth2, eth3, eth4, eth5, and ppp0. The listing must be placed in quotes and values should be separated by spaces.
vlan1ports	<ports>	A list of interfaces assigned to VLAN 1. Valid values for <ports> include (but are not limited to) eth1, eth2, eth3, eth4, eth5, and ppp0. The listing must be placed in quotes and values should be separated by spaces.

Wireless

NVRAM variables relating to wireless networking and encryption appear in Table A.4.

Table A.4 Wireless Networking and Encryption NVRAM Variables

NVRAM Variable	Expected Value	Description
wl0_ssid	<text>	Sets the SSID (network name) for the wireless network, where <text> = up to 64 alphanumeric characters.

Continued

Table A.4 continued Wireless Networking and Encryption NVRAM Variables

NVRAM Variable	Expected Value	Description
wl0_txpwr	*<number>*	Adjusts the wireless transmit power in mW. Valid values for *<number>* = 1 through 251.
wl0_radio	*<number>*	Enables or disables the wireless capabilities, where *<number>* = 0 for disabled or 1 for enabled.
wl0_country_code	*<text>*	Sets the wireless country code, allowing for specific wireless channel sets to be enabled. Values for *<text>* are: *AU* = Worldwide, channels 1–11 *TH* = Thailand, channels 1–11 *IL* = Israel, channels 5–7 (see note below) Note: w10_country _code when set to IL for Israel only enables channels 5-7. In December of 2005, by order of the Isreali Prime Minister, channels 1-13 are permitted for use. *JO* = Jordan, channels 1–11 *CN* = China, channels 1–11 *JP* = Japan, channels 1–14 *US* = USA/Canada/New Zealand, channels 1–11 *DE* = Europe, channels 1–13 *All* = All channels, 1–14
wl0_mode	*<text>*	Sets the wireless mode. Valid values for *<text>* are: *ap* = wireless access point *sta* = wireless client *wet* = wireless Ethernet bridge
wl0_akm	*<text>*	Selects the Wi-Fi Protected Access (WPA) mode. Can be a quoted, space-separated list for WPA, personal or enterprise method. Valid values for *<text>* are: *none* = no WPA *psk* = WPA preshared key *psk2* = WPA2 preshared key *wpa* = WPA Enterprise *wpa2* = WPA2 Enterprise

Continued

Table A.4 continued Wireless Networking and Encryption NVRAM Variables

NVRAM Variable	Expected Value	Description
wl0_wpa_psk	*<text>*	Defines the WPA or WPA2 preshared key. Valid entries for *<text>* are alphanumeric characters, from 8 to 63 characters in length.
wl0_crypto	*<text>*	Defines the WPA underlying crypto-graphic method. Valid values for *<text>* are *tkip*, *aes*, or *tkip+aes*.
wl0_closed	*<number>*	Enables or disables SSID broadcasting, where *<number>* = 0 for broadcast-enabled or 1 for broadcast-disabled (cloaked network).
wl0_wep	*<number>*	Enables Wireless Encryption Protocol (WEP) encryption, where *<number>* = 0 for disabled or 1 for enabled.
wl0_key	*<number>*	Primary WEP key index. Chooses the appropriate WEP key as defined by the *wl0_key<N>* NVRAM variables. Valid values for *<number>* are 1 through 4, depending on the desired *wl0_key<N>*.
wl0_key<N>	*<text>, s:<text>*	Defines a WEP key. *<text>* should be composed of five characters, or 10 HEX digits for 64-bit WEP, or 13 char-acters or 26 HEX digits for 128-bit WEP. *<text>* must be in hexadecimal formatting, unless the *s:* prefix is defined. Valid values for *N* are 1 through 4.
wl0_macmode	*<text>*	Sets wireless Media Access Control (MAC) access control list. Valid values for *<text>* are: *disabled* = disables MAC filtering *allow* = allows only the MAC addresses defined in *wl0_maclist* *deny* = denies only the MAC addresses defined in *wl0_maclist*
wl0_maclist	*<text>*	A quoted, space-separated list of MAC addresses to allow or deny access via wireless. MAC addresses must be listed in the xx:xx:xx:xx:xx:xx format.

Continued

Table A.4 continued Wireless Networking and Encryption NVRAM Variables

NVRAM Variable	Expected Value	Description
wl0_radius_port	<number>	Sets the Transmission Control Protocol (TCP) port number to be used for authentication to a Remote Authentication Dial-in User Service (RADIUS) server for WPA/WPA2 Enterprise, where <number> = a valid TCP port number form 1 to 65536.
wl0_radius_ipaddr	<ip address>	Sets the IP address of the RADIUS sever for WPA/WPA2 Enterprise, where <ip address> = a valid IP address in x.x.x.x format.
wl0_radius_key	<text>	Defines the shared key for authentication to a RADIUS server. <text> should contain an alphanumeric string of 1 to 64 characters.
wl0_auth_mode	<text>	Sets the authentication mode for WPA. Has been depreciated by wl0_akm, but will not damage any other settings by defining this variable, and some installations require it. Valid settings for <text> are: psk = WPA or WPA2 preshared key radius = WPA or WPA2 Enterprise
wl0_antdiv	<number>	Sets the wireless antenna diversity. Valid values for <number> are: -1 = auto-select 0 = main antenna (near Reset button) 1 = auxiliary antenna (near power connector) 3 = diversity, uses both antennas On WRT54G models pre version 2.0 and WRT54GS pre version 1.1, the auxiliary and main antennal physical locations are swapped.

File System

NVRAM variables relating to the flash file system (JFFS2) appear in Table A.5.

Table A.5 File System NVRAM Variables

NVRAM Variable	Expected Value	Description
jffs_mounted	*<number>*	Automatically mounts the JFFS2 file system, where *<number>* is 0 = not mounted and 1 = mounted. Only utilized under DD-WRT.
enable_jffs2	*<number>*	Enables the JFFS2 file system, where *<number>* is 0 = disabled and 1 = enabled. Only utilized under DD-WRT.
sys_enable_jffs2	*<number>*	Enables the JFFS2 file system at the system level, where *<number>* is 0 = disabled and 1 = enabled. Only utilized under DD-WRT.
clean_jffs2	*<number>*	Maintains the JFFS2 file system at the user level, where *<number>* is 0 = disabled and 1 = enabled. Only utilized under DD-WRT.
sys_clean_jffs2	*<number>*	Maintains the JFFS2 file system at the system level, where *<number>* is 0 = disabled and 1 = enabled. Only utilized under DD-WRT.

Miscellaneous Hardware and Custom Software Options

NVRAM variables relating to other miscellaneous hardware options appear in Table A.6.

Table A.6 Miscellaneous Hardware and Custom Software Options NVRAM Variables

NVRAM Variable	Expected Value	Description
boot_wait	*<text>*	Enables the boot wait option to pause booting in order to be able to recover from failures. Valid values for *<text>* are: *on* = enabled *off* = disabled
wait_time	*<number>*	Amount of time in seconds for *boot_wait* to wait before continuing to boot, where *<number>* = 1 through 65,536 (recommended is 30).
NC_LeaseFile	*<text>*	Specifies the location of the DHCP lease file, where *<text>* = the full path to the DHCP lease file. Only used by NoCat under Ewrt.
NC_binary_name	*<text>*	Specifies the NoCat executable, where *<text>* = full path to the NoCat executable file. Only used by NoCat under Ewrt.
NC_binary_path	*<text>*	Specifies the location of the NoCat binaries, where *<text>* = the full path to the directory containing the NoCat binaries. Only used by NoCat under Ewrt.
NC_DocumentRoot	*<text>*	Specifies the location of the Web pages for NoCat, where *<text>* = the full path to the NoCat document root. Only used by NoCat under Ewrt

Appendix B

Hardware Hacking Parts

Solutions in this chapter:

- Antennas
- SD Card
- Serial Port
- JTAG
- Alternative Power

Introduction

In this appendix, we list the parts used in each hardware hack outlined in Chapter 7. The supplies we indicate may not be available in all areas, but the information provided will allow you to find a reasonable replacement through a distributor of your choice.

Antennas

Table B.1 lists the parts used in the "Fun with Wireless Antennas" section of Chapter 7.

Table B.1 Antenna Parts List

Description	Part Number	Vendor
2.2dB Omnidirectional antenna	N/A	Included with each WRT54G
7dB Omnidirectional antenna	HGA9T	Get More WiFi (www.get-morewifi.com)
9dB Omnidirectional antenna	HGA7T	Get More WiFi (www.get-morewifi.com)
9dB Yagi	ANT-9Y-NF	Netgate (www.netgate.com)
12dB Yagi	ANT-12Y-NF	Netgate (www.netgate.com)
24dB parabolic dish	PG2424-F-1	Antenna Systems and Solutions (www.antennasystems.com)
RP-TNC to N male pigtail	CBL-RPTNC-NM-NF	Netgate (www.netgate.com)

SD Card

Table B.2 lists the parts used in the "SD Card" section of Chapter 7.

Table B.2 SD Card Parts List

Description	Part Number	Vendor
SD Card connector	HR845CT-ND	Digi-key (www.digikey.com)
Floppy edge connector	CC2204	MC^3 LLC (www.mc3llc.com)
Ribbon cable	MC14G-X-ND	Digi-key (www.digikey.com)

Serial Port

Table B.3 lists the parts used in the "Serial" section of Chapter 7.

Table B.3 Serial Port Parts List

Description	Part Number	Vendor
2-by-5 pin header	WM8123-ND	Digi-key (www.digikey.com)
2-by-5 socket connector	MSC10K-ND	Digi-key (www.digikey.com)
2-by-5 socket connector strain relief	MSSR10-ND	Digi-key (www.digikey.com)
Ribbon cable	MC14G-X-ND	Digi-key (www.digikey.com)
AD233BK serial converter kit	AD233BK	Compsys Workbench (www.compsys1.com/workbench)
9-pin male solder D-Sub connector	276-1537	Radio Shack (www.radioshack.com)

JTAG

Table B.4 lists the parts used in the "JTAG" section of Chapter 7.

Table B.4 JTAG Parts List

Description	Part Number	Vendor
2-by-6 pin header	WM8124-ND	Digi-key (www.digikey.com)
2-by-6 socket connector	MSC12K-ND	Digi-key (www.digikey.com)
2-by-6 socket connector strain relief	MSSR12-ND	Digi-key (www.digikey.com)
Ribbon cable	MC14G-X-ND	Digi-key (www.digikey.com)
25-pin male solder D-Sub connector	276-1547	Radio Shack (www.radioshack.com)
25-pin D-Sub hood	276-1549	Radio Shack (www.radioshack.com)
100 ohm resistors (package of five)	271-1311	Radio Shack (www.radioshack.com)

Alternative Power

Table B.5 lists the parts used in the "Powering Your WRT54G with Alternative Sources" section of Chapter 7.

Table B.5 Alternative Power Parts List

Description	Part Number	Vendor
N-type solder connector	274-1573	Radio Shack (www.radioshack.com)
8 AA battery holder with snap connector	270-387	Radio Shack (www.radioshack.com)
9 volt snap connector	270-324	Radio Shack (www.radioshack.com)
Li-ion battery 2200 mA 7.4 volt	L18650-2200-2	Tenergy Corporation (www.all-battery.com)
Li-ion universal charger	TLP_2000	Tenergy Corporation (www.all-battery.com)
Sealed lead acid battery, 12 volt	NP18-12	Pacific Battery Systems (www.pacificbattery.com)
Solar panel, 12 volt, 1.26 watts	SP60-12	BatteryStuff (www.batterystuff.com)
USB connector, 4-pack	925K-ND	Digi-key (www.digikey.com)
FireWire 400 connector	928K-ND	Digi-key (www.digikey.com)
Ethernet jack, Leviton	8552W	Smart Home (www.smarthome.com)
Ethernet wall jack plate, Leviton	85593	Smart Home (www.smarthome.com)
N type power jack	274-1576	Radio Shack (www.radioshack.com)
Cat 5 cable, solid core	8493BLU	Smart Home (www.smarthome.com)
Surface mount electrical boxes	8594DW	Smart Home (www.smarthome.com)
Velcro, industrial-strength	N/A	Home Depot (not available online)

Index